ONE HUNDRED CUPS

100 CUPS

THE STORY OF THE SCOTTISH CUP

HUGH KEEVINS & KEVIN McCARRA

MAINSTREAM
PUBLISHING·EDINBURGH

in
conjunction
with

Scottish Brewers

First published in 1985 by
MAINSTREAM PUBLISHING COMPANY (EDINBURGH) LTD.
7 Albany Street
Edinburgh EH1 3UG

Scottish Brewers have a long standing and happy relationship with football and football supporters all over Scotland through sponsorship at national and local level. Their McEwans and Youngers ales and lager are drunk wherever football is talked about before and after the match.
Scottish Brewers are therefore delighted to support and to be associated with a book about one of our oldest and most prestigious competitions.

Our thanks are due to the following who helped, in various ways, to make this book possible: Doug Baillie, Tommy Bryceland, John Byrne, Gerard Cairns, Bobby Collins, Jim Craig, Alan Cunningham, Alex Ferguson, Tommy Gallagher, David Hay, Jim Hossack, Sandy Jardine, Bob Laird, John Litster, Robert McElroy, Donald MacLeod, Bob McPhail, Jack Murray, George Oliver, Forrest Robertson, Brian Stewart, Willie Thornton, Pat Woods, Dumbarton District Library, Mitchell Library (and the staff of the Glasgow Room), SFA (Marjorie Nimmo), Scottish League (David Thomson)
We are indebted to the *Glasgow Herald* and *Evening Times* who are the greatest single contributor of photographs to this book. We also wish to thank *D.C. Thomson* and *The Scotsman* for granting permission to reproduce photographs.

ISBN 0 906391 85 7 (cloth)
ISBN 0 906391 86 5 (paperback)

Typeset in 11 point Andover by Studioscope in conjunction with Mainstream Publishing.
Printed and bound by McCorquodale (Scotland) Ltd.

Contents

For Janet and Susan

Inventing the Cup

SINCE THERE were no suitable trams or train stations south of the river you would probably have decided to walk to the ground on that blustery March day in 1874. Going down the Saltmarket, past the prison and court house, and crossing the Clyde on the Albert Bridge you were heading in the same direction as Glasgow itself. With the rise in population, the land to the south of the river was gradually being developed. Around Cathcart Road the empty spaces were beginning to fill with tenements and terraces. The venue was appropriate, for the game itself was a new phenomenon in the world. Hampden Park, at Crosshill, was the right place for the first Scottish Cup Final.

The ground was a neat one with a little pavilion which had cost £21. There was no running water or toilets till the following year, and no grand stand until 1876 but Queen's Park were right to be proud of having their own home. The views of the Clydesdale player who called the site a 'kailyard' were doubtless tinged with malice.

On the hill which rose to Hampden Terrace on the South-East of the ground a sizeable number was settling, without the trouble of payment, to look down on the match. Two or three thousand had chosen to view the game from more honourable positions inside Hampden and that was a pleasing crowd in times when professional athletics, a well-established sport, would attract 5,000 to a good meeting. Admission cost 6d (2½p), which was dear enough in days when a man working in the solid profession of bookkeeper earned only 25s (£1.25) per week, but 6d was only half what it had cost to get in to the first international in 1872, and the charge was a positive bargain when compared to many other entertainments. If you had gone on from the game to Mr and Mrs Haigh's 'IMPERSONATIONS of Yankee and Negro Eccentricities' at 'Hengler's Grand Cirque' it would have cost 3s (15p) for a good seat.

With the amateur's studied disdain for those who merely watch, the teams — Queen's Park and Clydesdale — emerged onto the pitch twenty minutes after the advertised kick-off time of 3.30 pm. How had they got there?

The story of the Scottish Cup begins in Dewar's Temperance Hotel in Bridge Street, Glasgow. There, on 13 March 1873, eight clubs attended a meeting called by Queen's Park. The previous year the Crosshill club had organised, and provided the players for, an international with England. Although Queen's Park exercised power well, and were to go on to hold a position in football comparable to the MCC's in cricket, it was clearly time to establish a national organisation. At that meeting the SFA was formed and the Scottish Cup instituted. Queen's Park could look forward to more frequent fixtures and more worthy challenges in future.

Fifteen clubs subscribed towards the purchase of the Cup. Of the sixteen clubs who entered the first round, Southern do not seem to have contributed but they avoided recriminations by scratching to 3rd Lanark Rifle Volunteer Reserves (to grant them their full name). Queen's Park, in appropriately regal manner, contributed £5 — more than double the average contribution. The trophy itself and a set of medals cost £56 12s 11d (£56.65). This price may have been something of a bargain since, in one of the earliest moments in the dance of football with commerce, it was displayed in the window of its makers, Messrs George Edward & Sons of Buchanan Street, in the week prior to the Final.

The competition got underway on 18 October 1873 and one of the ties played that day demonstrated the need for a standardised, nationally-organised sport. Kilmarnock, who had sufficient troubles at the outset since only ten men had turned up, were soon to have their problems compounded in their match against Renton in Glasgow. Some of their players seemed to be not totally weaned from Rugby and consistently gave away fouls by handling. Renton won 2-0. Kilmarnock appear to have been sluggish students. Two years later they brought a full complement of footballers to Glasgow for a Cup-tie with Clydesdale but their boots had bars instead of studs on the soles. On the wet surface these were next to useless and they lost 6-0.

There was a sense of occasion about Queen's Park's entry into the competition on 25 October, for on that day they opened Hampden Park — the first of their grounds to bear the name. A newspaper of the day advertised it as Hampton Park. Queen's Park, resplendent in the black and white hoops which they were wearing for the first time, certainly amazed Dumbreck as they ran up a 7-0 score. By following that with victories over Eastern (1-0) and Renton (2-0) they reached the Final. These games were little more than exercises for Queen's Park. In the Renton match their keeper only touched the ball three times.

Clydesdale found life à little more difficult. It took them three games to eliminate Third Lanark in the second round but by the time they reached the last four their play had begun to flow. There they beat Blythswood 4-0 but the margin could have been greater. From the reports, it sounds as if the fight was stopped to prevent further injury: '. . . the umpires agreed to cease hostilities as the light was very bad'. Umpires were the predecessors of linesmen and one was appointed by each side.

The 1874 Final was the first match between Clydesdale and Queen's Park and that in itself made the outcome uncertain. What made it even more intriguing was the fact that most of the significant Clydesdale players were drawn from one source. They were ex-Queen's Park players. The stringency of the challenge Clydesdale posed was largely of their opponents' making. Fred Anderson (a forward) had resigned his membership of Queen's Park late in 1873 and gained a cap against England in 1874 while with Clydesdale. Internal politics saw three other players follow his example. Robert Gardner was a founder member of Queen's Park and the greatest goalkeeper of his day. He also had a keen taste for legislative work. He chaired the meeting at which the SFA was formed, selected the first Scotland team (including himself), and was an enthusiastic representative of his club on the SFA committee. It was Queen's Park's proposal to replace him in that last position which led to his departure in February 1874. Two of the Wotherspoon brothers who had been pillars of the club in its earliest years followed him. David Wotherspoon, who was chosen for Clydesdale in the Final, had played in that first international and was the man who persuaded Queen's Park to give up their dark blue jerseys in favour of the black and white hoops.

Queen's Park must surely have been irked by the opposition of players they had nurtured, while Gardner and Wotherspoon would have been attracted by the prospect of revenge. Gardner's presence as an umpire in a match between Queen's Park and Wanderers in 1875 suggests that the breach was not great but it was sufficient to make the Final a tantalising prospect.

Queen's Park, the first Scottish Cup-winners
Back row left to right: A McKinnon, J Dickson, T Lawrie, C Campbell, R Neill
Front Row: R Leckie, J Taylor, H McNeil, J Thomson, J Weir, W McKinnon
Charles Campbell went on to set the record of eight winners' medals in the competition

Queen's Park won 2-0 with both of their goals coming in the second half. The *North British Daily Mail* gave the following descriptions:

> . . . a run was being made by the Queen's Park up to the Clydesdale fortress, where, at twenty minutes before time was called, Mr Wm Mackinnon finished a splendid piece of dribbling by sending the ball clean through the Clydesdale goal, over the keeper's head . . .
> . . . W Mackinnon piloted the ball well up, passed it over to Weir, who in turn sent it to Leckie, and the latter adroitly put it through the goals with his left foot.

It should be remembered that sports journalism of the time largely consisted of arcane columns about horse racing headed 'Sporting Intelligence'.

The controversial turning point occurred in the first half. James Lang, who, it is reputed, later became the first Scot to go South with the express purpose of playing football there, gave the following account of it:

> I drew the Queen's Park defence not long after the start and slipped the ball to Fred Anderson, whose shot, taken on the instant, beat John Dickson, the Queen's Park goalkeeper, and struck the knee of a spectator who was

standing behind the goal. There were no nets and the onlookers were close up to the goal and touchlines.

There was no doubt in anyone's mind that it was a goal. Dickson immediately walked down the field to the other posts, for in those days we changed ends when a goal was scored. We lined up and just as Billy McKinnon the Queen's Park centre was about to kick off, the referee, James McIntyre, said: 'If I had been appealed to, I would have given no-goal.' Now the referee had no right to say anything of the sort. It was his place to wait for an appeal and in this case there was none up to then. But McKinnon was quick to see his opportunity. He picked the ball up, placed it under his arm and ran over to Mr H N Smith, the Queen's Park umpire, to whom he told the good news.

On appeal, the goal was disallowed and the now unfamiliar laws in force in that first year made the decision an even greater blow than it appears:

We had a great chance of winning had the goal been allowed, for an equalising goal by Queen's Park would have given us the wind back in our favour and that was important. But the rule was that if no goal was scored in the first half, there could be no change of ends in the second ... The team that had faced the wind all through the first half was entitled to have the benefit of it for the whole of the second half. Queen's Park got two goals after the interval.

The umpire who had allowed the goal wrote to the papers stating categorically that the ball had 'dribbled' from the keeper's hands through the goals. In tones which suggested that the culprit be left alone in the drawing room with the pearl-handed revolver, one Francis Geitner, of Crosshill, called on Dickson to confess the truth of the matter to the Queen's Park members. In the beginning was controversy.

Queen's Park were the most accomplished and imaginative team in Britain and their character was very different from their chief English rivals'. The Glasgow side were middle-class in origin, their players of the time tending to be either businessmen or skilled tradesmen. At the meeting in the offices of *The Sportsman* in 1871 at which the FA Cup was born, all the delegates were the products of public schools. Having seriously strained their finances by contributing one guinea (£1.05) to the cost of the trophy, Queen's Park took part in the first FA Cup competition (1871-72) and drew 0-0 with Wanderers in the semi-finals. There had been much agonising within the club about the outlay of so much hard-won money on a journey to the capital and Queen's Park could not afford to stay for a replay. There is no record of Wanderers (largely Old Harrovians) striving to extend their visit. Wanderers went on to take the trophy.

Queen's Park achieved that draw although missing the injured J J Thomson and despite seeing Edmiston incapacitated in the first few minutes. English players drew their approach to the game from the form of football they had known at their public schools. In those games players were encouraged to dribble with the ball. As a result of this, in the games played as adults, teamwork was felt to consist of positioning oneself to pick up the play once one's teammate had lost possession. Queen's Park developed a more intelligent strategy. They saw football as a true team game in which passing should be used to press home the advantage. Dribbling was employed where the situation warranted and not as a matter of general policy. This should not be taken to suggest that they were above the rough and tumble of play or that individual brilliance was prohibited.

One of their backs, Phillips, was prone to view attacks by the other team as positive incitements. In one game, he 'seized the opportunity afforded of knocking the old Blythswood forward to the ground, and returning the ball'. With strangled admiration, a Vale of Leven supporter described J J Thomson as 'the greatest and roughest half-back that ever entered a football field'. The star forward J B Weir combined aggressiveness with as much individuality as anyone could wish. An opponent ascribed his phenomenal dribbling to the fact that his mis-shapen legs and feet formed a 'crab-like' circle from which the ball could not be extracted.

Queen's Park had been formed in 1867 and another of their chief advantages lay in their experience. In its earliest days a club is no more than the sum of the men who play for it. Queen's Park, however, had learned how to replace players while retaining standards. The defections to Clydesdale, which would have been the death knell of a lesser club, left Queen's Park comparatively unscathed.

In the second competition Queen's Park's chief difficulty lay in eliminating Clydesdale. In the second of three matches they were behind and were only saved 'through the instrumentality of Highet'. With the aid of an own goal they won the third match. The other Finalists were Renton who were described as 'excellent trippers and hackers' who suffered from 'a want of combined action'. Queen's Park scored a 3-0 victory and their second goal typified the contrast between the sides. Following the kick-off after the first goal, Brown of Renton ran off in an individual attempt to level the score. Phillips dispossessed him and put his team on the attack. A crisp series of passes ended with Highet scoring the second. The fact that Renton were 'refreshed' by their admirers at half-time did not seem to put new spirit into them.

Queen's Park started season 1875-76 in fine fettle. In October they briskly thrashed Wanderers 5-0. As one reporter gleefully wrote: 'This was now coming it rather strong — three goals, and half-time not yet called.' The game showed that football had taken a sure hold of the public's interest. In and around the ground there were fifteen thousand people and the papers dwelled on the fact that the city was full of errand boys forming clubs with high sounding names and playing in 'coups and vacant railway arches'. The effect of the sport on 'Young Glasgow' was wittily recounted: 'a vulgar cad, addicted to smoking and playing billiards, went into a blue jersey, and donning knicker-bockers proved himself a true Scotchman with a genuine love of good manly exercise. . . '

The crowds of the time do not seem to have appreciated the sanctity of the turf and were in the habit of straying onto it. There were only ropes to discourage them from doing so. So common was the practice that one corres-pondent remarked, in the tones of a parent congratulating their child on stopping short of arson, on the 'exemplary' manners of a crowd which 'never once attempted to invade the ground'. In another match they put any visiting forward 'who was well placed into a dilemma as to whether he should continue'.

Queen's Park limbered up for their third round tie with Clydesdale by playing a charity match against Rangers. The game, along with such other entertainments as a concert by the mesmerist J W Jackson, was arranged to aid a specific appeal. A thousand people had been thrown out of work when a fire which started in a spinning mill spread quickly in the tinderbox of Glasgow's East End. The occasion was not without humour — one family pushed a piano to 'safety' from their top-floor window while another man rejected those who wished to save his property. Locking his door behind him, he announced 'I am insured'. Thirty thousand, including pickpockets, watched the entertainment from Glasgow Green. Nonetheless, it is right to recognise the true harshness of the event and of the world which welcomed football so passionately.

Rangers had been unlucky in the Cup. In the first year they had, because of an administrative error, been too late in applying for entry and in the second they lost to Dumbarton by dint of a disputed goal. The third Scottish Cup was even more unfortunate for them. They beat Third Lanark 1-0 but were forced to replay when their opponents successfully appealed on the grounds that Rangers had taken the kick-off in both halfs. Rangers lost the second match and, in turn, appealed. Their main arguments were, firstly, that the Third Lanark goalkeeper (a late replacement) was wearing working clothes and could not be distinguished from the crowd close behind him and, secondly, that the game had finished seven minutes early as the result of a crowd invasion. Amazingly, their appeal was rejected. For connoisseurs, this was the Golden Age of the appeal since there were few precedents and the future of almost any protest was difficult to predict.

Third Lanark, picking up momentum from their luck, went on to give Queen's Park the hardest test they had yet faced in the Cup. The military side were resilient and had some alarmingly simple tactics. Prior to the introduction of the penalty kick in 1891 a foul in the goalmouth led only to a free-kick. In such situations one of the Third Lanark backs, Hunter, would gather his men around him and, amidst the pack, try to drive over the line with the ball at his feet.

Queen's Park were beginning to stumble under the burden of their success. On 5 February 1876 an era came to an end as they lost 2-1 to Wanderers at the Oval in London. It was their first defeat. When the immediate pain had faded, Queen's Park must have felt glad that so much strain had been relieved. Their continuing excellence was not in doubt. In March, three of their players were carried shoulder-high from the pitch after scoring the goals in a 3-0 victory over England.

In the semi-final of the Cup they played Vale of Leven at Hampden. A huge crowd of 10,000 was boosted by the fact that a special train had been run from Alexandria. One stolid reporter suggested that prices be raised to reduce such worrying attendances. He would doubtless have been happier at the other semi-final which was taking place only a few minutes walk away. A crowd of 60 watched Third Lanark play Dumbarton. At Hampden, some fans, desperate to gain admission, had pulled out the paling and used it as 'vaulting poles'. They committed a greater offence than they realised. At first, the ground had been surrounded only by a hawthorn hedge on three sides and was open to Cathcart Road on the other. The necessary fence was erected without charge for labour or materials by Phillips and J B Weir, who were both joiners. Those who called Weir one of the builders of the game did not know just how accurate the description was.

Queen's Park won a heated match 2-1 but the sides were on good enough

Johnny Ferguson (left) and Bobby Paton of Vale of Leven

terms to spend the evening at the Atholl Arms. Perhaps the Vale were there soothed by the fine tenor voice of Queen's Park's W McKinnon. The *North British Daily Mail* teemed with letters from the opposing sets of supporters who remained unreconciled, each accusing the other's team of thuggishness. The names have changed but the correspondence has continued ever since. How familiar is the letter which complains that Queen's Park behaved in an unseemly manner in enthusiastically celebrating their goals. A more absorbing letter accuses the Vale's forwards of stopping suddenly so that pursuing defenders ran into their backs, thereby affording the Vale players the opportunity of bending over and allowing their opponents to be thrown over their shoulders. It would have been worth a great deal to have seen it!

Significantly, there was a grand stand at the 1876 Cup Final at Hamilton Crescent and the match started on time. Football had begun to acknowledge its need of support. Third Lanark committed *lèse majesté* by scoring straight from the kick-off. Queen's Park fought back ferociously but, finding no rhythm, could only draw 1-1. It was the second half before Highet equalised Drinnan's opener. Queen's Park's team selection was almost symbolic of the difficulty they were to have in adapting to the ever-increasing competitiveness of football. They unwisely looked to a man who had served them well in the past but who was scarcely a credible candidate for the match of 11 March 1876. Angus McKinnon had retired in 1875 as a result of illness but was recalled for the Final. He was not a success.

In choosing their side for the replay Queen's Park turned instead to the future and selected youngsters Hillcote and Smith. They were rewarded with a performance which recalled their years of absolute dominance and the Rifle Volunteers' insurrection was smartly put down. Highet opened the scoring and followed that with a shot which knocked the bar off (whether as a result of its power or of negligent carpentry is not clear). A further goal was added by him in the second half and Third Lanark were comprehensively outplayed.

It was a splendid final act by Queen's Park but Scottish football was to have rather more complex plots in future. Nonetheless, the disappointments they had in the following seasons bore tribute to their open-handed and intelligent encouragement of the game. Scottish football and the Scottish Cup are the inventions of Queen's Park.

Down in the Valley

For want of a nail the shoe is lost, for want of a shoe the horse is lost, for want of a horse the rider is lost.

A LL GREAT events have their origins in matters which seem unworthy of notice at the time. The fact that the Leven is a fast-flowing river (said to be the second fastest in Scotland) might be thought only of importance to the compiler of a gazetteer but in the nineteenth century it changed life in the valley through which it runs. Those clear waters were of great importance to the dyeing trade which, from its small beginnings in the eighteenth century, came to be the chief source of employment in the area. Alexandria was once called 'The Grocery' after its single shop but by 1851 the population of the parish was 7,643 and the area was beginning to be linked with a larger community. In 1850 a railway line was laid between Balloch and Bowling and in 1858 the same connection joined Bowling to Glasgow and Dalreoch to Helensburgh. Gas lighting came in 1855, although we know that it was slow to demonstrate its usefulness since pedestrians still felt the need of lanterns in 1864 and a certain Thomas Blackstock, failing to discover Bonhill bridge one evening in 1876, walked straight into that brisk river. In the midst of all this expansion there appeared a football team.

Football, in general, was adopted with great enthusiasm throughout Dunbartonshire. Forty-nine teams entered the Scottish Cup of 1875-76 and amongst them we find Renton, Alclutha, Dumbarton, Lennox, Helensburgh, Star of Leven, Renton Thistle, Vale of Leven Rovers (Glasgow Section), Vale of Leven Rovers (Alexandria), and Vale of Leven. The press, on the whole, was slow to register this and tended to think that these sides could be tagged simply as 'country folk'. The last named of those clubs was to force a different assessment.

The fortunes of Vale of Leven and Queen's Park were tied from the start, since the Alexandria club's first match was against them in Glasgow in December 1872 and they again met in their first home fixture in March of the following year. The second of those games may have left the Crosshill club with some slight stirrings of disquiet since they could only draw 0-0. The fact that the game had to be stopped on a number of occasions in order that the finer points of the rules might be explained to the former rugby and shinty players does not entirely explain the result.

Vale of Leven's progress was vexingly impeded by the fact that they were forced to withdraw from the first two Scottish Cups as a result of protests by their opponents concerning the brilliant forward Johnny Ferguson whom they accused of being a professional. His club argued that he was not supported by football and that 'he wrought in the Vale from one year's end to the other'. That, however, was scarcely the point at issue and it was his sorties out of the area, such as the one he made to win a mile event (in 4 minutes $16\frac{1}{2}$ seconds) at Powderhall in January 1872, which caused the problem. He had undoubtedly been a professional runner. Eventually, he was saved by the fact that the SFA's strictures regarding professionalism did not, at that time, state whether they applied to payments in football or to sports in general. In any case, the SFA, having chosen him for the England game of 1874, were scarcely in a position to ban him from the sport thereafter.

McGregor of Vale of Leven was the first man to score against Queen's Park, although the game in question was abandoned after his side refused to accept the legitimacy of their opponents' second goal, and the improvement in his team was to culminate in the Crosshill club's first defeat by another Scottish side. That extraordinary match took place in the fifth round of the Scottish Cup at Hampden in December 1876 during torrential rain.

It was clear from the start that the game was unlikely to proceed in a calm manner. The *North British Daily Mail's* reporter was, for example, evidently piqued by the low company which he was being forced to keep. The 2000 of the 'football daft' who watched this 'scramble for the Cup': 'Yelling, hooting, and calling out the players by cognomens were nothing compared to the coarse and vulgar pleasantries indulged in. Happily no ladies were present in the vitiated atmosphere, or they would have been compelled to retire long before the game was over'. Given the prevailing weather, however, he might have paused simply to admire their ardour.

Thirty yards from one goal a 'water hole' formed and the ball almost disappeared from sight on landing in it. Indeed, a new, dry ball was required for the second half and it was hardly surprising that at least one of the umpires used an umbrella. Queen's Park went one up and seemed set to go further ahead when J B Weir unleashed a goal-bound shot. A goal was prevented by the fact that the ball was deflected over the bar from the umpire's umbrella and the Vale's greater strength eventually told as they won 2-1. The pitch was unplayable and the game a bruising trial of strength but that did not constrain the delight in Alexandria. 'The play of the Vale was the finest ever seen,' wrote 'Porkie', rather implausibly, to one newspaper. Another composed a celebratory poem, bizarrely modelled on *The Charge of the Light Brigade*, which included:

Flashed the red stockings there
Flashed as they spun through air,
Beating the stunners there,
Conquering the champions — while
All the West wondered.

Stormed at with shot so well,
The Hampden Park heroes fell,
Thrashed by the valiant Vale —
   Left cupless and sundered.

Queen's Park reacted rather differently. On finding on the Tuesday after the game what they took to be spike marks on the pitch (spikes were strictly illegal) they sent two representatives to Alexandria to examine the boots of the Vale's players. Naturally, they found no improper footwear and the whole exercise was both futile and inflammatory. One Vale supporter said that he and his friends would have thrown the Queen's Park men into that speedy river had they known of their mission to Alexandria. In a more charming, if unconvincing vein, 'Justice' wrote to a newspaper offering an explanation of the marks:

> I saw the ground on Sunday, 31st, when it was not frost-bound, and beheld an impudent black crow waddling over the ground, and ever and anon plunging his spiked beak into the soft ground. Now sir, imagine a dozen of these sable gentlemen pursuing their investigation over Sunday, and would you wonder if the frost-bound ground was completely riddled with small spiked holes?

More common were the impassioned epistles of such as the pseudonymous 'Corporal Trim' which voiced suspicion regarding Vale of Leven's ability to avoid slipping on the surface: 'The rarity of such occurrences amongst the lads from the "Grocery" was something marvellous.' Others, more resigned, were keen to rescue something for the Glasgow club and one suggested that a banquet be given in Queen's Park's honour, acknowledging their great role in the game's growth.

Queen's Park took matters badly but that historic result stood. With wicked humour, the Vale of Leven captain insisted on inspecting the boots of his own team and of Ayr Thistle before their sixth round tie. They went on to win 9-0 and reached the Final where they were to play Rangers.

Rangers were a lithe, young team but they showed in their passage to the Final that they could meet fire with fire. When drawn away to Mauchline they found themselves faced with a team of brutally rustic approach and a crowd which appreciated such play more than thoughtful football. Rangers coped:

> In the midst of a scrimmage Hill got in on the goalkeeper and sent him through, while Watson performed the same service for the ball.

Vale of Leven, though, were overwhelming favourites to take the Cup against opponents generally regarded as inexperienced.

The behaviour of underdogs tends towards extremes: they are either consumed by nerves or filled with a blithe insouciance. Rangers, happily displaying the latter quality, turned their youth to advantage as they ran all over their opponents. Vale of Leven were further troubled by the fact that one of their half-backs, Jamieson, played although not fully recovered from illness, and a forward, Baird, was hampered by an early injury. Rangers, although playing uphill in the second half, equalised in that period with the aid of an own goal.

Three weeks later the teams again met and produced the same result. Dunlop opened the scoring for Rangers but McDougall, who had scored the own goal in the first Final, displayed an improved sense of direction and equalised. The two sides agreed, with much inventiveness, to play a further thirty minutes and it would appear that this was the first match ever to have extra-time. The full period was not taken up because a crowd invasion followed an argument in which Rangers claimed that a Dunlop shot had crossed the line.

The quality and balance of the Rangers side had become apparent. As well as exciting forwards such as Moses McNeil and Peter Campbell, they had stern competitors such as Tom Vallance, who was a gifted athlete in a number of sports. The venue for the third match shifted from Hamilton Crescent to Hampden and, for the first time, a Final was replayed on a weekday evening.

The game kicked off in the early evening of Friday 13 April. Interest in it was great and one report described a scene which was to become part of the very fabric of the game:

> Thousands of the working classes rushed out to the field of battle in their labouring garb, after crossing the workshop gate when the final whistle sounded at five o'clock.

It was an ill-tempered, enjoyable game with arguments, off-the-ball incidents, and a fluctuating scoreline. Vale of Leven were 2-1 down after their keeper aimed a dismissive kick at a poor shot and missed the ball altogether but they displayed real stature in maintaining their pattern and tempo in that situation. They equalised; and scored the winner when a clever break by Ferguson and Baird set up Paton.

Great were the celebrations when Vale of Leven returned to Alexandria and they toured the area in an open carriage, accompanied by the Bonhill Instrumental Band. Cannons were fired, pipers were 'discoursing Highland music', and the Smollet fountain was switched on. The Scottish Cup spent the year in the dining room of Cameron House, the family estate of the Smollets (whose most famous member was Tobias, the eighteenth-century novelist), and was relentlessly shown by Alexander Smollet, Honorary President of Vale of Leven, to all guests.

The next season began with intimations of a new era for Vale of Leven as they opened a 'commodious pavilion' at the Gasworks corner of their ground and played a conciliatory friendly with Queen's Park. The game ended in a diplomatic 1-1 draw and the teams concluded a merry evening at the Bonhill Inn by singing *Auld Lang Syne*. Their progress to the Final was equally harmonious for they lost only one goal and easily dismissed the previous season's finalists in the fourth round.

Third Lanark struggled rather more and even exercised the SFA committee. Following a defeat by Western, they protested that the pitch had not been roped off and capitalised on the SFA's decision by winning the replay. The ruling body, however, penalised them when it was found that the Third's secretary had tricked a referee of his choosing into controlling their tie with Renton rather than applying to the SFA to have one appointed. Those who live by the sword, it would appear, suffer no great penalty, because Third Lanark won the replay which followed Renton's protest. No reference to the rule book was necessary, however, when Third Lanark knocked out Queen's Park.

The way in which Third Lanark had developed was indicative of changes in the game as a whole. When previously reaching the Final they had displayed more raw muscularity than science but now strength and knowledge were more effectively balanced. Resolute defenders such as Hunter remained and his club's motto of 'defence not defiance' seemed suitable, but they were also capable of economic and decisive attacking. In their first match with Renton their opening goal had its origins in their own penalty area and was the product of three good passes. Understanding of the game's rhythms and angles was no longer Queen's Park's exclusive property. Third Lanark's team had also been strengthened by the acquisition of the experienced James Lang (of the 1874 Final) who had returned to Scotland after a brief spell with Sheffield Wednesday. That particular sojourn in English football seems only to have suited him to the extent that he was able to conceal the fact, common knowledge in his native land, that he only had one eye. The other had been lost in a Clydebank shipyard.

The Final was a tousy, inglorious affair and its only goal matched the occasion — a long shot by McDougall deflected off Hunter leaving the keeper stranded. In Alexandria the fountain was once more restored to life and a local poet had it complain that it was only used:

> To signalise some great event
> That's happened to the Vale!
> Some victory of a football team
> Or some such silly tale.

Sandy McLintock of Vale of Leven, here seen in his later days with Burnley

Having quelled the nation, the following season's ties saw Vale of Leven impress the fact on their neighbours. With the sharp venom we reserve for kin, they beat Alclutha 6-0, Renton Thistle 11-0, Jamestown 15-0 (how had they even got to the third round?), Dumbarton 3-1, and Helensburgh 3-0. McDougall scored hat-tricks in the first and second rounds and four in the fourth (an 11-0 victory over Govan). The third round match with Jamestown seems to have defeated reporters with the enormity of its result and no record of scorers survives but it is tempting to suppose that McDougall notched a hat-trick or better in four successive ties. He confined himself to a brace in both the fifth and sixth round matches and left the opposition unmolested in the last two rounds of the competition. McDougall was also the first man to score a hat-trick against England. He did so in the 7-2 victory of 1878, perhaps invigorated by a desire to rid himself of the multi-coloured ball which was used on that occasion.

The most interesting moment in Vale of Leven's season came when they indulged in a spot of 'night life' on the eve of that second round tie with Renton Thistle. On the evening of Friday 25 October 1878 they played at Third Lanark's ground in the first floodlit football match to be played in Scotland. The machinery did not work properly and eventually a single beam was employed from a platform fifty feet above the pitch. This was moved around to follow the action but occasionally the spotlight was poorly directed and the significant play would then be conducted in darkness. As the 11-0 score indicates, Vale of Leven showed no signs of tiredness in their Cup-tie the following day.

Once again their opponents in the Final, who had played that year's David to the Queen's Park Goliath, were Rangers. The Cup Final was now a thoroughly established social occasion, a fact clearly indicated by the newspaper advert of a St Enoch Square Restaurant which announced its services, adjacent as they were to a horse cab service, as being particularly suited to football fans in need of pre-match sustenance.

As in 1877, Rangers proved something of a quandary for the Alexandria side. Struthers scored for Rangers and seemed to have added another when he headed in a Dunlop cross but, to his side's rage, the goal was disallowed for off-side. Vale of Leven struggled to accomplish even the simplest of moves but, with only a few minutes left, Ferguson snapped a low cross beyond goalkeeper Gillespie, one of the club's backs in the 1877 Final, who seemed to believe he was ushering the ball past the post.

After the second game of the 1877 Final Rangers had considered refusing to play the third match and this time, an appeal to the SFA about the referee's decision having been rejected, adopted that course of action. The Cup was awarded to Vale of Leven but Rangers' pain was slightly relieved by a victory over their technical conquerers in the Glasgow Charity Cup Final.

Aside from forwards like Ferguson and McDougall, the Vale possessed, in Sandy McLintock and Andy McIntyre, defenders of dispiriting force and strength. McLintock was one of those individuals whose natural level at any sport was excellence for he was also outstanding in running, jumping, rowing and shinty. His sporting careers provide us with a clue as to the causes of his club's superiority. He was, in the range if not the success of his sporting enthusiasms, an unremarkable product of the area. The achievement of Vale of Leven had much connection with the near-fanatical interest in sports of all kinds which existed in the district. One member of the football club was James McLeavy, a great professional runner who won three races billed as 'British Championships' at one mile, four miles, and ten miles on three successive Saturdays in 1876. He died at the age of 34 in 1884. Another successful sportsman was Robert Walkinshaw who won the World Quoiting Championship and £200 in 1870. Boat racing, too, enjoyed great popularity. A special train run from Dumbarton swelled a crowd of several thousand which watched a race between Vale of Leven and Dumbarton sides on Loch Lomond. A boat, the *Prince Consort*, was used to carry the most committed of spectators.

The team also benefited from the strong sense of common identity which inhabitants of the Vale possessed. There was even a club for those who travelled on foot to Dumbarton each day to work (1872 miles per year), while the Highland Association which was started in Alexandria in 1873 predates the formation of An Comunn Gaidhealach by eighteen years. The presence of so strong a Highland influence meant that a knowledge of the principal sources of team strategy was developed through shinty. As early as 1858, the *Dumbarton Herald* complained that Helensburgh children were in the habit of playing shinty in the streets. The Vale of Leven football club sprang from the shinty team and several players competed in both sports. As well as winning a Scottish Cup-winners' medal in 1877, Davie Lindsay also turned out for the shinty club in a prestigious match with Inverary in February of the same year. Both sides claimed prior to the match that they had never been beaten but it was Vale of Leven who maintained their record, winning by four hails to one.

There was tremendous cohesion in the Vale of Leven team itself. For one thing, many of them were totally devoted to living in the area. Wood worked for twenty-five years in the dyeing trade while McGregor made that seem like temping by spending fifty years with a local firm. McGregor was also a founder member of the football club and accordingly bore the nickname of 'The Patriarch'. McGregor was one of three members of that first team who went on to win Cup-winners' medals with the club. This was a remarkably high number when one considers that those players were, previously, more or less unversed in football matters.

Vale of Leven rode out the storm of the early years when they were invariably accused of violent play and persevered in developing the skill and understanding of their players. The fierce sense of common cause which those players had can be seen in the fact that they held annual reunions till well into the 1920s. The pretext for the revels was the passing on for one year of the commemorative 'loving cup', presented by local businessmen to mark those three Cup wins, from one player to another.

Accounts of their visit to London to play Wanderers in April 1878 offer an appealing insight into the idiosyncratic but effective *ésprit de corps* which informed the team. They left Alexandria by train in their own special coach on a Thursday evening. It was not long before messages and refreshments were being passed between compartments. 'The right wing passed well to the centre, who, in turn, passed to the left wing, in the most unselfish manner.' One player wore a striped night-cap, another was dressed in a tiger skin rug and worsted tam o' shanter and a third distinguished himself by smoking a pipe which had been curiously carved from the branch of a tree. With the aid of a penny whistle an impromptu concert was held on the platform at Edinburgh, while a reel was danced at Berwick. At two o'clock in the morning a party composed of those who had been born in the Vale met the train at Newcastle.

A seedy-looking and tired team toured the Tower of London and Madame Tussaud's on the Friday in an attempt to renew acquaintance with their legs. These preparations for Saturday's game were vindicated by a 3-1 win in which Ferguson scored a hat-trick. The Hon A F Kinnaird conceded that the Vale excelled not only at the passing game, which was to be expected given their nationality, but also at the dribbling game.

After the 1878 Final had been won, one of their supporters, noting their victories over Queen's Park, Rangers and Third Lanark, thought he heard the death knell for football in Glasgow:

> Toll for the teams,
> The teams that are no more,
> All beaten by the boys
> From Leven's winding shore.

Wrong. Not dead, but sleeping.

The empire strikes back

IN THE LONG run no team can survive its own success. As the expectations of victory are being nourished by it so the players' taste for it is increasingly sated. To help an unfavoured club challenge a great one is to court triumph, but to defeat one's inferiors is workaday toil. Inertia dictates that a winning team be left intact, even though it grows older, but its rivals are free to experiment and rebuild. It was Dumbarton who did for Vale of Leven.

The rise in numbers (the SFA listed 117 member clubs in 1879) and considerations of economy had led, from season 1876-77, to the early rounds of the competition being organised on a regional basis. An exacting local derby was a likely prospect in the first round, and so it was that Vale of Leven found themselves playing in front of 4,000 at Boghead, Dumbarton on 20 September 1879. The Alexandria club were always straining to stay on the required pace and it was the kind of game where quirks in style cost them goals. Goalkeeper Parlane was caught off his line and so gifted Dumbarton a third goal and a 3-1 lead. In the midst of a bland series of notes on leading players the SFA annual for 1880-81 remarks stonily of him: '. . . his practice of leaving his goal and following his backs is a dangerous one, and should be strictly avoided'. Instinct drew Vale of Leven back into the match and they went on to level the score but another goal in the 85th minute parted them from the Cup which had almost begun to seem part of their domestic *bric á brac*.

The prime beneficiaries of their demise were Queen's Park. On the same day they were drawing with Rangers but they found that a little luck attended them when their opponents were forced to enter the replay without the services of Tom Vallance. Against a side thrown out of kilter they ran up a 5-1 score. The malaise was over, the convalescence completed, and Queen's Park went on to play as if they felt their powers rising within them once again. 14-1, 10-1, 15-1 — the bell rang out on the 'Test Your Strength' machine.

Their team contained several new faces but good clubs seem to proceed according to laws of genetic inheritance and the Queen's Park side possessed the same nice blend of intelligence and resolution which had previously taken the Cup to Hampden. They continued to command the services of five of their players from the triumphs of the 1870s (Neill, Campbell, McNeil, Highet and Weir), and the new recruits matched their standards. An element of cool calculation can be detected in this since two of the newcomers chosen for the 1880 Final had previously won international caps while with other clubs and it is likely that the attack on the practice of acquiring a good team from the ranks of one's rivals which the SFA annual for 1880-81 contains is aimed at them. They could, however, regard their home-grown products with pride. George Ker had played with other clubs but it was with Queen's Park that he really developed. At first he followed the example of his elder brother William, who had played for them between 1870 and 1873, and filled the full-back position. In 1878, though, he was converted to centre-forward and his stinging, accurate shooting brought him many goals. He shares the record for the highest number for Scotland against England — seven in three jousts with them.

The regional organisation of the Cup ensured that weaker areas of the country were guaranteed representatives in later rounds of the competition. Queen's Park's opponents in the Final of 1880 were Thornliebank. They had begun their campaign in the Renfrewshire section and it was the fourth round before there was much chance of them being taxed. The confidence gained through the victories then stood them in good stead. In the last eight of the competition they played Third Lanark. A virtual hurricane forced the abandonment of the first match and difficult conditions hampered play in the second. With the score at 1-1 the teams, in a spirit of self-preservation, decided that twenty minutes of extra-time would suffice. With five minutes remaining the invigoratingly named Wham scored the winner for Thornliebank. In the semi-final Pollokshields Athletic were beaten 2-1, the winner coming, according to the *Glasgow News*, in 'most scientinc' fashion.

In the other semi-final Dumbarton manfully left the Hampden pavilion to enter a wintry scene shared by 8,000 indomitable fans. Peering through the snowflakes they noticed that Queen's Park had not joined them on the pitch. It was not any deference to the thermometer which kept them indoors but the fact that one of their players had not yet arrived. Battle was eventually joined and a single goal by Ker took Queen's Park through. It is possible to understand the rules of football too well and Dumbarton were lambasted for the manner in which they played: '. . . they lose the sympathies of many friends by attempting to steal a march on the enemy in connection with "off-side"'.

In the Final, Thornliebank proved to be little more than guests of honour at an awards ceremony for Queen's Park. Praised for their sporting play earlier in the competition, exasperation led them from the true path on the great occasion: 'One of the Thornliebank men fell on top of Ker, and, amid some hissing, kept him pressed down in the mud, apparently with the intention of temporarily depriving him of his breath.' Ker scored one of the goals in a 3-0 win.

In the following season of 1880-81 Dumbarton again proved the chief rivals to Queen's Park. Their semi-final was against Vale of Leven and, for the occasion, the Alexandria club abandoned the attempts at rebuilding which had occupied them that season and re-instated, with the exception of Ferguson, all the leading figures from their Cup wins. The events of the match showed that Vale of Leven had mistaken unthinking conservatism for prudence. The ease with which Dumbarton cruised to a 2-0 win was as dismissive as any crushing scoreline. The excitement about the tie which had led one paper to carry reports on it from Glasgow, Alexandria, and Dumbarton correspondents was quickly dissipated.

The Final with Dumbarton was the first test Queen's Park faced in that year's competition. A crowd of 10,000 was drawn to Rangers' ground at Kinning Park and gate receipts totalled £475. The financial benefits to the clubs were all the greater in those days because the SFA did not take any share of the income until 1886. McNeil scored an early goal in the match with a long shot which 'to his and everybody's amazement took effect'. Before half-time McAulay took advantage of an error by A H Holm and equalised. With scant regard for those who require longish intervals in order that fresh oxygen might be taken on board, the second half commenced three minutes after the conclusion of the first. Kay, of Queen's Park, went on to convert a cross for the game's decisive goal. Or so it seemed.

Prior to the 1890s and the widespread employment of banked terracing the fact that only ropes stood between fans and players meant that there was bound to be much pushing at moments of excitement. An SFA annual quotes the shame-faced admission of a former player, turned fan: 'Old Anderson . . . charges me with digging my thumbs into his ribs, and nearly strangling his youngest son at every scrimmage near goal.' Crowd encroachment on the pitch was an inevitability.

The cross which led to Kay's winner had been hit from amongst spectators and it was impossible to tell if the ball had crossed the bye-line before it was played. Dumbarton appealed to have the game replayed and their protest was upheld. This was an astonishing decision by the SFA since crowd conditions had been accepted at the outset by both teams. In ordering a replay they were also encouraging the dangerous belief that crowd intervention might rescue a lost cause on the field. Queen's Park considered withdrawing from the SFA but eventually agreed to play again, albeit under protest. The saddest part in the affair lay in the fact that Harry McNeil, who had scored in the first match, was injured and unable to play in the second. He was a popular figure whose dynamic style, pleasingly at odds with his slight build, won him warm praise. 'That little, fiery, furious, flying fellow' was one description, while his selection for the game against England in 1881 caused the *Glasgow News* to announce that he was 'For the sixth time chosen to baffle and mystify the English backs'.

Crowd control for the replay exercised the minds of many. One correspondent suggested that a single row of benches be placed around the pitch so that those sitting on them might form an 'immobile barrier'. He thoughtfully suggests that such positions should be cheaper than stand seats but one suspects that actual remuneration would have been necessary to persuade anyone to act as a crush barrier. More tellingly, another writer advances the idea that ropes be arranged in a large sweeping oval around the pitch since the greater the perimeter, the less the crowd density at any point on it. It is this principle which was to lie behind the design of grounds such as the present Hampden. The SFA's response was comprehensive. They employed 51 members of the Renfrewshire constabulary, under the command of a certain Captain Hunter, erected boarding to restrain people, and built a platform on three sides of the ground so that raised positions were available to those who might otherwise have seen little. By these tactics the non-combatant status of the spectator was ensured. Queen's Park won 3-1 in that newly-tempered atmosphere.

In 1881-82 the Crosshill club provided further evidence that they had quelled all unrest and regained their empire. The scores from the Cup-ties had all those who believed in the brotherhood of man flinching. 14-0, 9-0 (after a draw, ridiculously enough), 3-1, 10-0, 15-0 were the scorelines of their first five ties. One newspaper, bearing in mind Queen's Park's nickname, printed a spoof report of the last of those games as 'The Spiders v The Flies'. The acknowledgement it made of Queen's Park's excellence had a sting in the tail. Of their superiority it said: 'No one could dispute that, and, above all, did they not know the fact themselves with marvellous accuracy.' The flies, with their 'feebleness of wing', were no match for opponents who 'desired not only to defeat, but to effect the complete extinction, of the hopeful and harmless race of Flies'. Dumbarton, once again, inched their way towards the Final, having to bear such tribulations as a replay with Rangers when it was discovered that their first victory had occupied only eighty-five minutes.

Difficulties with the adjudication of matches continued to abound. In 1880 one restless intellect addressed itself to the problem of umpires whose arms tended to raise the flag to stop the game without first consulting their owners' brains. His idea was that umpires should be issued with whistles or horns since a conscious decision would have to be made before either could be sounded. Eventually, of course, whistles were universally used, but by referees and not linesmen (umpires). The idea of horns being employed is a particularly attractive one. The grizzly, rebarbative contests of the time would surely have produced a 'soundtrack' like a river-load of ships on a foggy night.

It was Queen's Park who suffered from suspect refereeing in the 1882 Final. After taking a two-goal lead they conceded one in a perplexing incident. The ball hit the Queen's Park bar and bounced over and out of play, but a Dumbarton forward, following up, ran through the goals and headed the ball. The referee and umpires, stout gentlemen who were not in the vicinity, gave a goal. Queen's Park, understandably perturbed, then lost an equaliser. The auguries for the game had been bad for them from the first since their great half-back, Charles Campbell had, as the result of a sore throat, been unable to play. They recalled David 'Iron Horse' Davidson in his place but the pistons had obviously rusted and the pressure dropped since his retirement the year before. He was a woebegone figure by the end of the match and it was apparent that his mind had returned to the pavilion some minutes before his body was permitted the same sanctuary. Surprisingly, he kept his place for the replay while J W Holm, who had played in every Cup-tie that season was dropped to make room for Campbell. There was little room for doubt or creative refereeing at the second time of asking. Queen's Park scored in the first minute and won 4-1. It was the considered opinion of the club's committee that their side of 1882 was the finest they had ever fielded.

Dumbarton were to reveal that childhood lessons concerning Bruce and the spider had not been wasted on them as they gamely continued to confront those other 'spiders'. Perseverance saw them into the sixth round of the 1882-83 contest where they were drawn to play Queen's Park. That fixture, as we have seen, tended to constitute the terminus in Dumbarton's Cup journeys but on this occasion they managed to shred that itinerary. They were perhaps encouraged by the fact that the game saw Queen's Park's first visit to Dumbarton. It was a venue which they had been accused of avoiding and the ensuing match provided much evidence to justify any wariness.

Queen's Park were met by their opponents at the station and the afternoon seemed to be proceeding in a pleasant vein when Kay scored for them after ten minutes. Before half-time, though, 'Brown (1) amidst a scene of the wildest excitement made the score equal'. It should be explained that there were two Robert Browns in the side. Number 1 was Robert 'The Sparrow' Brown, a winger whose fragile appearance concealed a zest for hurling himself upon lofty opponents. The other, also to become an international forward, was Robert 'The Plumber' Brown. Another five minutes and 'The Sparrow' had crossed for McKinnon to score a further goal. With only a minute of the second half gone Dumbarton paid a further premium on their insurance policy against a malign fate by scoring a third, again through McKinnon. The match ended in a 3-1 victory.

Dumbarton perhaps believed that they were now in the happy position of needing only to mind where they put their feet in order to win the Cup. Their game with Pollokshields in the last four disabused them of such notions. They won by a solitary goal and even that, the papers insisted, had actually gone wide. Goalnets, it should be remembered, were not employed until 1892. There were requests that they should replay the match and in one of the noblest moments in football history they agreed to do so. Most clubs, had they experienced the previous travails of Dumbarton, would simply have viewed that goal as a down payment on long overdue good fortune. Happily, their virtue was rewarded by a 5-0 victory.

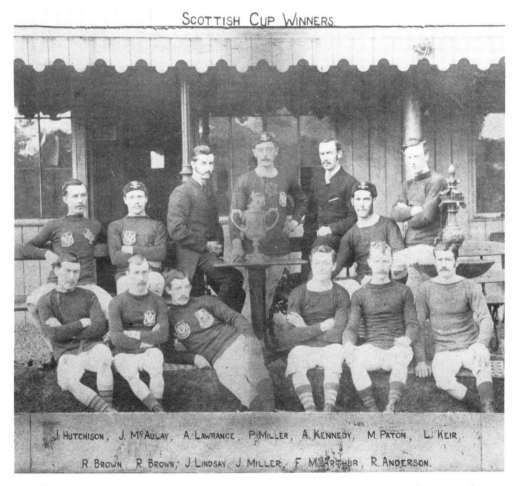

The men who gave Dumbarton their only Scottish Cup success. The club has appeared in six Finals.

In the Final they faced local rivals Vale of Leven and adopted an unusual formation of 2-3-5. That system, in varying interpretations, was to remain in use until the 1950s, although it was only in the 1920s that the third half-back was converted into the purely destructive centre-half figure who is the very stuff of nightmare. In an exciting match, a goalkeeping error permitted Vale of Leven to scramble a 2-2 draw. With Lang injured, Dumbarton introduced a

27

second string forward, Anderson, and so reverted to 2-2-6 in the replay. In the second half of the match Anderson, exemplifying beginner's luck, scored with a shot which deflected off the post. 'The Sparrow' added a second and although Vale of Leven were permitted to leave their impression on the scoreline, Dumbarton won with assurance. The grail was at last attained.

Amongst a clutch of international players, the most interesting member of the Dumbarton side was James McAulay. He had, at first, been understudy to centre-forward Joe Lindsay and, although he had scored in the 1881 Final, was a lesser light in the team. All that changed when he went over to the 'enemy' by becoming a goalkeeper. Perhaps he was aided by the knowledge he had gained of forward play for he became the most authoritative keeper of the day, the first in Scotland to be awarded the title of 'Prince of Goalkeepers'.

Queen's Park shook off their disappointment and reached the 1884 Final with laughable ease, playing not a fixture of any competitive note. Any problems they faced were of a purely administrative nature. They had been forced, by railway development, to leave their ground in 1883 and they did not move into Second Hampden, later taken over by Third Lanark, until October 1884. Home fixtures were played at Titwood Park in the intervening period of homelessness. The other Finalists were, once again, Vale of Leven, but the game never took place. On the Wednesday before the match Vale of Leven asked that the game be postponed as they would be without four players (three through injury and one through family bereavement). The SFA business committee refused to rearrange the match at so late a stage and, when Vale of Leven did not appear, the Cup was awarded to Queen's Park. On the day of the match Queen's Park played Third Lanark at Cathkin, the intended venue for the Final. Amongst those who received Cup-winners' medals in these most

The Queen's Park men who won the trophy by default in 1884. Those events brought Walter Arnott (back row, fourth from left) his first Scottish Cup-winners' medal and Charles Campbell (back row, sixth from left) his seventh. The other trophy is the Glasgow Charity Cup.

restful of circumstances was Walter Arnott, later recognised as the greatest full-back of the age and famed for his long, controlled clearances.

In the same season Queen's Park came close to attaining a staggering double, for they reached the Final of the FA Cup. There they played Blackburn Rovers and, wounded by controversial refereeing, lost 2-1. The Glasgow club was hampered by the fact that the side fielded was not their strongest and by difficulties in travel arrangements. Some of the players could not leave Glasgow until the Friday evening, along with 500 of their supporters, and so reached London only on the morning of the match. Blackburn Rovers faced no such obstructions for they were, to all intents and purposes, a professional side. The financial inducements they could offer brought a sheen of excellence to the side in the form of Scottish players such as Fergie Suter and ex-Rangers men Hugh McIntyre and John Inglis, the latter having been imported only two months before the Final. Suter, an early example of the footballing soldier of fortune, had been a stone mason in Scotland but is said to have claimed that the hard English stone he worked on was so painful to hands and arms that he was forced to earn his living in football instead.

The SFA annual for 1880-81 speaks of 'the professional football "loafer", who does not work, but preys upon his fellow members', but hard words do not alter cases and the steady flow of talent to England increased with the legalisation of professionalism there in 1885. In that same year, Queen's Park again played Blackburn Rovers in the FA Cup Final but this time left London with the sour consolation that they had deserved no better than second prize. In 1887 the SFA forbade its clubs membership of other associations and the chance of an FA and Scottish Cup double disappeared.

Queen's Park now towered over every other club in Scotland but their campaign of 1884-85 was to emphasise that a Cup competition, capable as it is of being utterly re-shaped by the peculiarities of a single match, is more than the equal of any side. Having glided to the third round they were drawn to play away to Battlefield but their opponents agreed that the game be switched to Queen's Park's ground and so ensured that they took part in the first Scottish Cup-tie at Second Hampden. Queen's Park's confidence was understandably high and they fulfilled a fixture against Lancashire side Darwen in England on Thursday 23 October, only two days before the Cup-tie. Some of their players returned to Glasgow as late as the morning of the match.

There was little interest in the game and only a small crowd was present. Despite having an early lead cancelled out, Queen's Park must have been happy enough with the half-time scoreline of 1-1 for they knew that they would, on the resumption, be playing with the wind at their backs. The sheer quality of Battlefield's play reduced that fact to a meteorological nicety and they eventually recorded a 3-2 win which was met with incredulity throughout the city. It was, it should be said, a time of turmoil for the losers and four players, including Walter Arnott, briefly left them for Pollokshields Athletic that season.

Queen's Park protested the result on the grounds that some members of the Battlefield club were not properly registered. Prior to this, however, little attention had been paid to such matters, indeed it was quite normal for a player to be a member of more than one club. In 1880 Star of Leven lost a Cup-tie to Jamestown but protested that the referee, the Vale of Leven player Paton, was also a member of their conquerers. The SFA rejected the protest since no trace of his name was to be found in Jamestown's books. Paton, however, went too far when he played for Jamestown, along with three other Vale of Leven players, in a later tie. Jamestown were ejected and the teams they had beaten reinstated. In such an anarchic climate it was difficult for the SFA to control the sport adequately. The following opinion, to be found in the SFA annual for 1881-82 could only be met with derision: 'The referee is the "king's eye", and the king is the Scottish Football Association, to whom your remarks to the referee, should they savour at all of disrespect, will be most assuredly reported'. As the case of Paton indicates, it was not always so easy to tell whom one's referee owed allegiance to.

The defeat by Battlefield forged a curious link between the clubs and a number of their players later came to be associated with Queen's Park. William Sellar, a Queen's Park member even while with Battlefield, went on to play for them and attained the office of president in 1894.

A month after the Battlefield tie, a Cup shock of equally seismic force appeared to have occurred. On 15 November Rangers lost a tie at Arbroath but protested that the pitch was two feet short of the minimum fifty yards. 'Beaten on a back green,' said the furious telegram sent after the game. The SFA at first decided to let the result stand but, following renewed protests by Rangers, it was compelled to recognise its own rules and ordered a replay which the Glasgow club duly won 8-1. These events would appear to have been traumatic for Arbroath since they were to wait ninety years for their next 'success' against Rangers, a 3-2 win in a League match. The SFA decision allowed Rangers to put a figure to the cliché about being 'inches from disaster' — 24 to be precise.

Rangers' opponents in the sixth round were Renton, who had survived a more mundane protest about refereeing by St Mirren. The Glasgow side lost 5-3 on a strength-sapping, muddy field. In similar conditions Vale of Leven held off Thornliebank and, a further round having been negotiated, the two Dunbartonshire sides turned the Cup Final into a local derby.

Vale of Leven had not entirely replaced their former stars, indeed they summoned McIntyre from retirement for the Final, but quality was to be found in their ranks. Their full-back Forbes was both stylish and single-minded, the latter trait being evidenced by his retirement from Blackburn Rovers while at the peak of his powers, the subsequent establishment of a successful gentleman's outfitting business, and the final achievement of a directorship with the Blackburn side. For Renton, the greatest days lay in the future. Seven members of the side would later gain international honours. Among that number was Andrew Hannah, a full-back given to demonstrating his suppleness by kicking the crossbar.

In the first attempt at deciding matters both sides failed miserably to contrive a goal and the progress of the match offered the spectators little enough distraction from the by now traditional arctic Cup Final weather. Renton recorded an assertive 3-1 win the following week but few had been persuaded that these were the country's best teams. The splendidly gossipy sports paper, *The Scottish Umpire*, started in 1884 and depending on a growing public interest in the background to matches, was more interested in after-match events in Ancell's restaurant. There the humdrum spirit of goodwill was shattered by the aggrieved behaviour of two of the Vale of Leven players who insisted on directing 'caddish insults' towards the referee and linesman.

Renton's first Cup-winning team.

Events lapsed back to normality, however, and the Renton players returned to the bonfires, fireworks, and music of their celebrating village.

Queen's Park's progress to the 1886 Cup Final met with more opposition from the elements than from the abilities of their challengers. In the semi-final they played at a wintry Cathkin. By the interval three of the Third Lanark players had been rendered virtually inoperative by the cold while 'restoratives' were given to one of the Hampden men in an attempt to kick-start his system for the second half. Queen's Park would not agree to abandon the match because of fears over fixture congestion. They therefore took the field alone and ran the ball through the unattended goal to indicate their willingness to continue. The three thousand 'ardent souls' present surrounded the pavilion and 'howled and hissed out their displeasure'. Queen's Park were awarded the tie.

The victims in the Final were Renton, the trophy which had been on loan now being reclaimed by its rightful owners. While 1-0 ahead, Queen's Park were forced to endure a little pressure and the spectators were treated to 'a most exciting bully right in the mouth of the goal'. Gillespie, the former Rangers keeper, 'Rugby fashion, went under, but stuck to the ball, and although 20 eager plungers struggled over his prostrate body he eventually got into touch'. In the second half Kelso, an international right-half who eventually took the road South, equalised for Renton but that was no more than a fluctuation in the general trend and Queen's Park won 3-1. Both sides spent the evening at the Grand Theatre where a song alluding to the afternoon's contest was part of the musical entertainment. With this victory Charles Campbell gained his eighth winners' medal — the record for the competition to date. In winning five out of seven Scottish Cup competitions Queen's Park regained and perhaps, given the improving standards, even enhanced their early glory.

In the FA Cup semi-final of 1885 they met Nottingham Forest in a replay at the Merchiston ground in Edinburgh. A crowd of 10,000 watched the match and although so vast an attendance was a compliment to Queen's Park's fame it also indicated that Edinburgh might be more, in football terms, than just a satellite state.

Willie Groves, the crucial figure in both the 1887 competition and its aftermath

In the money

O N THE CARRIAGE used to transport Hibs from Waverley Station, where two thousand people had gathered, to the celebrations at St Mary's Street Hall in Edinburgh's Canongate there was a large banner. On one side it bore the orthodox message 'Welcome, Hibernians, winners of the Scottish Cup, 1886-87' and on the other the more striking legend 'God Save Ireland. Hurrah for the green jerseys'.

The club was begun by the poor Irish community in Edinburgh. The immigrants to Scotland, driven here by famine, were not easily assimilated into society and found themselves subject to a wide range of criticisms. They were generally feared as disease carriers (likely enough given the slums they were compelled to live in), robbers of jobs which rightly belonged to the natives, and worshippers in a superstitious creed. Little wonder that those people strove to establish their worth by identification with the fortunes of a football team.

In Hibs' early years the Catholic influence was all-pervasive. The first person to act as manager was a certain Canon Edward Hannan and the club signed only Catholics, indeed one player's chances of joining them disappeared when he betrayed an unfamiliarity with proper practice at Sunday Mass. This identity did not endear them to everyone in football and when, shortly after their formation, they applied to join the SFA they were rejected on the grounds that they were not really a Scottish club. Their eventual admission was a grudging one and they were not permitted to participate in the Scottish Cup in their first season of SFA membership. By the 1880s they had become a team of some substance and reached three successive Scottish Cup semi-finals in the seasons preceding 1886-87.

Hibs were a mercurial team whose fans accepted that the players' entertaining individuality was paid for in a fair measure of inconsistency. Despite that the feeling grew in the Autumn of 1886 that this was to be their year. The disquieting prospect of a tie away to Third Lanark proved to be less intimidating in reality and Hibs advanced to the semi-finals where a favourable draw gave them home advantage against Vale of Leven. The last minute postponement of that game, due to icy conditions, and the loss of a goal in the early stages of the tie when it was eventually played must have brought an excited Hibs side to the verge of panic. They retained faith in their own abilities, however, and eventually scored three times to gain a comfortable victory. A victory, incidentally, watched by a grateful press who had recently been given a table in the stand.

Paralleling Hibs' run to the Final were Dumbarton, whose opponents presented them with some unorthodox problems. In the fifth round, the Harp club of Dundee were drawn to play them at Boghead and decided to scratch from the competition on the understanding that Dumbarton would come to Dundee for a friendly match. Six thousand people eventually watched a 2-2 draw between the teams at East Dock Street, Dundee. This presented certain problems, for Harp had advertised the match locally as if it were the Cup-tie. What about the replay?

Harp asked Dumbarton to play again, promising that they would be allowed to win and offering a substantial guaranteed income. Dumbarton would have nothing to do with such deception and Harp were left to explain their behaviour to their supporters as best they could. In a curious epilogue to this, Dumbarton came to play Harp in a friendly at New Year 1887. On arrival they went to a hotel for lunch and only then discovered that their opponents had fixed a bizarre kick-off time of 12.15. It was too late to meet this and Dumbarton were forced to leave Dundee, having wasted a day and without the expected share of the gate money.

In the semi-final Hurlford insisted on the replay of their tie going ahead on a pitch at Boghead which both Dumbarton and the referee considered unplayable. As well as losing, the home side saw W Keir badly injured in a fall on the ice. The inevitable replay which the SFA ordered ended in a comfortable win for Dumbarton.

As if all this were not enough, they proved adept at perplexing themselves. Goalkeeper McAulay, an engineer, announced his intention of emigrating to Burma to take up a position with the Irrawaddy Steam Navigation Company and further revealed that he would be leaving on the day before the Final. Happily, he was persuaded to adopt a less damaging timetable and did play in the match.

The Final aroused great interest amongst a Hibs support which had, in any case, little taste for the phlegmatic approach. They had managed to bring to an early end, that season, a fixture against Airdrie in which one of their players was badly fouled even though the game was actually being played at Broomfield. In the Final with Dumbarton partisanship was, for the first time, clearly visible; the Hibs committee wore the team colours and their supporters put cards in the bands of their hats inscribed 'Hurry up, Hibs'.

Hampden was a distant venue for the Edinburgh fan since the Caledonian Railway's fine service (65 minutes at peak times) was only available to those who could spare 4s (20p) for a seat — the third class price. Many of the unemployed solved the problem by walking, leaving Edinburgh on the Thursday evening. They, presumably, were later amongst the two or three thousand who were thought to have climbed into the ground.

Hibs were a delicate side and even their strengths, such as the sinuous front running of Groves and Reynolds, had a fragile quality. In the defence the skills of McLaren had to overcome the restraints of his sportsmanlike, dispassionate personality. Dumbarton were aware of this and set out to play the match at the kind of hectic pace which diminishes the importance of individual players. Even late on the game was said to proceed while three or four men lay injured. Hibs, in their first Final, were flustered and deservedly went behind early in the second half. The would-be emigrant, McAulay, sabotaged his team's efforts by gifting Hibs the equaliser. The winner for the Edinburgh side came either from a great solo run by Groves or, depending on which newspaper one reads, from an offside position.

It is ironic that at their most glorious moment Hibs should go on to assist in their own destruction. Immediately after the match Hibs attended a banquet at St Mary's Hall, Calton, in the heart of the community in which Celtic were to be formed later the same year. Hibs even went on to open Celtic's ground in 1888 with a friendly against Cowlairs. The financial drawing power of Celtic enabled them, however, to acquire some of the Edinburgh side's best players

— Groves, McLaren, McKeown, and Gallacher. It is understandable that Hibs fans rioted when Celtic came in October 1888 to play the club they had ransacked. In truth, however, Celtic were simply mimicking Hibs' policies on a larger scale. The Edinburgh side had themselves, presumably through financial inducements, persuaded players of other clubs, notably those of Lugar Boswell, to join them. Such matters were to be clearly exposed shortly after the Final.

Robert Kelso. One third of the Renton half-back line in the club's triumphs of 1887-88. After a spell in England he returned to play for Dundee.

With the aid of a private detective named Morton the beaten semi-finalists, Vale of Leven, had been able to accuse Hibs of professionalism, claiming that the team regularly dined together at a hotel and that Groves, an apprentice stone mason, was grossly over-compensated for time lost through football activities. Accounts of the SFA's enquiry make it clear that Hibs were guilty. Although earning only 8 to 10s (50p) per week Groves received 3s 6d (17½p) compensation from the club for taking a Saturday morning off work and, indeed, he had not been seen at his place of employment in the three weeks prior to the Vale of Leven match. McFadden, the Hibs secretary, stated, with near-suicidal honesty, that Groves was a good player and that the club was disposed to be liberal to its footballers. Two votes were taken on the matter but on each occasion there was deadlock and it took the casting vote of the chairman, the SFA president R Browne of Queen's Park, to ensure that Hibs retained the Cup. Perhaps the committee could not face the confusion which would have entailed had Hibs been thrown out for all the teams they had beaten in the Cup would logically have had to be reinstated. Hibs were given the benefit of a non-existent, but administratively necessary, doubt.

It is right to consider what the extra cash meant to Groves. An interesting light is cast on this by an Edinburgh court case which took place in the same month he was preparing for the Vale of Leven match. Two children of Patrick Laven, a stone mason like Groves, and Mary Higgins (or Duffy) had been charged with begging from train passengers near the station. In their defence Laven said that he could exercise little parental control since he was required to work from morning till night while Higgins, rather contradicting her common law husband, claimed that the begging of the children was simply a necessary source of income. For Groves football may, at the time, have been no more than a means of rising a little way above subsistence level. The number for whom a football career led to the higher echelons of society was still small and Groves, when his career had ended, spent the remainder of his life drifting towards the murderous poverty in which he died at the age of thirty-eight.

For the Hibs fan in February 1887 there was a simple relief that the SFA had not repossessed his club's glory. One was to write in the SFA annual:

> 'Did not the representatives of the Vale of Leven hold up their hands and cry aloud: "These Hibernians are guilty of an unclean thing; they are not of the true field; beware of them for they are like unto 'wolves in sheep's clothing'; for did not our trusty *detective* discover that these Hibernians eat their dinners heartily, and some other body *paid for them?"* . . . And the chief scribe of the SFA did send a summons to the scribe of the Hibernians, and to that player of the Hibernians whose name reminds one of that place where lovers delight to meet, commanding them to appear before the Chief Priest and the scribes (and Pharisees) of the SFA to answer the charges made against them. And they appeared and were examined, and several of the scribes (AND PHARISEES) stood up and said these men are guilty, and other some said they were not guilty. And then the Chief Priest stood up and said they were not guilty, and so the Hibernians were acquitted.'

Hibs went out of business in 1891 and two years passed before they were restarted, this time on non-sectarian lines.

Renton, to their credit, managed to avoid a quick knockout in their fight against the lures of richer clubs, even if the eventual verdict was entirely predictable. In part this may have been due to failings in their opponents. An agent of a Lancashire club had taken Kelso and Hannah of Renton for drinks in an attempt to persuade them of the richer pickings to be had South of the border. His panicky search through numerous pockets which ended with his producing a lonely sixpence to pay for the beverages left the players sceptical about the prospects he outlined. Some of the Renton players retained an amused contempt for those who sought their services so feverishly and both McCall brothers rejected all blandishments and spent their entire careers with the club. One of the players was able to write of a New Year tour in England:

> Beds damp, blankets scarce, whisky bad . . . Might as well have taken a trip to Hades. McCall has been offered a public-house, a preaching tent, a hot potato cart, and a blushing young maiden thrown in to make life a pleasure, if he remains here. McCall has been praying over the offer all day. The blushing young maiden squints and that may settle him.

Renton entered the first round of the 1887-88 competition in fine fettle.

That first round saw the by-now expected event of Arbroath wreaking havoc on hapless Aberdonians. On 3 September 1887 they beat Orion 18-0, the margin of humiliation only being checked by a 'really brilliant goalkeeper'. Perhaps Orion (later to be one of three clubs who merged to form Aberdeen) had him to thank for the improvement on the 1886 Cup-tie scoreline of 20-0 to Arbroath. Worse still for the Granite City had been the results on 12 September 1885 when Harp (of Dundee) beat Aberdeen Rovers 35-0 while Arbroath were surpassing even that margin by beating Bon Accord 36-0. Bon Accord had unwisely chosen to waive their right to home advantage. By 17 December 1887 Arbroath's chastisement of their neighbours in numerous Cup-ties and friendlies that season had, it was reported, allowed forward Stephen Buick to accumulate 88 goals. In the early rounds of the competition Partick Thistle also made a substantial, if less readily quantifiable, impression by putting out Rangers.

The truly crucial struggles took place elsewhere and Renton announced their intentions by beating Queen's Park 4-1 in a friendly early in the season. The opposition most feared by the clubs that season, however, may well have been the SFA. Responding to the Willie Groves case, the ruling body decided to take action and peremptorily gave those clubs three days in which to submit their account books for scrutiny. Most of them managed to cobble together some plausible records and only Queen of the South Wanderers were found out and suspended. The SFA was beginning to adopt a more interventionist policy in its control of the sport. Earlier in the year they had prepared a carefully vetted referees list and had set fixed tariffs for those gentlemen's expenses. The referee would receive a minimum of 5s (25p) for journeys of up to five miles and a maximum of 17s 6d (87½p) if he had travelled between forty and fifty miles. In the event of a journey of such epic proportions as to be outwith the guidelines he was left to arrange suitable payment himself.

The Cup draw took Renton into forbidding territory — Paisley. An 8,000 crowd watched them play St Mirren at Westmarch and too many of them took up positions on the roof of the dressing room hut. The structure gave way and several people fell through and found themselves trapped inside since the door had been locked. Renton lost a two goal lead — 'Old men on the verge of the grave leaped and shrieked in their ecstasy of joy' — but eventually recovered to win 3-2.

Another Paisley side, Abercorn, reached the semi-finals and were drawn to play Cambuslang. Once again a large crowd attended, this time at Blackstoun Park, and football fever had palpably taken over the town. A placard at the pavilion read 'Go in and win, Abercorn'. The hat-band cards with the same message revealed a local tendency to hero-worship for they also bore a photo of Martin, the club captain. The ball had to be recovered from a frenzied dog which had run on and taken it before the game could begin and the players themselves, over-conscious of the crowd, betrayed signs of nerves. When the ball was crossed to James Buchanan of Cambuslang, standing virtually on the goal-line, he aimed a frantic swipe at it, missed altogether, and landed a resounding kick on the goalpost. The match resulted in a draw. Abercorn ended the replay with some players fighting amongst themselves and others disdaining to participate. They lost 10-1 — a record for a Scottish Cup semi-final.

Renton comfortably qualified for the Final and were 'full of running and as nimble as cats', having been trained by a redoubtable man named Peter Campbell. Above all, they seemed unified as a team, indeed it was said that goalkeeper Lindsay was a much reduced figure when, in internationals, he lacked the Renton full-backs Hannah and A McCall in front of him. The names of the half-back line — Kelso, Kelly and McKechnie — tended to trip off their fans' tongues together as if the players involved had no independent lives, existing only in relationship to each other. In the forward line McCallum, McNee and J McCall subjected opposition defences to a particularly stylish form of torment.

Cambuslang had enthusiasm and fitness to offer. John Buchanan revelled in his ability to run the heats and finals of quarter mile events at athletic meetings while also taking part in the four-a-side football tournaments which were popular at such gatherings. His side showed early resilience and one of their players even managed to burst the ball — a waste of 8s 6d (42½p) — in heading determinedly clear. In the long run, however, they were no real match for Renton who ended the game playing purely for the aesthetic pleasure of themselves and their supporters. 6-1 was the score — a margin of victory which is yet to be bettered in a Scottish Cup Final. The Renton fans, striving for new ways to express their ecstasy, unyoked the horses and drew their team's brake through the village themselves. And the season was not finished.

May of 1888 was a month of marvels in Glasgow. An international exhibition of true Victorian ebullience was opened by the Prince of Wales. The main building, with its red and yellow decor, cost £50,000; £20,000 had been spent on laying out the gardens at the Kelvingrove site; and an exact copy of the Bishop's Castle which had stood on the banks of the Molendinar was erected for use as a museum of Scottish antiquities. As well as the expected displays of art and machinery and foreign culture 'Henri Balleni, aeronaut' offered flights in his tethered balloon, a height of 1000 ft. being attained. In the first fifteen days 557,891 people saw the exhibition. For the true football fan, however, all that was nothing more than a distracting entertainment prior to the month's true event.

On 19 May Renton played FA Cup-holders West Bromwich Albion in a match which the Dunbartonshire side had unilaterally billed as the 'Championship of the World'. The English side were firmly defeated 4-1 but although Renton 'simply waltzed round their opponents like a cooper round a cask' the match was rather over-shadowed. That day a terrifying storm swept across Scotland and there was great destruction and some loss of life. Two boys, watching a company of volunteers at drill on Glasgow Green, had been killed by lightning and two adults elsewhere in the city met the same fate. As 'Heaven's artillery roared overhead' West Brom had pleaded that the match be abandoned but their opponents, 2-1 up at the time, would not hear of it. Renton, their reputation boosted still further by a victory over Preston North End in Walter Arnott's benefit match, affixed a sign to their pavilion which read 'Renton FC — Champions of the World'. In the entire season they had lost only one match. That text was more eulogy of the past than standard for the future as the day of the country clubs was, in reality, coming to a close since their rivals in the industrial centres had begun to tap their huge potential audience. Foremost in this process were Celtic, who had not stopped at Hibs players but also drew to their ranks Kelly and McCallum of Renton.

Sketches of the first match of the 1889 Final, won by Third Lanark

With a core of players from the 1887 and 1888 Cup-winners, Celtic were widely expected to appear in the Final of 1889. They did so, but only after appealing successfully against a defeat by Clyde. The game had ended in darkness and Celtic argued that this was a result of a delay caused by some of the Clyde players attempting to start the match in illegal footwear and being forced to change. It was a case for the SFA to resolve but, in the end, Celtic were permitted a replay and signalled their relief by winning 9-2.

The opponents in the Final were Third Lanark and enthusiasm for the sport touched new heights. Football by then had a sufficiently lengthy lineage to have acquired a certain romance, a fact indicated by the *Scottish Umpire's* publication of a love story based around it. Eleanor wishes to marry Jack, a Queen's Park player, but her father intends that the junior partner in his business become her husband. Fortunately Jack wins an international cap, so becoming a fit suitor, and all ends happily. A man, a woman, Hampden Park — what heart could remain untouched?

There was little pretence of amateurism and the intensive training of both teams for the Final was widely reported. Peter Campbell of Renton was said to have sent a tin of chicken broth to the Third Lanark camp. Renton used to explain the standards attained through illicit professionalism by saying that they trained their players on 'chicken bree' and the matter became a standing joke.

On the day of the match one supporter was observed on his way to the ground at 9.15 am and around seventeen thousand others followed his example at a more civilised hour. Several hundred climbed in despite the attempts of the police to discourage them by use of batons. Had the crowd known that the game they were to see was not a *bona fide* Cup Final it would have taken something more than lengths of wood to restore order. A snowstorm had made the pitch unplayable and the presidents of both clubs signed the following document which had been drawn up by a lawyer in attendance:

> Brown, on behalf of 3rd LRV FC, and Glass, on behalf of Celtic FC, agree to play a friendly game instead of a cup tie, the ground and weather being unsuitable. Both clubs concur in requesting the Association to fix a new date for the playing off of the final tie.

Somehow no-one thought to inform the crowd but it would not have been difficult to tell that something was amiss. The two sides warmed up by having a snowball fight while, in the game itself, some players temporarily ceased play to join the crowd in singing *Two Lovely Black Eyes.*

The stars were mostly on Celtic's side and Third Lanark had had their troubles. A Thomson played although not fully recovered from a fractured collar bone but another player, W Thomson, had recently sustained a knee injury which threatened to end his career. The latter problem, however, did little harm to the team. It allowed John Oswald to join his elder brother James in the side and he scored two of Third Lanark's goals in their 3-0 victory over Celtic. The match had been something of a fiasco with the thick carpet of snow preventing the ball from rolling across the surface. The SFA could have confirmed the official status of the match but chose to sanction a replay. The second match confirmed Celtic's feeling that the weather was mirroring their fortunes and they lost 2-1 although they had seemed on the verge of taking the initiative when they levelled the score at 1-1.

Third Lanark had been formed at a meeting of some regimental enthusiasts in the orderly room at Howard Street immediately after the first international in 1872. The journey to the pinnacle of the game had taken seventeen years and the successful campaign of 1888-89 had stretched through ten matches. It was understandable that their players sought to ensure regular celebrations. They chose four gentlemen to take turns at custody of the trophy on the understanding that each of them would invite the team to dinner.

For Celtic's impassioned support the disappointment was vast. Many sought the traditional solace. A newspaper quoted one fan climbing into a cab and announcing to the driver, 'Jist dhrive us to the nearest Public, me bhoy'. Less forgivably, John Glass, the Celtic president, churlishly refused to admit the superiority of Third Lanark over the two matches.

The first game of the Final had produced gate receipts of £920. The banns of marriage between football and commerce had been read and soon scrutiny of the bank balance would provide the best guide to a club's prospects. That new world would suit Celtic very well.

Arrivals and Departures

BEHIND CLOSED doors, in the early months of 1890, the blueprints of the future were being drawn. The major clubs were meeting to bring about the formation of a Scottish League, having become aware of the need to safeguard themselves against the financially damaging uncertainties of the Cup. A League allows for a fixed number of matches arranged months in advance and, as such, is close to the heart of any treasurer; such gentlemen preferring regular income to intermittent Cup windfalls.

At the AGM of 1890 the SFA rejected, by a margin of 105 to 31, a motion from the League cabal which required that the sixteen top clubs be exempted till the later stages of the Cup. The first League competition nonetheless began in 1890 and in 1891 the motion which had been defeated the year before was passed. The big clubs held only a trifling number of votes but their less significant brethren could not afford to disregard their wishes since there is always the danger that, under such provocation, UDI might be declared.

Queen's Park, staunch defenders of the amateur principle, remained aloof from the League until 1900 but continued to build for the future in their own inventive way. In 1889 they expanded their pavilion, installing for the use of members a gymnasium, the construction of which was supervised by one Mr Benson of Glasgow University, and a reading room. Queen's Park seem to have been the first to learn that a club must offer more to the public than the fortnightly opportunity to contract pneumonia on the terracing. All of £1100 was spent on the development. They were not, however, retiring from 'public life' and they dominated the Scottish Cup of 1889-90. In the fourth round they travelled North to beat Aberdeen (predecessors of the modern club) 13-1. The aristocratic ambience obviously proved too much for the sons of the 'Granite City' who revealed 'a large sprinkling of funk'. Behaving with wayward humility, their umpire even failed to appeal against two of the goals which were visibly off-side.

In Dunbartonshire the footballing tradition continued to be grittily upheld. Vale of Leven beat Third Lanark 5-0 in the semi-final, having been inspired by the presence in the crowd of ten of the Cup-winners of the 1870s. Contemplation of a glittering past was not the Vale's only resource, however, and the more mundane light cast by paraffin lamps allowed them to train three evenings a week. Away from the track their players followed their own individual regimens. Osborne neither smoked nor drank and took to his 'virtuous couch' at the regular time of nine o'clock. Wilson favoured eggflip and milk as a substantial part of his diet. More vaguely, and suspiciously, Whitelaw eschewed the 'virtuous couch', preferring to take the air around Loch Lomond at night. Around this time one of the committee members decided that a walk round his greenhouse should be part of the side's preparation but the introduction of these footballing bulls to his horticultural china shop proved unwise and several pots of choice leeks were knocked over.

The Final was to be held at Ibrox but the football fans awoke on the Saturday morning to find that the streets were clogged with the kind of dense, freezing fog which would have set Conan Doyle thinking of Holmes, Watson, 221B Baker Street, and evil goings-on in remote country houses. The inevitable call-off was slow in coming and, when it did, one frustrated supporter who felt the need to express his anger left a message for the football press at their table in the stand. In the frost which had formed on its surface he scratched the words 'DEAD HEADS'.

On the next day the weather almost led to a tragedy for one of the Queen's Park players. George Gillespie's mother was seriously ill and he made his way to Gourock in the hope that someone would row him across to the family home at Kilcreggan. The weather deterred the locals and Gillespie set out to make the crossing through the fog on his own. He was nearly capsized by a passing steamer which he heard but barely saw and later had to use his hat to bale out his leaking boat. The journey took two hours.

The following Friday SFA officials played a practice match on the pitch and decided the game could go ahead. A Glasgow printer, impressively enough, was able to run off posters that afternoon and the good news quickly spread.

The 'DEAD HEADS' had a new recruit to their ranks for the match since the *Glasgow Evening News* decided to carry an account by a lady reporter. The hand of the Victorian chauvinist can be detected in the fact that she was given a seat beside a window opening onto one of the dressing rooms. It was said that she had written her report in advance and anyone who reads the piece, lacking as it is in detail and filled with a twittering delight at being given access to the world of manly endeavour, is likely to believe it.

The application of fourteen cartloads of sand to the pitch to make it playable had been required and polo on camels would have been a more suitable contest. Vale of Leven took the lead through a goal by McLachlan and with a minute to go Osborne must have been toying with the idea of extending his self-imposed curfew that night or, who knows, giving the 'virtuous couch' a miss altogether. Then, the simplest of moves — a free-kick from Smellie turned in by Hamilton — levelled the score just as it appeared that the Queen's Park cause was lost.

The replay ran along similar lines with Vale of Leven taking a first half lead, through Bruce, and ranging nine of their team in front of their majestic custodian Wilson in an attempt to hold it. This time the ceaseless Queen's Park pressure brought a goal, again from Hamilton, with all of ten minutes to go, and a winner from Stewart in another five. A local auctioneer named Chisholm had put forward a gilt clock to be presented to the winners, but Queen's Park seem to have decided that it was no more than a lot which had never reached, and would never reach, its reserve price and, deciding that the Scottish Cup would suffice, politely refused it.

The AGM of the SFA which closed the season revealed that footballers were not always so ascetic when it came to 'gifts'. At the meeting a splendid balance of £2363 was announced but some members were perturbed by the cost of the dinner which had followed the recent international with England. The bill of £80 15s 6d (£80.77½) included a conspicuous £33 for champagne. An embarrassed Charles Campbell, who had risen high in the SFA by this time, admitted that he had, at the dinner, grown tired of being asked by waiters if more alcohol might be served and had unwisely said that those present were to be given everything they asked for.

On their way to the Final, Vale of Leven had knocked out Heart of

OUR ARTIST AT THE FINAL.

Cartoonist's view of the first, somewhat drab and wet, match of the 1890 Final.

Midlothian by a margin of 3-1. The subsequent protest by the Edinburgh club reads like the perennial grouch of the terracing tricked out in Sunday best:

> We protest the result of the tie as given by the referee, Mr Walker, because of his utter incapacity to act in such a responsible position owing to the physical infirmity of defective eyesight.

Hearts wisely decided to withdraw it but the irate referee insisted on submitting a medical certificate in his own defence to the SFA. A Vale of Leven representative noting that Hearts had queried two of his side's goals, asked why they did not go further and discount the third as well, so making themselves winners of the tie. Behind all this was the resentment of Hearts at the way in which they were regarded by those in the West, amongst whom they included the SFA establishment. Generally, and with some justification, the press dismissed them as a team adept at thrashing local rivals but always likely to falter when faced with a serious challenge.

Hearts understandably lacked little in resolve as they fought their way through the competition of 1890-91, determined to confound their critics. Their poor fortune in the draw compelled them to take the 'scenic route' to the Final and they played ties in Ayr, Greenock, Falkirk and Glasgow. Even a home tie with Methlan Park (of Dumbarton) in the third round was played at the unfamiliar venue of Meggatland in Edinburgh as part of the programme for an Electrical Exhibition. For Hearts, though, the Cup was much more than a sideshow and they moved impressively onwards. In the sixth round they were to make a notable, if unfortunate, contribution to the development of the game. While beating East Stirling, one of their players punched a dangerous ball out of the goalmouth, conceding, under the rules of the time, only a free-kick. A riot followed and the SFA seem to have been persuaded that the creation of the penalty kick was necessary and agreed to its introduction prior to season 1891-92. The scribes of the West, however, reckoned that nothing could save Hearts when they were drawn to play Third Lanark at Cathkin in the semi-final.

Everything about the day seemed designed to deter them and their support. Industrial action, or inaction, meant that the train took four hours to carry the fans to Glasgow and the engine was uncoupled at one point while it was supplied with water. The afternoon was stormy and four League matches were cancelled within a ten mile radius of Cathkin. Playing with the wind behind them Hearts established a 3-1 lead by the interval but Third Lanark suspected that they would claw that back in the second half. Hearts dispelled the illusion by scoring again immediately after the changeover and their opponents went meekly to defeat.

Hearts had, in 1884, been the first club to be punished for professionalism but the suspension imposed on the club and the players involved was swiftly lifted. They had had little option but to struggle to retain their better performers for they seem to have been particularly attractive to English scouts. Of the fifty-seven players listed as having gone South that year ten had been on their books. In the school of hard knocks, however, Hearts proved to be dux and fought back vigorously. Four of the players in the 1891 Cup team were from the West of Scotland. Scott had been brought from Cowlairs to form a classic left-wing partnership with Baird and their left-half Hill had been lured from Hampden by the offer of the captaincy.

Dumbarton, who were then on the way to sharing the first League championship with Rangers, not only reached the Cup Final but were also unbeaten that season. Earlier they had recorded a 3-1 win over Hearts and would go on to beat them 4-0 at Tynecastle later in the season. The pundits favoured them heavily and the Edinburgh club could not easily have taken issue with the judgement.

Dumbarton, once again finding the Final to be a foreign country whose language and customs they could not grasp, did not, in the event, manage to reach even moderate form. Hearts were little better but pertinently managed a goal through Davie Russell. This extraordinary player, later moved into the half-back line, had two spells with each of his first-class clubs — Preston North End, Hearts and Celtic — and won Cup and League-winners' medals with all three.

It had been an extremely assertive performance by the winners and their spirit was typified by forward Mason who played despite a long-standing and serious injury. He had consistently refused to see a doctor, presumably on the grounds that there is no ailment so severe that it cannot be worsened by the intervention of an experienced physician. When he finally went to Edinburgh's Royal Infirmary on the Monday after the Final astonishment was expressed that he was even able to play. The injury, indeed, effectively ended his career.

The Edinburgh club's joy was intoxicating and Hill accosted one of the 'Selecting Seven', as those who picked the international team were nicknamed, and informed him that he was looking forward to the game with England in

April. His wish was granted and he, and the white handkerchief he always carried, appeared in Scotland's 2-1 defeat. Hearts had made their point, and their victory, along with that of Hibs four years previously, firmly dispelled the idea that the Scottish Cup was only a regional competition trading under false pretences.

An infectious excitement surrounded the players as they made their way homewards. A newspaper report informs us that the driver of their train was allowed to enter their carriage to inspect the trophy but fails to tell who was left to control the vehicle. Hearts reached Edinburgh safely, though, and it is likely that the greatest health risk was being run by supporters flirting with alcoholic poisoning. When the result reached the capital, via the telegraph service, three cabmen abandoned their horses and carriages in Princes Street, knowing that the proprieties demanded their instant attendance in a nearby hostelry.

The much-travelled Davie Russell. His goal brought Hearts the Cup in 1891.

For Celtic supporters the Hearts victory was one more postponement of success they felt to be rightly theirs. The East End club had everything in their favour and had managed their affairs with spectacular single-mindedness. The team required a full-back? The response was to bring Dan Doyle from Everton. The means of doing so was, as with James Kelly, the offer of the tenancy of a pub, worth £5 a week in this case, and the payment of a set fee for each match played. Celtic's terms made the move a desirable one, for Doyle had earned only £3 a week with the professional Merseyside club — 'amateurism' with Celtic was a much more alluring prospect.

For a large number of people a Celtic match was the event around which the rest of the week revolved. A Nottingham Forest scout had written to Neilly McCallum arranging to meet him after a particular match in order that a move South might be discussed. McCallum's landlord, however, had opened the suspicious envelope and communicated its contents to the Celtic president. When the agent appeared at the appointed time he was captured by some Celtic representatives and warned off. Celtic had to go to great lengths even to ensure his safe departure for his presence had become widely known and a large crowd was toying with the idea of tarring and feathering him. Celtic only allowed the player to leave when his services were no longer required, at the end of season 1891-92. The case was not unique, for in the same year Johnny Madden was brought back from Yorkshire where he had gone to sign for Sheffield Wednesday, his whereabouts having been made known by a local priest who obviously regarded Celtic as his church's footballing order. A similar series of events took place when Sandy 'The Duke' McMahon attempted to sign for Nottingham Forest. Celtic staged something of a 'commando raid' into the South and persuaded him to return home, there to be cheered by a large crowd wondering at his restoration to his 'duchy'.

The heroic spirit which was to generate such deeds had, prior to season 1891-92, succeeded only in winning one paltry Glasgow Cup. More and more the club had come to resemble a triumph looking, with ever-increasing desperation, for a place to occur. Such frustration had pumped emotions higher and higher and the club's appearance in the 1892 Scottish Cup Final against the arch-representatives of the old order, Queen's Park, threw Glasgow into a state of hysterical excitement.

It was as well that an almost entirely reconstructed ground was available to contain such a game. Clubs had become aware that there was much profit to be made in hosting the major matches and Rangers invested large sums of money in making the Ibrox of the time a fit crucible for those heated encounters. Their new steel-structured stand, which had cost £1300, was available if not quite completed, in time for the match. A vast, record crowd of 40,000 — 12,000 decamping at Ibrox station alone — was attracted and the gates were opened at twelve o'clock, a full four hours before the game's scheduled kick-off.

With so much time to pass people were left to amuse themselves as best they could but one wonders what the popular reaction was to the man who whiled away the hours by giving vocal impersonations of the sound of the violin. Those who attempted to steal the money-bags from the pavilion might well have claimed, in mitigation, had they been caught, that the noise had temporarily parted them from their normal, law-abiding dispositions. The use of cudgel and water hose by the zealous guardians of the takings was, in any case, sufficient to drive them back to the company of such as the human violin.

The only concession to the past in a ground offering the services of its own telegraph office to the press was the absence of goal-nets. They had become widely used throughout the Scottish game in the first few months of the year but Queen's Park felt that they were likely to induce claustrophobia in goalkeepers and refused to have them. In May, 1893 they were made compulsory for semi-finals and Finals.

Perhaps it was a similar psychological ailment to that being risked by keepers which caused the crowd to spill over from the terracing and interfere with play

Johnny Campbell, scorer of two of Celtic's goals when they won their first Scottish Cup by beating Queen's Park 5-1 in 1892. After three years with Aston Villa he returned to the Glasgow club.

on the pitch. After twenty minutes the two captains informed the referee that they did not think the conditions suitable for a Final and did not wish it considered as such. Their request was later granted and Celtic's victory was immaterial. A newspaper of that day announced in its classified ads that both teams would be attending a performance of *A Midsummer Night's Dream* by Mr Benson's company. It seems appropriate that they should have left chilly Ibrox, having passed a frustrating afternoon, to watch a play in which conflicts are resolved by magic in the course of a balmy night.

Four weeks passed before the replay took place — the Saturdays being required for the trials and international with England — but that was only a deferment of sentence for Queen's Park.

The international was a cruel experience as England crushed Scotland 4-1 at Ibrox. Representatives of both Finalists tasted the lees of defeat and the elder statesmen of the two clubs, Arnott and Kelly, gave particularly poor accounts of themselves. The week which followed, however, saw their fortunes diverge widely. 'Erysipelas' (a fever with accompanying skin inflammation) affected Arnott, who had been absent from the first match of the Final and was in generally poor health at the time, and he missed the game. Illness also accounted for the other full-back, Smellie, and the finest division of the Queen's Park side was wiped out. The club worsened the position by drafting the forward Sellar into the position and he was to look every bit as lost as commonsense suggested he would.

Kelly, in contrast to Arnott, shrugged off the disappointment of the international and rolled back the years to give a dynamic and dominant performance in the replay. Injury had robbed his side of Johnny Madden, who was later to play a crucial role in the growth of football in Czechoslovakia, but the loss was far less grievous than those sustained by their opponents. Waddell opened the scoring for Queen's Park but Celtic treated that as no more than the report of the starter's pistol and spurted away from opponents who were made to look as if they might have been playing for their club since that first Final of 1874. A brace by both McMahon and Campbell and an o.g. gave them the five goals which swamped Queen's Park.

Near St Mary's Hall that night a vendor of ice-cream, the food of celebration, placed in his window a 'transparent picture' of Celtic with a sign giving the score and then, presumably, prepared himself for a sharp improvement in his 'cash flow' situation. Football was good business.

'Old money' was represented at the Final by Lord Kinnaird, a Scot who helped create football in England, but he left for his Perthshire estate at the interval. Accompanying him at the match was Professor Drummond, author of *Natural Law in the Spiritual World*. In more material attendance and, like the ice-cream magnate, conscious of the game's financial significance, were striking East End weavers with collection boxes.

A sober student of the newspapers, however, would rightly have concluded that 'real money' was still the property of a class which was in general only distantly aware of the game's existence. The first game of the Final had produced receipts of £1,800 but the *North British Daily Mail*, around this time, noted that a certain Mr Wells had ended a poor run by winning 150,000 francs (£6000) in one day at Monte Carlo.

Glory, and not vulgar finance, was sufficient incentive for Queen's Park the following year as they strove to erase painful memories. There was a crowd of 15,000 to watch them hold the home side to a 1-1 draw at Tynecastle in what was an exacting, if sloppy, match. The size of the crowd was particularly impressive for another 10,000 sports fans had imprudently gone to watch Scotland lose to Wales at rugby elsewhere in the city. In drawing, Queen's Park seem to have sensed that they had weathered the storm and sailed into clear water. At Hampden the following week they beat Hearts, whose poor fortune featured a thunderous own goal by Begbie, 5-2.

By rights they should have feared an encounter with Celtic in the Final but the younger club had lost something of its impetus in the early months of 1893. Since the previous year Celtic had been playing matches at their new ground. It was built on the site which they occupy to this day but few clubs would even have considered it. The land in question included a disused clay quarry, filled with water to a depth of forty feet in parts, and it took 100,000 cartloads of material simply to level it for building. The spirit of enterprise, however, was not steadily mirrored in actual performances.

Waddell (top) and Gulliland (bottom).
Queen's Park's right wing partnership when they last won the Cup in 1893.

On the Saturday before the Cup Final they lost to Rangers for the first time. This shock defeat was viewed by some as evidence of the debilitating effect of the Turkish baths which some of the side had been taking. The players trained hard and were kept at room temperature in the days which followed, causing many *aficionados* to believe that they would return to form on the big occasion.

The assembly point for Queen's Park players on the day of the match was St George's Place and for those who predict results by reference to signs and portents this was a poor choice. It was from there that the more significant funeral cortèges commonly left. The match gave those who harboured superstitious beliefs little inducement to adopt a more rational outlook since Celtic scored the only goal of the game through Towie.

Ibrox was a fine place to watch a game for Rangers had, by this time, completed their main stand (the takings from which were entirely theirs at such matches) and had built much-improved, banked terracing but, despite this, the fan was still exploited. For the second time in succession, and for the third time in five years, the spectators were to discover that what they took to be the Final was, in fact, nothing more than an expensive dress rehearsal. This time the players had agreed that it was not meet that they should contest a Final on so frozen a pitch and decided to play a friendly instead. It is not surprising that the Finalists in 1896 were to think it only honourable to agree in advance that no protests of any sort would be made.

Back came the fans, in significantly smaller numbers, a fortnight later. It was a wretched, stormy day and wind tore to tatters the League flag which Rangers had won two years previously. The game was reduced to a contest in which the teams discover who can best harness the wind. Queen's Park had that ally in the first half. The veteran Sellar gave them the lead but the fulcrum of the match was his second goal. It was claimed in the midst of a scrimmage and Celtic were insistent that the ball had not crossed the line. They evidently took the referee, the vice-president of the SFA, to be something of a retiring soul since they felt Sellar's cry of 'It's a goal, Mr Harrison, it's a goal' had unreasonably affected his judgement.

The incident brought to light the curious associations people make between football and politics. One Celtic fan is said to have announced philosophically that good refereeing and Home Rule for Ireland could not be expected in the one year. Gladstone's bill was, at the time, making its passage through the House of Commons and it was only in September that the Lords threw it out.

Two behind at the interval, Celtic might reasonably have hoped to level the score in the second half but the disputed goal seemed to break their concentration and a determined Queen's Park team — Willie Maley ended the match with a mouthful of blood and teeth — confined their opponents to a single score.

It was their last victory in the competition. In the same year professionalism was finally legalised in Scotland and Queen's Park became a glorious anomaly. Of the twenty Scottish Cup tournaments played in the era when clubs professed to share the amateur creed they had won ten.

Tales of two cities

A S THE NEW season began to take shape in September 1893, Swami
Vivekananda was addressing a 'Parliament of Religions' in Chicago on the
subject of Hinduism. His career as an enthusiastic and prolific communicator
increased the understanding and respectability of his faith throughout the
world. One of his most idiosyncratic and appealing traits was his passionate
espousal of football as a key to the development of the individual's body and
spirit. The game was truly making its way in the world, having touched even
the religion of the mysterious East.

Not that it was in any danger of drifting away from those who had nurtured
it in its first decades. In the decidedly less mysterious West (of Glasgow)
football compelled attention as Rangers began to make their mark in the Cup.

They had first to pass through a troubled adolescence, however, before
reaching the commanding position of their maturity. During 1882-83 their
president, George Goudie, had been required to loan £30 to the club to ensure
its existence for a little longer, and even at the end of the season the wolf was,
if not at the door, at least in the neighbourhood, with Rangers still owing £100.

The next few years brought recovery and Rangers took a share of the first
League Championship, with Dumbarton, in 1891. At the time the very worth
of that fledgling competition was proper material for discussion in the bars of
Scotland and success in it brought nods of approval rather than jigs of joy. It
was perhaps only in 1956, when the League Championship became the
passport to the European Cup, that it achieved its present eminence.
Previously, the Scottish Cup was invariably, indeed compulsively, described as
the sport's 'blue riband'.

Rangers had painstakingly assembled a team of great cohesion and fitness.
At full-back, Smith and Drummond appear to have been the templates used in
modelling the future, traditionally unyielding inheritors of those positions at
Ibrox. They were an enervating sight for opposing wingers and must have
made the bye-line seem like a mirage — visible but unattainable. That season,
their League form, despite such foundations, was curiously variable and they
were to finish only fourth. All of which made their Cup semi-final with
Queen's Park of even greater import.

Hopes that Queen's Park might buckle under the stress of playing at Ibrox
were swiftly dashed when they took the lead. David Boyd hit back for Rangers
but they could make no further improvement to the scoreline and were left to
ruminate on a visit to Hampden the following Saturday. Queen's Park's
previous opposition to goalnets may, the course of this match suggests, have
had something to do with a certain solicitude for goalkeeper Baird. He seems to
have been one of that breed who are picked on by inanimate objects and is said
to have been prevented from saving Boyd's effort by the fact that he had his
hand caught in the rigging at the time.

Queen's Park welcomed back Sellar and J Lambie to their side for the replay
and were close, the newspapers suggest, to making a further, truly
sensational, addition. It seemed for a time that C B Fry of Corinthians might be

prepared to play in the tie and the Cup would certainly have been honoured by his presence. His achievements over the course of his life are scarcely credible to the modern mind, attuned as it is to the idea of specialisation. A brilliant scholar, he equalled a world long jump record, played association football and cricket for England (captaining the latter), was a member of Southampton's side in the 1902 FA Cup Final, refused the offer of the throne of Albania (the wretched nation had to make do with Ahmed Bey Zogu/King Zog I), and served at the League of Nations. At rugby he was only good enough to play for Blackheath and the Barbarians. Physically, he resembled a Greek god.

Lucky Rangers, they would surely not have had the impiety to score against, never mind defeat, a team brandishing him. As it was the match was illumined only by run-of-the-mill daylight and Rangers opened the scoring through a long punt by Nicol Smith. Although Queen's Park equalised, the Ibrox side scored twice more, so winning their place in the Final.

Their success in the semi-final replay had been achieved without the assistance of Boyd who had been injured in a fall at work and was to miss the Final itself. Interestingly, he worked as a joiner in a shipyard and so was a member of the 'constituency' from which his club were always said to draw their support in the decades prior to the de-industrialisation of Clydeside.

It was the first 'Old Firm' Cup Final and Celtic must have suspected that the fates did not intend them to remember it with affection. The weekend before the match a storm had damaged the grand stand at Celtic Park and blown debris into Janefield cemetery. One press diarist responded to a wild rumour that Celtic players had been trapped at the ground and imagined the following events:

> Search party organised. McMahon carried from beneath the medicine chamber holding onto Blessington's whiskers. Maley affectionately embracing Cullen . . . Doyle lost and found.

There was little humour in it for Celtic and there was even talk of their being sued because of damage done to the graveyard.

Poor judgement increased Celtic's problems. Campbell was selected although he had not played for twelve weeks and despite the fact that Divers would have been a very able replacement. Willie Maley also turned out although he had been ill and weakened by diarrhoea.

Rain had fallen continuously in the thirty hours prior to the game and Rangers looked, from the early stages, more methodical and resilient and far more likely to thrive in the sapping conditions. Somewhat optimistically, hay seed was spread to improve the surface. Celtic's first half vigour proved to be no more than bluster. H McCreadie, Barker and McPherson all notched a goal apiece in the second half and even Maley's solitary counter for Celtic was tinged with dubiety.

The Final was now more of an occasion than ever and the country was in the habit of coming to town on the big day. *Scottish Sport* mocked yokels enraged, reasonably enough, at being given tickets marked 'Crosshill' when they had asked for Hampden and puzzled by the fact that Queen's Park was not the correct station to disembark for the ground owned by the club of the same name.

The Final had marked the conclusion of the twenty-first competition for the Scottish Cup and Rangers too had reached their majority. Even an eminent supporter such as Bailie Primrose, later to be Lord Provost of Glasgow and chairman of the club, could not forbear to give raucous acclaim. Later that day he apologised for the hoarseness of his voice to those at the Christian Institute about to attend to his illustrated talk, 'Rambles With A Camera'.

Cold figures also announced success. In 1889 Rangers' income for the season had been £1240. In 1894 it was £5227. A three guinea bonus (£3.15) for winning the Final was of personal significance to Nicol Smith and Robert Marshall who both married soon after.

Rangers' first Cup-winners, 1894

Rangers too were entering into new relationships in the months which followed the Cup victory. In April they signed Alec Smith who was to emerge as the greatest outside-left of the age and who possessed a seemingly inexhaustible array of trickery which included the ability to hit discomfiting, low crosses. He was a single-minded individual who had, as a virtual unknown, turned down an offer of £2 10s (£2.50) a week from Sunderland because they paid £3 a week to their first team regulars. Rangers met his terms and found they had tapped a deep well of loyalty. He created a club record for the time by staying at Ibrox through twenty-one seasons.

At the end of the year Neil Gibson signed and was introduced to the side. The half-back was an extremely confident crowd pleaser who found the display of his talents irresistible no matter the context. The effect on the life-expectancy of spectators occasioned by his habit of employing flicks and backheels in his own goalmouth must have been considerable. Within a few months of making his debut he had, despite that, established himself in the Scotland team. Cup glory, however, was denied these players in the short term as Rangers lost out to Hearts in the first round of the following season's competition.

St Bernard's, from Edinburgh, had hitherto seemed little more than an engaging side with an aptitude for enjoying life. The rigours of their social programme had once led to their centre-forward falling asleep during a match at Aldershot and their small bow-legged forward Barney Crossan had, on another occasion, amused himself by pretending to be an Oxford professor.

The club's greatest achievement in the sport itself had been to take third place in the First Division in 1894.

Their journey to the Cup Final of 1895 was, then, unexpected enough but the conditions under which it was made give it the air of the miraculous. They pieced a team together as they played their ties. Cleland joined them from the Minerva club at New Year and obligingly scored two goals on his debut. Change continued to be the order of the day and another signing, A Christie, injured his arm in a match at Cathkin and missed the Final.

Some of the other members of the team had arrived there under puzzling circumstances. Tom Robertson had been a member of the Queen's Park Cup side of 1893 but had drifted away from Hampden into a virtual retirement punctuated only by his Cup appearances for St Bernard's. Glasgow had been a rich vein for the club and four of those who appeared in the Final had once been Third Lanark players — Cleland, Crossan, Murdoch and Oswald. The latter, a restless individual, seemed at the turn of the year to be using matches as recreation between instalments of a dispute with the St Bernard's committee.

The club was also shaken by a tragic event in February of that year. Their full-back Cowan was struck a fearful blow on the head by the handle of a crane he was operating. *Scottish Sport*, revealing the widespread level of medical ignorance at the time, announced that he had fallen into an extremely deep sleep and expressed the hope that he would be much better when he wakened. It was almost certainly a coma for Cowan's death was announced only a fortnight later.

A saddened St Bernard's maintained their Cup campaign, continuing where team selection was concerned, to make it up as they went along. Combe Hall came from Blackburn Rovers to join them and appeared in their semi-final replay with Hearts. St Bernard's, against all expectations, had drawn 0-0 at Tynecastle, so ensuring a replay on their own ground. Hearts were unable to make much headway against a side grimly holding on to their vision of the Cup Final but it remained difficult to see how the underdogs could achieve more than simple resistance. A stroke of good fortune gave them the opportunity to consult the railway timetables for Glasgow. A long shot by George Murdoch seemed unlikely to take effect until it deflected off Hall's head and beat the Hearts keeper.

After knocking out Celtic, Dundee were favourites to reach the Final but they too 'received their quietus', their particular nemesis being Renton. The Dunbartonshire club were, by this time, in grave decline and drastic remedies such as amalgamation with Vale of Leven and Dumbarton or transportation to Glasgow cropped up frequently on the sports pages. Dundee felt confident of their ability to beat their Second Division opponents but their faith was to prove unfounded.

The tie threatened to turn into football's answer to the One Hundred Years' War. The match had been scheduled to take place at Carolina Port, Dundee, on 2 February but scuba gear would have been necessary to make a proper pitch inspection and the sides played a friendly instead. The tie itself was twice drawn when it did get underway and the teams met at Hampden for the second replay on 9th March. Dundee were unable to adapt to the muddy, cloying conditions on the day and persisted in trying to employ a short, passing game on a surface definitively unsuited for the purpose. Pragmatic Renton, aided by a display of clumsy goalkeeping, won 3-0.

REFEREE ROBERTSON IN THE NET.   PRYCE ATTEMPTS TO PULL SNEDDON THROUGH.   CLELAND HEADS A BEAUTY.

St Bernard's shock triumph in 1895

St Bernard's entered the Final in their customary disarray. Brady and Wilson did not recover from injuries in time, while the club captain, Baird, was ruled out because of an inflammation of the lungs. The team, with the exception of Tom Robertson, had spent the week at Burntisland, secluded both from their fans and the sight of a football. Robertson, who trained at Hampden, seems to have missed out on some vital discussion for he took the pitch wearing dark-blue shorts while the rest of the team wore white ones. His were deemed to clash with Renton's colours and he changed at half-time.

Their play, in contrast, displayed a great deal of co-ordination and Renton were made to appear ponderous and mechanical throughout. The Dunbarton-shire side never came to terms with the adroit tactics which saw Cleland loitering with intent on the left and making searing runs onto the ball played through the middle. He opened the scoring and three minutes later added a second. Renton's only reply came through Duncan.

The Edinburgh side could look forward to even greater standing in the capital and for Barney Crossan, in particular, there was the likelihood of still further reductions in his cost of living. A cobbler had once slashed his price from 4s 6d (22½p) to 1s 6d (7½p) on learning that the damaged guttapercha training shoes presented to him customarily adorned the feet of the esteemed forward.

St Bernard's made a stout defence of their title but the semi-final proved to be a precise reversal of the previous year's. This time it was a fortuitous goal for Hearts which determined the result. In the other semi-final Hibs beat Renton, so ensuring the only all-Edinburgh Final the competition has ever known. Sensibly, it was decided that the match should be played in Edinburgh and St Bernard's ground, Logie Green, was chosen. For the first, and only time to date, the Final was played outside Glasgow. But hard though the hosts worked to improve conditions there, Logie Green was widely suspected of being too small for such an event. Fearful for their safety, the Edinburgh public stayed away and the eventual attendance fell four thousand short of capacity.

That Final was also subject to problems of a more fundamental nature for it seemed until almost the last moment that it might have to be postponed. Renton had convincing evidence that Robertson of Hibs had breached the regulations governing professionals by playing for a small Lanarkshire side the previous summer and had in consequence been ineligible for the semi-final. Although losing their appeal before the SFA committee, Renton felt that the matter should not be allowed to rest and called a Special General Meeting of the game's ruling body to consider fresh evidence concerning what they claimed to be the perjured testimony of some of those who spoke at the first enquiry. Although the meeting refused to re-open the matter, Renton continued their fight.

The Dunbartonshire side seem to have felt that Stair's *The Institutions of the Laws of Scotland* should be considered the necessary companion to the SFA annual on every secretary's desk. In 1890 they had been suspended for playing against a professional side but had forced the SFA to reinstate them by instigating legal action which looked likely to succeed. Now, in 1896, they sought an interdict against the playing of the Cup Final and their case was heard by Lord Low in the Court of Session on the day before the tie. The judge, however, refused to prevent the playing of the Final because the Renton evidence, as presented to him, did not demonstrate that the SFA had acted wrongly. Renton waved goodbye to £104 of legal fees and attention turned to the healthier strife of the football field.

Hibs, in their second incarnation, had swiftly made their way back to the centre stage in the game. They had finished top of the Second Division in both 1894 and 1895 although they only gained promotion after the second success. It should be explained that promotion was determined by the votes of the First Division clubs and the automatic system which operates today was only introduced in 1921. Second Division success was not the key to the door but simply a brisk knock on it which might or might not be answered. In 1896, however, Hibs completed their re-establishment by finishing third in the First Division.

Although their fixture at Tynecastle had been lost in September of that season, Hibs claimed a division of the spoils by winning at Easter Road three months later. Despite due consideration of those results, the members of that élite who have, as a favoured form of isometrics, the exercise of keeping their faces straight while impoverishing bookmakers would still have been quietly betting on Hearts. Few clubs have ever been able to show the adaptability they did in the first half of the 1890s.

Hearts had wasted little time in regretting the rootlessness of the new breed of professional footballer. Only four players in their 1896 side had played in the Final five years previously, and of those Russell had spent two of the intervening seasons in England and was now a centre-half, while Baird had side-stepped from outside-left to inside-right. But Hearts were not disconcerted. In filling the vacancies they displayed a dexterity which would have had them hailed as colleagues by the showmen who work the three shell trick in the 'bunko booths'.

At full-back Mirk had been brought from Paisley; Hogg, from Mossend, completed the country's most authoritative half-back line; and John Walker had joined the club from Armadale. The centre-forward was Michael, scorer of the semi-final's only goal, but his style was more controversial than that of the other famous names in the side. An early historian of the club says of him, 'He would have charged a stone wall and risen up, rubbing his cranium. Then, spying the ball at a distance, he would have gone for it as a terrier goes for a rat.' An approving nod would certainly have been forthcoming from the modern day manager who was heard to laud one of his players for 'going in where the noses get broke'. On his off-days, however, all of Michael's aggression resulted only in a string of fouls and the vexed fan would begin to wonder if he might not be some sort of double agent. For all that, he consistently exuded a sense of menace and Hearts' Cup-tie astringency depended on it.

The Hibs team selection was, in comparison, ill-conceived. Willie Groves had returned to the club and a good performance in the early stages of the semi-final had misled a management which should have noticed instead the tiredness which latterly saw him slip back into an anonymous midfield position. The twists and surprising feints were still evident in his play but although still in his twenties his body could no longer carry them out at such pace and the tricks were, accordingly, no longer conclusive. Once he would have gone clear of a defender, but now the trailing leg just made contact with the ball and ended the move he would earlier have completed. A gruelling career had caught up with him and he was even rumoured to be suffering from a heart condition. There was to be no 'Indian summer' for him in the Final.

At the beginning of the match Hearts too seemed to find it difficult to accomplish the ploys they intended. Nervousness in their play meant that they took one touch too many to control the ball and consequently found themselves struggling for space. The impression was given that they had mysteriously been placed on a pitch drastically narrower than regulation size. Helping them through this spell, however, was the soothing thought that they were 1-0 ahead, a Baird free-kick after only three minutes having gone in off a defender.

Hearts v Hibs at Logie Green, Edinburgh in 1896. The only Final to have been played outwith Glasgow.

Eventually the pitch assumed its normal girth and Begbie, Russell and Hogg, with a blend of attacking skill and defensive capability, put their half out of bounds to the opposition. Walker responded to their influence by scoring once and creating another for Michael. The consolation goal for Hibs suggested only that McCartney and Mirk had grown forgetful concerning the defensive duties expected of backs.

The Easter Road side, despite the defeat, at least had the consolation of knowing that they had once again placed their name amongst the country's serious contenders for honours. They had truly risen from the grave in 1893 and were not to disappear, like so many Hammer vampires, when faced with prolonged exposure to the light of day.

In Glasgow, football clubs would have been more irritated by the existence of a Cup Final contested by Edinburgh sides than interested in its outcome. On the day of the Cup Final, Hampden was even reduced to being the venue for Scotland's 11-0 rugby victory over England. The errant trophy was soon persuaded to return 'home', and was then confined there for four seasons, presumably to teach it a lesson.

The first to take their turn at custody were Rangers. Their triumph was the result of the kind of clear thinking which saw Thomas 'The Boy' Low installed at outside-right during season 1896-97. As far as full-backs were concerned he had an unhelpful habit of skipping wide of tackles which would, had they made contact, have reduced him to a more sedentary pace. While on trial with Blackburn Rovers in October 1896 he had given Drummond of Rangers an extremely disquieting ninety minutes. Scything through the problem presented by this, Rangers cheekily signed him, ensuring that the number of those who troubled the full-back did not increase. Low did not develop quite as expected but in the short term he enjoyed a meteoric rise. He played against Ireland in March 1897 and so added a cap to the Cup-winners' medal he had won the previous week.

The route to the Final had included only one game to seriously concern Rangers. Dundee were widely regarded as the coming side in Scottish football, having acquired ready-made experience in the form of Kelso, who had appeared in two Cup Finals with Renton, to place beside a considerable number of able performers. Playing the quarter-final at Dundee's waterside Carolina Port ground, Rangers failed to find the net in the first half and turned round to face a howling wind knowing that the Cup might well be on the point of slipping away from them. Strangely, it was everyday logic that was blown away as Rangers were seized by a welcome goal-scoring mania which produced a 4-0 lead in a hectic seven minute spell.

The semi-final — a 7-2 victory over Morton — was noteworthy only for the fact that the Greenock side included at right-half a player who, when he stepped back, would place himself in the forefront of the domestic and international game. A couple of months later Harry Rennie began to play in goals and so properly embarked on a career which saw him play with Hearts, Hibs, Rangers and Kilmarnock and win thirteen caps.

The Ibrox side seemed barely able to stifle a yawn at the prospect of a Cup Final against Dumbarton, who were to finish bottom of that season's Second Division. Centre-forward James Oswald was allowed to play, and score, for Scotland against Wales on the same day. The absence of that experienced attacker, who had joined Rangers shortly after St Bernard's Cup win, blunted the side's attacking edge not at all. With a minimum of effort a 2-0 lead was established through Miller and Hyslop but Rangers' idyll was briefly interrupted by a Dumbarton goal. W Speedie, whose younger brother Finlay was later to play for the Glasgow side, celebrated by joyously shaking the hand of Rangers' full-back Drummond. Perhaps Speedie was acting out of some form of prescience for Rangers soon had much cause for real celebration. In

Neil Gibson, Rangers' right-half in their comfortable Cup success of 1897

the space of five minutes they scored a further three goals, so threatening the record margin set up in 1888.

At Ibrox the quest for improvement continued apace and they made one of their best signings in the summer following the Cup success. R C Hamilton had come to Glasgow to study at the University and had played for a season with Queen's Park before joining Rangers. He was very much the finished article and scored two goals in a debut which took place at the opening of Partick Thistle's Meadowside ground. His height gave him the smooth pace of the classic sprinter and he was able to capitalise on the room created by use of a crashing right-foot shot which seemed to have strayed from some schoolboy's daydream of glory.

The hours before a Final are said to pass slowly for those about to take part in it but that was one problem Hamilton did not have to face in 1898. It may be assumed that he felt fully absorbed by the three hour examination he had to sit on the morning of the match.

On their way to the 1898 Final the club had also faced a severe examination. In the first match of the semi-final Third Lanark had held the lead and, aided by two penalty misses, were once again in a commanding position in the replay. The fact that both games were nonetheless drawn disgusted the Cathkin side and a 3-0 defeat in the third match left them to repent their leniency at leisure.

The Final of 1898 was a great deal less exacting, especially so for Nicol Smith who entered the fray with all the freshness of a man who had not played in a single Cup-tie that season. He replaced Crawford, who had filled the right-back position in all the games Smith missed. Kilmarnock had won the Qualifying Cup in 1896-97 (it had been introduced the season before that to add point to the scramble for entry to the Cup itself), and would be promoted to the First Division in 1899 but their achievements were minor when compared to those of their exalted opponents. They were, however, capable of cramping Rangers' style and the Ibrox side were roundly castigated for a truly wretched performance which brought them only a 2-0 victory. A certain chumminess between the sides may have been responsible for defusing the confrontation. Sixteen of the players were from Ayrshire, Mitchell and J McPherson of Rangers had been with Kilmarnock, and McCallan and D McPherson had travelled the same road in the opposite direction. The opposing McPhersons, incidentally, were brothers.

A lacklustre victory would, when soberly considered, have been viewed by the club's support as infinitely superior to the kind of experience Celtic had endured the year before.

On 9 January 1897 Celtic travelled to play Arthurlie, a non-League side, at Dunterlie Park. They had refused their opponents' offer of switching the tie to Celtic Park, presumably because Arthurlie would have expected, as was common till World War Two, compensation for doing so. To say that the pitch was uneven would be to understate matters enormously; its astonishing collection of humps and hollows might have generated employment for a whole team of ordnance survey cartographers.

Celtic's performance was diabolical. Hannigan scored a glorious hat-trick and his side were never behind. Only a late, disputed goal by Celtic narrowed the margin to 4-2. The Arthurlie victory ranks with Battlefield's over Queen's Park in 1884 and Berwick's over Rangers in 1967 among the competition's greatest shocks.

Prior to the match a local draper named Andrew Cairnduff had offered to give each member of the Barrhead side a new hat if they won. He was as good as his word and had the date and result recorded on the inside of each of them. They were treasured possessions and Sandy Tait, a successful heavyweight boxer as well as a footballer, took his with him to Canada when he emigrated.

Andrew Cairnduff wasn't the only one in the market for new purchases as Celtic began to cast a critical eye over the situation within the club. It had been clear for some time that their hopes were being impaired by tensions and resentments. In November 1896 Meechan, Battles and Divers refused to play in a match with Hibs unless a journalist whose newspaper's reports they objected to was removed from the press box. Rather than give in, Celtic began the match with only ten men. The players in question were suspended and were not in the team which lost to Arthurlie. Disciplinary action was also taken after the defeat in Barrhead. Doyle, who had failed to turn up for the match, was fined £5 and others found their wages reduced.

Some of the malcontents were unloaded and the club followed its traditional pattern by turning to England for replacements in the summer of 1897. Campbell and Reynolds returned from Aston Villa and Welford came from the same source, Orr and Henderson were parted from Preston North End, and Allan and Goldie left Liverpool and Everton respectively. 'When is this migration of Villa players to the crack Celtic club going to cease?' lamented Birmingham's *Sports Argus* when Celtic extracted yet another player from that nursery the following season. The situation becomes even more astonishing when one recalls that Aston Villa won both the League and Cup in 1897. Welford had no cause to regret the move for he later became the first, and so far only, Englishman to hold FA and Scottish Cup-winners' medals.

As Celtic set their sights on the 1899 Final they were under the command of Willie Maley who had become the club's first manager in 1897. The effects of his influence were slow to be noticed in an era which thought little of managers and it was only his great successes of the 1900s which fixed him firmly in the minds of the public. Celtic, however, seemed more settled from the moment he took charge.

It was a comfortable passage to the Final for them and their 'replay' with Queen's Park in the third round was the result of bad light bringing a premature end to the first match rather than of any severity of challenge. The fact that Rangers also reached the competition's final stage ensured that Celtic could not win the Cup without facing at least one taxing game.

The encounter was predictably dominated by nerves and the pattern of play was dictated by the behaviour of defenders. They took an unfortunately reductive view of their duties and confined themselves to extraditing the ball from their half in as basic a manner as could be contrived. Those who believed in such pastimes as passing or running with the ball were made to look entirely superfluous to requirements. Celtic's left-winger Bell, in particular, was placed firmly on the margins of the game by a stern challenge from Nicol Smith. He spent the remainder of the match limping and sporting a bandage round his knee. Since the result was impossible to predict, however, the crowd of 25,000 remained entirely occupied by the spectacle.

In Old Firm games the crucial moments always seem to be haunted by the ghosts of events which might just as easily have taken place. In this case Rangers felt seriously aggrieved at having a goal chalked off just over ten minutes into the second half. From the free-kick Celtic broke swiftly and gained a corner. Unusually for a man of such delicate touch Sandy McMahon was an extremely dangerous player when the ball was in the air. Rangers' concentration seemed to have been broken by the referee's decision and McMahon was allowed to meet the corner and plant a firm header into the net. With a quarter of an hour remaining Hodge ran away from the waving palms of Rangers players claiming off-side and confirmed the Cup's destination.

1900. R S McColl of Queen's Park dashes through at Celtic keeper McArthur.
The stand (extreme left) at the new Ibrox was not completed in time for the Final.

The chance for revenge came in the semi-final of 1900 at Ibrox the following season. When the match's oscillations died down Celtic had emerged with a 2-2 draw. The nerve of Campbell had been vital to Celtic for it was he who levelled the score at 1-1 early in the second half. The goal came from the spot and an attacker had, prior to the rule change in 1929, to face some extremely bizarre attempts to unsettle him. Goalkeepers were allowed to move before the kick was taken and Dickie was said to be executing a savage dance as Campbell ran up.

The match took place in front of a crowd whose mind may well have been fixed on a more grievous conflict. In describing a period of Celtic dominance, one reporter wrote, 'McArthur's citadel looked as distant as Bloemfontein'. After several months of the Boer War, Britain had only just succeeded in taking that town. The news of the fighting was particularly important to Glasgow for many members of the Empire's 'second city' were amongst the Scots who constituted ten percent of the British forces.

Celtic easily won the replay and faced their old rivals Queen's Park in the Final. The Crosshill club was no longer a major force but Celtic would have been extremely wary of centre-forward R S McColl, who would soon move on to Newcastle and whose name is perpetuated in the business he started. 'Toffee Bob', as he was universally known in the days after the establishment of his sweet shops, scored a hat-trick at Celtic Park in Scotland's 4-1 victory over England the week before the 1900 Cup Final. That same Spring the readers of *The Scottish Referee* rated him the country's most popular player; he received more than three times as many votes as the runner-up, Alec Smith.

It was fitting that the SFA, standing as they were on the verge of the new century, should choose a new ground at which to play the match. The new Ibrox, on the site occupied today, had only been opened at the very end of 1899 and vied with Celtic Park as the country's most impressive venue. The choice of that ground meant that the subway was, for the first time, the obvious means of travel to a major match in Glasgow. It had taken a little time to establish its credibility. On its first day of operation, in December 1896, the inner circle was closed after a car went off the rails in Buchanan Street. Service continued on the outer circle for the rest of the day, until it too was closed following a collision beneath the Clyde. More than a month passed before a service of any sort was resumed. In 1900 it cost 1d ($\frac{1}{2}$p) for trips of up to four stations and 2d (1p) for longer journeys.

Queen's Park were seriously disadvantaged in terms of ability and, as in 1892, the fact that they scored the first goal meant little. Like a warm-up comedian, it did little more than tune the audience's attention for the main event. Celtic built a 3-1 lead and were never caught although Queen's Park struggled proudly. The 4-3 victory reads more excitingly in the record books than it appeared to the watching supporters.

The last Final of the nineteenth century had been played with no possibility of the Cup leaving Glasgow. The upheavals of two decades were now clearly visible in the Scottish Cup's roll of honour. It had been twelve years since the trophy had slipped from the hands of those clubs in the country's 'two capitals' — Glasgow and Edinburgh. More and more, success for the outsiders would be a triumph over not only ninety minutes of accomplished opposition but also the forces of population and finance.

Eminent Edwardians

IN GLASGOW, shortly after 7 pm on the evening of 22 January 1901, the shows were stopped at the Royal, Royalty, Grand and Princess's theatres and, following announcements from the stage, the audiences quietly dispersed and made their way home. In Edinburgh the bells of St Mary's Episcopal Cathedral and the other city churches rang out. In Aberdeen the local Liberal Association adjourned its annual meeting and joined the awestruck crowds on Union Street. In Osborne House, at 6.30 pm, surrounded by her children, Queen Victoria had died.

The funeral service took place on Saturday 2 February and the sense of being suddenly becalmed which the nation was experiencing seemed on that day to communicate itself to the horses whose duty it was to draw the gun carriage bearing the coffin in the cortège from Windsor Castle to St George's Chapel. On no account could they be persuaded to move and since the normal methods used in such circumstances would have been inappropriate to the occasion they were unyoked. Their places between the shafts were taken by a group of sailors who spliced the traces and pulled the carriage themselves. In Scotland, the preservation of the sense of solemnity was aided by the abandonment of the day's football programme.

A week later matters resumed their normal course and several of the second round ties in the Scottish Cup were played. To the new century, however, had been added a new monarch, Edward VII, and, as if prompted by this, the nation as a whole was beginning to enter years of unprecedented change. On 9 February the secretary of the SFA, J K McDowall, was seated in one of the principal agents in the restructuring of society — the motor car.

It was taking him from Glasgow to Edinburgh for the tie between Hearts and Queen's Park. He seems to have arrived there on time but his fellow citizens experienced rather more difficulty in getting to the ground. At the last minute the Queen's Park players finally managed to force their way through the crowd and made their way across the pitch to change in the pavilion. Eventually, they re-emerged and, wearing similar black armbands to those of their opponents, began the match in front of a large and excited audience.

The preceding months had been ones of dramatic change for Hearts but the underlying reasons were somewhat prosaic. They had begun the season ill-prepared, having just parted company with several of the 'old guard', and had finished second bottom of the League (that competition having, in this case, just come to a close as the Cup got into its swing). Houston and Bell were purchased from St Bernard's as they attempted to rebuild their forward line but the truly crucial addition to the side for the important Cup-ties came from within the club. After a period of injury the great Bobby Walker made his return.

A month after the 1896 Cup victory Hearts had spotted Walker playing for the Scottish juniors against an England side at Birmingham. By the turn of the century the inside-forward had convinced the nation that he was one of the greatest talents the game ever had, or would ever know.

Those who are proficient in juggling explain that the knack lies in the individual's sense of time. Most who attempt it have the impression that they are involved in a frantic and hopeless race to keep the objects in the air but the skilled juggler feels even fractions of a second to be lengthy periods. No sense of haste disrupts his rhythm because he knows in his bones that a single moment is ample for him to release one object before catching the next. Excitement is infectious but Walker, like a juggler, performed as if he had been inoculated at birth and could never be rushed out of his normal style. For him there was always time to control the ball, peruse the available options, and play the appropriate, frequently killing, pass.

Hearts beat Queen's Park (although they themselves had been soundly beaten at Hampden Park only three weeks before) and had the chance to unwind following that by comfortably ejecting Port Glasgow Athletic in the next round. The draw for the semi-finals gave them home advantage against local rivals Hibs and the problems regarding access to the ground were once again apparent. A crowd of 19,000 generated record receipts for an Edinburgh match where the normal admission charge of 6d (2½p) was being made and Harry Rennie, by this time the Hibs goalkeeper, had to climb over the palings to make sure that his skills were at the club's service. Hearts only managed to beat him once, through an irresistible goal by Mark Bell, and since Hibs themselves managed to score, Easter Road was also given the chance to face the happy problems occasioned by a large crowd. The 18,000 who attended, indeed, caused a section of the fencing to collapse.

For the replay Hearts pushed forward Charles Thomson, naturally a defender and ideally a centre-half, whose build made him look like a scale model of a particularly daunting mountain range. His bone-shuddering presence made every Hearts attack a matter for serious concern. The game's key goal, however, was a beautiful cameo of Walker's ability. With the score at 1-0 to Hearts, a piece of adept dribbling took him into the danger area. An alarmed Glen made a lunge at him but Walker had anticipated the move and turned it to advantage by lobbing the ball over the defender's head, stepping round him, and sending a curling shot beyond Rennie. Hearts won 2-1 and so entered the Final, where they were to meet Celtic.

On the face of it, Celtic should have been daunting for they had not lost a single goal in that season's competition and had the chance of registering a hat-trick of Cup Final wins. Hearts had nine players making their debut in a Final; the two exceptions were Hogg and, football's equivalent of the Scarlet Pimpernel, Baird, who now popped up in the right-back berth. Celtic included two ex-Hearts players — Dave Russell and Barney Battles — whose presence might have been expected to depress the club which had lost them.

Hearts, however, had youth and pace to offer against a side which included some whose experience was on the point of disintegrating into infirmity. With impressive practicality they dropped Clark, an accomplished forward, in order to create a better balance of pace and strength in the attack. Porteous, although not much admired by the press, was included because of the power of his shooting. Hearts meant business.

In Celtic's first real attack Philip, in goal, could only push out a McMahon shot but the ball ran to Walker, who dispelled thoughts of his club's limitations by coolly side-stepping the on-rushing Orr. Soon after, a Walker shot spun off McArthur's hands and into the net — the match was played on a greasy

Bobby Walker
scorer of Hearts' first goal in the 1901 Final.

Harry Rennie
Hibs keeper who played in the 1902 Final.

surface — and fears of inferiority turned to visions of triumph. Although Celtic equalised, Hearts re-established themselves by scoring after another mistake by the Celtic keeper led to a Davidson own goal. Davidson had been unwisely restored to the side for the Final in place of Storrier even though he had suffered 'a slight touch of concussion of the brain' in the semi-final with St Mirren. Hearts felt that they were near to closing Celtic out and mounted a ferocious assault at the beginning of the second half. Walker gathered his strength and launched into an elusive run which saw the ranks of Celtic jerseys in front of him dwindle quickly away. As Battles made a desperate attempt to stop him, he slipped the ball through to Thomson who ably converted the master's genius into a 3-1 lead. But it was not over.

Furiously, Celtic pushed Hearts back into their penalty area and when McMahon, following McOustra's second goal of the game, performed his party piece by heading in from a corner it appeared that Celtic had both levelled the score and brought the Edinburgh side to heel.

Perhaps Celtic felt they had earned the right to pause and catch their breath for they briefly dropped their guard and allowed Hearts the game's seventh and last goal. Once again McArthur failed to hold the ball and the sturdy Bell, who could run the 100 yards in even time, was first to the scene and joyously smashed the ball into the net.

Important though Bell's pace was, the most telling factor was pinpointed, again and again, on the way home. 'Bobby,' said Thomson, 'you're the best player in Europe.' The euphoria of the occasion had no doubt set him babbling but one suspects that he would, even on a wet Monday, have persisted in that assessment of Walker.

The bid to retain the trophy was unsuccessful when Hearts were defeated by Celtic in the third round of the 1902 competition and others were left to experience the heightened emotions of the Cup's final stages. Appointed to cope with and restrain that excitement were, as always, the referees. Amongst the many problems they faced was a widespread ignorance of the rules of the game. In the manner of a problem page the *Scottish Referee* offered a question and answer service to its readers and the difficulties which the fans were experiencing with the laws of the game were not always of a very sophisticated order:

Q If a player in an off-side position lets the ball alone, but plays an opponent, should he be pulled up for off-side?

A Certainly, a player in such a position can neither play the ball or an opponent.

The answer, rather worryingly, seems to imply that you are entitled to lay about an opponent provided you are not off-side. In such a climate it was certain that the referee's life would not be a happy one. The *Scottish Referee* noted that one such official had to be spirited out of the ground in a clothes hamper to escape the baying hordes. A cartoon and the following verse accompanied the story:

Lift him up tenderly, cart him with care,
Do not expose him too much to the air;
The crowd is awaiting inflated with ire,
Eager to order a funeral pyre.

The referees themselves could of course be incompetent. On 1 January 1902 Sandy McMahon was sent off for kicking the official after a controversial judgement. The Celtic forward escaped further punishment, however, because the referee failed to post his report to the SFA until five days later. By the time the ruling body received it, too much time had elapsed and no action could be taken.

Amazingly, the same referee, Mr Nisbet, was chosen to officiate at the semi-final between Rangers and Hibs at Ibrox and he appears to have had an undue effect on the outcome. He ignored the very reasonable claims for off-side by Rangers and allowed a goal by ex-Celtic player Divers to stand. An enraged and unsettled Rangers then conceded a penalty and although Divers missed it, Hibs' control of the game was established. McCartney later stole in behind Drummond, who seemed mesmerised by the danger Divers posed, to score the second. Shortly afterwards McCartney had the misfortune to break his leg as he made a hectic attempt to score his side's third and so the man who had started the month by winning his first international cap had lost his only chance of a Cup-winners' medal with the club.

Before the Final could take place the sport was shaken from top to bottom by the Ibrox disaster. Shortly after the beginning of the international match with England on 5 April 1902, a section of the newly-constructed west terracing measuring about 80 feet by 13 feet collapsed and 25 people fell to their deaths. The structure was flimsily composed of wood and had no supporting banking of earth beneath it. The medical resources at the ground were scant and the fragments of wood were used as splints while the longer lengths of plank were employed as stretchers. Almost 600 people would later receive compensation for injuries received. In the month prior to the international the Govan Burgh surveyor had put in writing his complete faith in the new structure and recorded that he had made several visits to Ibrox to observe its construction. Nonetheless, a later court case strongly suggested that the contractors had skimped on materials while building the west terracing.

The SFA dug deep into its financial reserves (as organisers of the match they bore much of the legal responsibility) and contributed £5000 to the disaster fund. Those present at the AGM later that summer heard that the SFA's finances were, as a result, dangerously disrupted and that the auditors had suggested that much economising would be necessary by the ruling body.

The venue for the Final was switched from Ibrox to Celtic Park and so Celtic were allowed home advantage in their confrontation with Hibs. In the wake of the disaster, all of Glasgow's grounds had been examined at the command of the city's Lord Dean of Guild and the new venue for the Final had not received an entirely clean bill of health. A degree of concern was expressed at the fact that wood was the material used at some key points where brick would have been more appropriate. The terracing at the South-East corner was closed off and the Final allowed to proceed.

ON THE LINE.

A GRAND WASHING.

The prolonged conclusion to the 1903 competition was not without its compensations for the clubs involved

It was decided that the takings from the stand should be donated to the disaster fund and the SFA accordingly waived its right to complimentary tickets for that area of the ground. £120 was raised from that source. A collection for the same fund was also made around the ground. Doubts about safety, however, kept the crowd down to around 15,000 and for that year at least the Cup Final was more an obligation to be fulfilled than a thrilling climax to the season.

For both sides, team selection was constrained by circumstance. Hibs, of course, were without McCartney, who attended the match on crutches, and Campbell was unable to play for Celtic. The home side found greater difficulty in adapting to enforced change and although they mounted a great many attacks it seemed unlikely that their territorial advantage would result in a goal. Once, a Livingstone shot rebounded off McMahon and on to a post and Celtic again hit wood later but Hibs too could complain of misfortune when an

Atherton 'goal' was controversially disallowed for off-side. It was perhaps inevitable that this crabbed match should be decided by a goal from a set-piece. A Callaghan corner went low across the Celtic goals and McGeachan was able to score with some ease at the far post, indeed some reports credit him with flamboyantly backheeling the ball into the net. There was little chance of Harry Rennie conceding a goal and a Hibs victory was assured.

The 1902 Final was conducted in an atmosphere of great gloom but the new Edwardians, in general, seem to have discovered a taste for frivolity. The popular *Daily Record and Mail* delighted in affording lavish coverage to the doings of the idle rich. One illustrated article informed the public of a new game being played in Paris in which toy cars, operated by long sticks, were raced round a complex course. The knocking over of any of the obstacles on it resulted in a heavy fine which was paid into a pool to be scooped by the eventual winner. The same paper also lingered lovingly over life in the ski resort of Davos in Switzerland where, apparently, the day began with a breakfast of 'rolls and coffee such as only the Swiss can produce'. In Scotland, however, snow was nothing but a damned nuisance.

It delayed Celtic's match with St Mirren and the players who had been taken to Seamill to prepare found themselves stuck at the Hydro for three full weeks before being loosed onto a football pitch once again. Even when the tie did begin the weather had not much improved and a veritable hurricane led to the abandonment of the third attempt to decide the matter and the collapse of the St Mirren player, Greenlees.

Rangers avoided the worst of these problems and quickly advanced to the third round, but they then had to wait for some time before discovering that they would be playing away at Celtic Park. Perhaps Celtic felt that they deserved the Cup for having overcome St Mirren and the Scottish climate. Rangers, however, who had previously played six Scottish Cup-ties with Celtic and had succeeded in winning only once (in the 1894 Final), easily disposed of them, establishing a 3-0 lead in the first half and coasting towards the semi-finals in the second.

The 1903 semi-final was more of an outing in the country than a voyage into the unknown for Rangers. The upright members of Stenhousemuir had rejected, by a margin of 105 to 5, a tempting offer to switch the tie to Ibrox, but, on an icy surface and surrounded by a crowd of 8000, most of whom could see nothing, Rangers won 4-1. Hearts beat Dundee in the other semi-final and had the encouragement of knowing that no Edinburgh side had ever lost a Final to one from the West of Scotland.

A spell of fine weather lifted just in time for the Cup's concluding act and the normal conditions of snow and gale pertained on 11 April. Both selections contained points of interest. For Hearts, Baird's tour through the various departments of a football team turned out to be a round trip and now, in his fourth Final, he appeared in the outside-left position he had occupied twelve years before. For Rangers, Drummond had the chance to maintain his record of having played in every Cup victory his club had enjoyed while James Stark — a marvellous, driving player and Rangers' greatest discovery in the early part of the century — was playing at centre-half and making his Scottish Cup Final debut.

Hearts were overly concerned to play through Walker and since he was suffering the eager attentions of Gibson, Stark and Drummond, Rangers held a tight grip on the match. Walker sustained an unpleasant head wound and attempted to leave the pitch but was intercepted by Orr who managed to persuade him to remain. On the other side, Jacky Robertson actually made it to the safety of the track and spent ten minutes having his wounds tended.

With eighteen minutes to go and with Rangers leading through a Stark goal everyone left the field because the weather had become insufferable — where the fans were supposed to find shelter is not clear. This unforeseen interval allowed Hearts to convene a council of war and re-adjust their approach to the game. On returning Baird went to full-back, Thomson trundled into the front-line and, even more importantly, Hearts had realised that something dramatic was required if they were not to go tamely to defeat. Walker provided it when he drilled into the core of the area, maintaining a precarious hold on the vertical as determined opponents tried to ground him, and expertly beat the Rangers keeper. This piece of plunder brought Walker more than the chance to appear in a replayed Final for shortly afterwards Hearts offered terms which were good enough to persuade him to reject Spurs' bid of £1-a-day plus a lump sum.

The replay was a monotone event with neither side managing a goal, and so the Final limped on into a third match. The training which prepared players for such challenges was still rudimentary. Prior to meeting Rangers, Hearts had done some climbing on Blackford Hill but, in general, they passed most of their preparation time in taking long walks. Led by their two trainers they were a peculiar sight in these sessions and one old woman is said to have observed them sorrowfully before remarking to her companion, 'Puir fellows, they are frae the asylum, and the twa in front are the keepers'.

In 1904 Jimmy Quinn scored the first hat-trick in a Scottish Cup Final. The response of his team-mates is every bit as demonstrative as would be that of their modern counterparts.

The third game of the Final must certainly have driven Hearts to distraction. Both sides had been forced to make changes and there was a feeling that this time something would give. The admission charge had been halved to 6d (2½p) for the second replay and 32,000 saw Mackie put Rangers ahead. The lead was made to look fragile when Drummond tore a muscle while trying to stop Hunter and had to go off. Rangers moved Finlay Speedie to left-back with some confidence for he had once excelled there when playing against Everton in Liverpool but they still had to face the problem of being a man short.

The burden of having so visible an advantage seemed to drain Hearts of creativity and they wasted much time in trying to force a breach in a grimly determined defence and eventually succumbed to a weakness of their own. With Buick missing through injury and Thomson thrown forward in the later stages Hearts were feeble through the centre since, as one forthright paper has it, the replacement centre-half was a 'third-rate substitute'. A through ball into that area was picked up by Hamilton and he stormed through for the game's decisive goal.

When Rangers next won the Cup, the country, having passed through the fires of World War One, was an entirely different place. In the short term, Rangers' pain at finding themselves blackballed from the game's élite was intensified by the fact that it was their greatest rivals who strained the ingenuity of the headline writers as they won the lion's share of the major prizes in the next decade. It was, typically, a Cup victory which ignited Celtic's lust for the whole range of domestic silverware.

The defeats in the Finals of 1901 and 1902 provoked them to a period of pained but fruitful self-examination and a clean break was made with the policies they had followed since their foundation. Out went the hired guns, the 'wild geese', and the soldiers of fortune and in, at Willie Maley's insistence, came an emphasis on raising one's own players and buying for moderate sums which has since become a major creed of the club's catechism.

The Celtic team which was about to emerge was built on axioms which every manager now regards as fundamental. The defence and half-back line, although fine players, existed to extract the ball from the opposition's clutches before passing it swiftly on to the highly creative attackers. Once it had arrived there the beleaguered opponents would have to face a lengthy period of shadow-chasing during which they could look back on the days when they had actually touched the ball with something approaching nostalgia. Nor were the forwards simply looking for points for technical merit; when the ball-manoeuvering had sufficiently discomposed a defence, an abrupt through ball would suddenly be played and a goal might result.

Admirable though such stratagems might be, the cloying surface played on in the Scottish winter often favoured those addicted to the 'alehouse ball' — aerial barrage directed towards a punitive forward. In the third round Celtic were one down to Dundee with three minutes remaining and even their equaliser had only been made possible by some absent-minded goal-keeping. Celtic clung on, praying for the conditions of Spring to arrive, and scraped a draw in the second game at Dundee, where they bowed to reality by choosing the square-rigged Gilligan in place of the more artful Bennett. A week later they found themselves at last playing on a true surface and won 5-0.

The 1904 Final, with Rangers, was the first to be played at modern Hampden, then the finest ground in the world, which Queen's Park had opened the previous October. Scotland had found its national footballing shrine and Queen's Park had discovered their vocation as the game's distinguished impresarios. The charge was kept at 6d (2½p) and the implicit economic sense of this was testified to by an attendance of 64,323.

The match itself was a tale of two centre-forwards, both of whom did not play. R C Hamilton dropped out shortly before through injury and was badly missed but the exclusion from the proceedings of his opposite number with Celtic, Alec Bennett, was much more mysterious. Shortly before the match the papers were carrying stories to the effect that a certain young Celtic player would be joining Rangers at the end of the season. After the Final Bennett's absence was not satisfactorily explained and his marked fondness for Rangers, allied to Celtic's irritation at such sensational matter reaching the press, would seem to account for his demotion to the rank of spectator. In 1908 Bennett finally made the move to Ibrox. In his place at centre-forward in 1904 appeared a man who normally turned out on the left-wing. In the course of ninety minutes Jimmy Quinn was to entirely re-shape his career within the club and within the whole of Scotland.

The game began well for Celtic with the ball being swung around enthusiastically among the forwards but, as every fan knows, the blunders of an individual are often more telling than the best efforts of his ten team-mates. Smith rounded McLeod of Celtic and crossed neatly to Finlay Speedie from the bye-line. The Rangers forward, surprised by the simplicity of the chance, could only head straight towards Adams but the goalkeeper allowed the ball to slip through his hands. Celtic could scarcely believe it but only a minute later Speedie ran through a distracted defence to increase the lead.

By half-time Quinn had put the teams on an equal footing and Rangers could make nothing of his persistent, momentous buffeting. Famed though he now is for the manner in which he burst through defences he was not fleet-footed. It was his taste for physical conflict, and his disdain of personal injury, which allowed him to drive into situations which others would have been glad to absent themselves from. He was built like a stevedore and permitted himself few delusions concerning matters of style; when presented with a sight of goal he would commit every ounce of muscle to the task of driving the ball at it. Occasionally some keeper would have the misfortune to block the shot but frequently the net would be left to receive the brunt of it. Rangers must have guessed that they were only to act as official observers in the second half and Quinn duly scored his third and Celtic's winner.

When faced with such a feat the jaundiced modern supporter is likely to muse that there is a tide in the affairs of men, which, when taken at the flood, leads on to a personal agent, a modelling contract, a lucrative career in sportswear advertising, and guest appearances on games shows. That, however, is an unduly limited view for there is no doubt that such a match can change the entire tone and meaning of a man's life at the very deepest of levels. Jimmy Quinn left the field to enter upon an entirely new world. In those times, only the Scottish Cup could have so transformed a man.

John Neilson, left-half in Third Lanark's 1905 success

Third Lanark's Cup-winners of 1905. Hugh Wilson (front row, third from left) scored two of his side's goals in the Final replay.

Running to riot

IT HAS TAKEN many years for the idea of imprisoning fans behind iron bars separating them from the pitch to become acceptable in Scotland. That attitude, however, may not stem so much from respect for civil liberties as from deeply engraved memories of a certain Old Firm Cup-tie in March 1905 where creative use was made of such a barrier.

The Celtic element in the crowd had made their way along London Road in good spirits for the superiority of their team was indisputable and they had beaten Rangers at Ibrox by the margin of 4-1 in a League match the month before. The first ever League and Scottish Cup double seemed at hand.

The stark meaning of a Cup-tie, though, concentrated Rangers' determination in the match, while for their opponents the afternoon provided the chance to compile a lengthy inventory of troubles. The Parkhead side were reduced to ten men by an injury to McLeod and fell two behind when their goalkeeper donated a goal to Robertson. It was not the referee's whistle, in the event, which ended Celtic's suffering. Furiously seeking to roll back the deficit Jimmy Quinn appeared to charge into Craig who was lying on the ground at the time. The referee sent him off and in doing so tripped the wire which detonated the Celtic supporters' store of frustrations.

A crowd invasion followed and the doughty referee, Tom Robertson (Cup-winner with Queen's Park and St Bernard's), was in serious danger. Only the intervention of Celtic's Hay, who extended his definition of defensive duties to include protection of officials, ensured that he reached the pavilion. The game did not re-start and Rangers were declared the winners.

This kind of thing should have been prevented by the presence of spiked railings but the enraged supporters, turning ploughshares to swords, wrenched them from the ground and added them to the arsenal of offensive weapons, which included the corner flags, already being employed. It is understandable that one of the papers should, later in the month, publish a cartoon mocking Lord Rosebery's dictum that 'Football makes for health, for discipline, for character, for manhood and for Empire'.

Manhood was certainly on parade in the other semi-final between Third Lanark and Airdrie at Cathkin but it was the foolishness of Thomson in attempting to play dodgems with the home side's centre-half Sloan which decided the game. Both were injured but Thomson had to leave the field, perhaps to consider the adoption of the pacifist cause, and Johnstone broke the deadlock to make the score 2-1 and ensure Third Lanark's place in the Final. Third Lanark were in the midst of one of those necessarily brief periods in which youthful enthusiasm stands in perfect balance with battle-scarred wariness.

The men who embodied that latter quality were the most significant members of the team. The goalkeeper, James Raeside, was one of those whose size allows them to fill the goal without too much recourse to leaping around. Any forward intending to dribble round him would have required a sextant to plot his course. Third Lanark were captained by Hugh Wilson who had returned to Scotland after many successful seasons with Sunderland. He had joined the English club in 1890, just before they were admitted to the League, and engineered their rise to the pinnacle of the sport. His signing by them had, in contrast, little glamour about it. He was seduced from Newmilns by the offer of a £70 signing fee, 25s (£1.25) appearance money, 5s (25p) for a win, and 2s 6d (12½p) for a draw. Curiously, he was also obliged to agree to obey the commands of Samuel Tyzack (club treasurer and coal magnate) and to play to the best of his abilities in all matches. It was not long, though, before he and the other players were earning a basic wage of £3 a week.

In the early 1890s Sunderland won the League three times out of four. The side which began the run, in season 1891-92, included ten Scots and the sole Englishman, right-back Tom Porteous, had been signed from Kilmarnock. The shrewd Wilson captained the colony from the right-half position. By the time Third Lanark signed him in 1901 he had slipped to the lower levels of the English game and might have been expected only to pass on a little of his knowledge to the Cathkin youngsters before drifting to retirement. Instead, Wilson, now playing at inside-left, seemed to grow stronger by the day and led Third Lanark to the League championship in 1904.

It was a markedly unsettled Rangers team which opposed them in the Final. Tragedy had struck at the New Year when Nicol Smith died of enteric fever soon after the same disease had killed his wife and only two days after Rangers and Queen's Park had played a benefit match for him. On the trivial level, R C Hamilton, having had a knee operation in January, was unconvincingly making a swift comeback. A comparative newcomer to the side was R S McColl who had returned to Scotland in 1904.

The first game of the Final, played at a Hampden which could now hold around 84,000, was lifeless and Rangers were able to maintain a goalless situation even though Hamilton went lame early in the game and had to drift out to the left-wing. He did not play at all in the second match and Thomas Low returned to the team. Rangers, however, were convincingly beaten and the long range shooting of Wilson proved decisive. It was he who lifted a period of siege in the first half by completing a sweeping counter-attack with an imperious 20-yarder. After Johnstone had capitalised on a poor clearance to increase the lead, Wilson built an unassailable advantage by hitting the target with another long shot, this time of a more speculative nature. A late Rangers goal did no more than provide substantive evidence that they had in fact turned up.

Any ladies present in the 95,000 or so who watched the two fixtures had been admitted free of charge. Any masculine twinge of envy over this practice — which was not uncommon in football before World War One — is dispelled by the evidence concerning the position of women which the newspapers of the time provide. The General Election of 1906 saw the *Daily Record and Mail* straining to find a feminine 'angle' on the event and producing an article of hints for woman canvassers: only thin gloves should be worn since writing may be necessary; do not be upset if the election agent neglects the usual courtesies, he has much on his mind . . . It was 1918 before women won the vote.

Third Lanark reached the 1906 Final but were there confronted not only by Hearts but also by the implacable forces of numerology. The Edinburgh club had won the Cup in 1891, 1896, 1901 . . . What could prevent the latest instalment in the five-year plan?

Charlie Thomson, centre-half in Hearts' Cup victory of 1906, their last for fifty years

The key result for Hearts was a 2-1 victory away to Celtic in the last eight. The Edinburgh side dedicated themselves to an afternoon of stern confrontation with a team widely regarded as too good for them. Although they opened strongly it was Celtic who scored first. Hearts refused to console themselves with the thought that their performance merited the title 'moral victory' (football's equivalent of fool's gold) and opened the second half as if they anticipated nothing other than success. Walker eluded Orr to score and although Celtic hit back energetically Hearts were not to be deflected from the next round and Menzies scored the winner.

The semi-final tie must have stirred different sorts of apprehension in Hearts for they were drawn to play a 'minnow' which had given evidence that it currently had the loan of a piranha's set of incisors. Earlier Port Glasgow had knocked out Rangers; although their goal had come after only twenty-five minutes there could be no equaliser against goalkeeper Ward who had strayed far beyond his normal capabilities. He was not, in the event, proof against Hearts' attacking and conceded two goals. Harrassed though the Edinburgh side were, they were sufficiently gifted to pass most of the game protecting the lead rather than seeking it.

The other semi-final saw Third Lanark and St Mirren circling one another intently but finding it difficult to land the telling blow. It went to three games and one scribe remarked, 'We are going to have the Cup allocated by degrees'. When that tie reached its conclusion it was Third Lanark who had won. In the last match, at neutral Ibrox, Johnstone scored a scrambled goal and his team hung on. In the late, desperate stages the veteran Wilson was seen energetically covering the length and breadth of the pitch, slamming doors in St Mirren's face.

Hearts were a much changed side from their previous Cup Final appearance in 1901. Buick had gone South in 1903 and, it is alleged, liked it so much that he persuaded four of his former team-mates to make the same journey the following year. The process of re-establishing the club was aided in 1905 by the flotation of Hearts as a public company and, in any case, their two greatest players — Thomson and Walker — remained; jointly forming the still centre of the transfer whirlwind. The new intake, however, was of an impressive standard. George Wilson was joined on the left-wing by his brother David; the blood relationship giving the fans a more than usual expectation of telepathic understanding. At centre-forward, Menzies was set for international honours.

Third Lanark's preparations for the Final, which included the occasional game of cricket, were disrupted when McGrain's nagging injury forced him to drop out. The Morton centre-forward Reid was obtained (apparently on loan) and made an unavailing appearance at Hampden. Later in the summer the Scottish League records note his transfer from Morton to Motherwell. The Cup Final was his only competitive appearance for the Glasgow club. Remarkably, he would, in 1909, again make his debut for a club (Rangers) in a Scottish Cup Final.

Glasgow was underwhelmed by the occasion and only 25,000 showed up to share the terracing with some foul weather. The players were also affected by the depression and performed as if living only for the moment when they could clock off from this assembly line of a game. It appeared that a spanner had been thrown in the works when Menzies had to leave the field for treatment but it was, strangely enough, in those moments when they were depleted that Hearts' superiority registered on the scoreline. Raeside made an ill-advised trek from his goal and lost the ball to Walker whose pass allowed George Wilson to shoot into the unattended goal.

Hearts might have agreed with the philosopher's statement that you can never step in the same river twice but could still have protested that there was no need for the forces of change to try so hard to drown them. Season 1906-07 suggested that Hearts should have considered changing their crest from a heart to a revolving door. Both Wilsons went to Everton and Menzies joined Manchester United. New recruits were Peddie, once of Third Lanark and with Manchester United prior to joining Hearts, and two Englishmen — Wombwell and Yates — who neatly filled the gap left in the attack by the brothers Wilson. As the days of the 1907 Cup competition ticked away, Hearts put the Final touch to their side by signing Henderson from Dundee in mid-April.

On the very eve of the Final, Hearts yet again found their plans disrupted by a cruel fate. Dickson, Peddie and, most seriously, Thomson were all unable to play. Matters almost took a further turn for the worse when, on the day, their goalkeeper Allan failed to arrive at Hampden at the specified time. He eventually appeared but the game kicked off fifteen minutes late.

Weakened and unnerved though Hearts were, their competitive instincts saw them give their opponents, Celtic, a difficult time. But once they had lost a goal to an unconvincing penalty the final verdict was totally predictable. The only point of interest lay in the fact that it was Peter Somers, not particularly regarded as a marksman, who scored the other two Celtic goals.

Celtic were in a glorious phase of their history and collected the League each season as casually as a housebreaker lifts the available baubles before looking for the real valuables. They made off with the Scottish Cup in both 1907 and 1908.

The great James McMenemy of Celtic caught the eye as the true successor to Bobby Walker, so great was his grasp of the science of game management. He was nicknamed 'Napoleon' and even his shooting bore a premeditated air. He was one of those who are said to draw no distinction between passing and shooting, simply seeming to roll the ball between the posts. With a defence which conceded little in adversity — only two goals were lost in the six matches required to dispose of Morton and Hibs in the 1907 ties — Celtic were supremely suited to Cup football.

Cartoon recording the Celtic dominance of season 1906-07. By winning the Glasgow Charity Cup Rangers prevented a clean sweep by their rivals.

St Mirren were the cannon fodder in the 1908 Final. The season began unhappily for them and the board expressed dissatisfaction with the players' performance and attitude. Right-back Tom Jackson was late returning from a holiday in America and went on to demonstrate that he was not only far-travelled but also wayward when he was censured by the club for being drunk. In the same season a referee making his way to the station from Love Street was pelted with stones and the SFA reacted by closing the ground for two weeks.

Tom Jackson would not have been surprised by the fact that so troubled a season could include a Cup Final appearance. Such contrasts, he had already discovered, could be experienced in a single day. On the morning of Saturday 9 April he was at home in Thornliebank when a telegram arrived asking him to go immediately to Celtic Park to play against England. The first choice, Andrew McCombie of Newcastle United, had been forced to withdraw. By

that evening Jackson was probably regretting having answered the door, for England ruined the occasion by beating Scotland 1-0.

Despite the presence in the side of Jackson and McAvoy, a survivor of the side's great half-back line at the beginning of the century, the Final was all too easy for Celtic. Bennett signed off in his last major match before joining Rangers by scoring twice in a 5-1 victory.

It was the team from Ibrox who stood between Celtic and a hat-trick of Scottish Cup victories in 1909. Rangers were not too far from producing the side which would break Celtic's League dominance and in that year's Cup competition they displayed an impressive cussedness in defence, losing not one goal on their way to Hampden. Considerable credit for that was due to keeper Harry Rennie whose travels had brought him to Ibrox in 1908, but it was he, paradoxically, who allowed Celtic back into the first match of the Final when all seemed lost for them.

As befits a team which has reached the ultimate stage by scoring thirteen goals, Celtic played with much pomp in the early stages and took the lead when Quinn managed to get his head to a long punt by McNair. With only eighteen minutes remaining Gilchrist, whose previously muted play in the match was attributed by one newspaper to nerves at the prospect of his graduation from Glasgow University on the Monday, equalised with a header. Rangers, believing that the balance was tipping towards them, played with a verve which made sure that it did. Three minutes later Alec Bennett gave an untouchable solo run its proper finale by swerving his parting shot round Adams, so putting his former club 2-1 behind.

There matters should properly have rested, for the fires of Celtic's invention had been banked by the goal. With the Rangers countdown to victory entering its last ten minutes, however, Munro fired the ball into the goalmouth with only the Micawberish belief that something might turn up to justify his action. Something did. Rennie grasped the ball but, in attempting to swing away from the on-rushing Quinn, turned over the goal-line with it. The referee was in no doubt that a goal had been scored and, according to the *Scottish Referee*, the Rangers players afterwards acknowledged that he was correct.

Rennie's curious error might well be explained in terms of his restless quest for perfection in goalkeeping. He viewed his work in the last line of defence not so much as a trade as a calling. When his playing days were over he occupied an unofficial position with Morton and continued his training programme at Cappielow, where he was observed using a technique which seemed to be based on shadow boxing. He would face the wall of the dressing room and, balanced on the balls of his feet, jump from side to side before, at irregular intervals, flinging himself full-length onto the hard wooden boards of the floor. Another element of his training involved running backwards at great speed since he believed that a keeper should, above all, be nimble and adaptable. The theoretical side of the job also fascinated him and he would endlessly discuss questions of positioning and angle. This expertise was eventually passed on to Morton's Jimmy Cowan and his performance in Scotland's 3-1 Wembley victory in 1949 was an animated tribute to the man who had first kept goal for Scotland forty-nine years before.

But in 1909 it cost Rangers dear. Goalkeeping is only an approximate science and the solitary requirement is that the ball be prevented from passing through a gap eight yards wide by eight feet high. The method matters little. With Munro's shot coming in and Quinn charging towards him, the goalkeeper should simply have met the ball with a meaty punch and cleared the immediate danger. In attempting to bring classic technique to the situation he sentenced Rangers to a replay.

The Cup Final and a League game two days later took its toll on Rangers and a much-changed team was chosen for the following week. Willie Reid, who made that fugitive appearance for Third Lanark in 1906, had been signed by Rangers shortly before and was once more making his debut in a Cup Final. Gordon, another replacement, gave Rangers an early lead with a finely angled shot but the inevitable Quinn brought matters back to stalemate in the second half. At the end of the ninety minutes several players hesitated on the pitch, unsure as to whether there might be extra-time. In doing so they provoked the greatest riot in Scottish football history.

The rules as they stood stated that the further thirty minutes would only be employed if a tie were still undecided at the end of the third match. Celtic and, to a lesser extent, Rangers were keen that every attempt should be made to produce a finish to the second encounter. There was much talk in the press of extra-time but no official approach was made to the SFA to have the regulations altered. It is doubtful, in any case, if they could have been at so little notice. The question was a heated one since there had been a recent history of draws between the clubs in Glasgow Cup-ties and, in consequence, there was much wild talk of replays being contrived to boost gate receipts.

There was no shortage of people on the terracing who felt they had been served a short measure. Some of them tried to take their case into the pavilion and although they were prevented from doing so the chain reaction was begun. Goalposts were torn up and one crossbar disappeared under the penknives of those seeking relics. Wooden barricades were dismembered and used to form a bonfire on the track beside the North terracing. There were one

1909. Pay-boxes on fire as the riot reaches its height.

hundred policemen on duty but that was sufficient only to initiate a battle and not to conclude it. A baton charge drove the incendiarists up Hampden's classic slopes but they simply made their way to the pay-boxes at Somerville Drive which were so efficiently set alight that all twenty-seven of the turnstiles contained there were destroyed.

The arrival of the fire brigade made no difference for the engines were attacked, the hoses cut, and the firemen stoned. There were reckoned to be 6000 involved but the ranks of the police were eventually swelled to 300 and the rioters were dispersed. Around one hundred people, mostly police and firemen, required treatment at the Victoria Infirmary.

The SFA accepted the request of Celtic and Rangers that the Final should not be played again. Had they not, it was suggested, the clubs would simply have refused to play in a further episode. Rangers, however, beat Celtic 4-2 at Celtic Park in the Charity Cup Final four weeks later.

Remarkably, this Old Firm riot featured no sectarian feuding and no division amongst supporters. It was prompted by little more than irritation with the SFA rules and regulations. A point, however deplorably, had been clearly made. The rules for the competition of 1910 allowed for extra-time at the end of the Final's second match.

The Scottish Cup is the oldest of all Britain's national football trophies, for the FA Cup currently in use is the third to have been employed. The first was stolen in 1895 and the second was withdrawn and presented to Lord Kinnaird in 1910 when it was found that duplicates were being used in local competitions in Manchester. It was only the actions of Willie Maley's brother Tom on that April afternoon in 1909 which ensured the continuation of that happy state of affairs. With admirable presence of mind he seized the trophy (along with some £1400 in gate money) and took it to the refuge of a nearby house.

The Scottish Cup would live to torment another day.

The last days

GREENOCK WAS Sugaropolis, Paisley was Cottonopolis, Dundee was Juteopolis. By granting such aliases when writing about places regarded as outposts of the soccer empire the press attempted to add a little colour to their reporting. In 1910, however, a growing interest by the people of Dundee in the commodity of silver gave them the chance to treat that city and its inhabitants in an altogether more serious manner.

The Cup is a pyramid in structure and as a team climbs the numbers gradually thin out until all attention is fixed on a single contest. Dundee's form in the first round of 1910 wrongly suggested that they firmly belonged in the sport's murky basement. They should have found their opponents a soft touch; the more so since Beith had sold their right to a home match and so played at Dens Park, but when a team carries so many advantages it often keels over under their weight. Beith were largely composed of potentially dangerous veterans, some of whom were suspected of being old enough to have gone 'avoyaging with Noah in the Ark', and further had that inevitable figure in supposedly unequal Cup-ties — the inspired goalkeeper. Indeed, Monteith's excellence led to his joining Airdrie later in the season. When Bellamy of Dundee lifted an early penalty over the bar with 'the utmost nonchalance' the suspicion grew that the tie would require more than one instalment. A 1-1 score ensured that it did and a 1-0 victory the following week was only contrived with difficulty.

The second round brought an apparently alarming tie with Falkirk who were maintaining a brave pursuit of Celtic in the League but the thrill of the chase seemed to deprive them of breath in the Cup and Dundee won 3-0, aided by a freak goal scored from the bye-line. On the same day, a 2-0 defeat of Rangers by Clyde introduced the element of unpredictability which is amongst a Cup contest's necessary credentials. Poor weather had disrupted the programme and Rangers had spent the fortnight prior to the tie at Troon. Preparations involved a fair amount of golf and the party on those occasions included Tom Fernie, Scotland's professional golf champion. More outlandishly, Rangers arranged a concert for their own amusement and players Galt and Hogg performed a burlesque of a wrestling match in which they impersonated the great wrestlers of the day, Hackenschmidt and Poluski. It appeared at Shawfield, though, that too many combative instincts had been left at the coast.

Clyde were drawn against Queen's Park who had recently demonstrated that they had lost none of their stern rectitude. They had offered £150 to East Fife to have their tie played at Hampden, but when their opponents held out for another £20 they refused to negotiate any further and rubbed salt in the wound by winning 3-2 at Methil. Queen's Park were an unblinking challenge to Clyde as well as the first two meetings were drawn 2-2. The Shawfield side won the third match in a midweek fixture but the League programme decreed that the teams should meet, three days later, for the fourth successive time. Once again the sides produced their favourite score of 2-2.

The draw for the Cup continued to ensure that there would be no danger of Clyde being required to make complex travel arrangements, even if replays were required. For the third tie in a row they found themselves opposed by local rivals. Celtic were weakened for the visit to Shawfield by an injury to McMenemy and they attempted to shore up the side by calling in Hamilton, even though he had not played for seven weeks. An even greater worry for them lay in the goalkeeping position where, remarkably for a club of such ostensible resources, they had no suitable deputy at hand for the injured Adams. With a considerable amount of imagination Celtic acquired the services of the Welsh international goalkeeper Roose for the match but they could not so readily build an understanding between him and his new defence.

This factor may have contributed to Celtic's downfall for he conceded an equaliser to Clyde when he was caught totally unsighted. Clyde scored twice more to complete an Old Firm Cup double. If the occasion was an unhappy one for Roose, he at least added to the dignity of the occasion by running to shake the hand of Clyde's centre-forward Chalmers after he had scored. A delighted board entertained the players at the Trocadero hotel on the following Tuesday and councillor Frank Cohen, in the days before the Scottish Health Education Group, presented each of them with a pipe.

As Clyde cruised joyously past Celtic, Dundee were toiling against Hibs in the other semi-final. In two games Hibs refused to concede their opponents' superiority and not a goal was scored. Dundee, however, had established a simple but repeatedly effective pattern of play in Cup-ties and in the second replay they finally imposed it on Hibs. Consistently that season, and particularly in their third round meeting with Motherwell, Dundee had been able to create the space for right-winger Bellamy to ply his trade. From his cross, John 'Sailor' Hunter (a nickname associated with his rolling gait rather than with years before the mast) expertly eliminated Hibs.

The Cup Final of 1910 was the greatest occasion the Dundee players had yet experienced but they nevertheless had good reason to think that they would be able to cope with the strain. Of the team which turned out against Clyde on 9 April all but two had experience of playing in English football and were unlikely to be alarmed by new experiences.

The game may be assumed to have been of particular importance to three of those playing for Clyde. For outside-left Booth it afforded the opportunity to add the Scottish equivalent to the FA Cup-winners' medal he had won with Manchester City six years before. For McCartney, who had broken his leg in the 1902 semi-final while with Hibs, it provided one last chance to regain redress from the Cup. McAteer's motives must have been acute, if less romantic, for he had once been on Dundee's books but had never quite been able to win a first team place. Now, perhaps, he could demonstrate his worth to his former employers.

It seemed for a long time that the Englishman, the veteran, and the reject would have their day. Although neither side could dominate, Clyde were at an advantage since their forwards were producing the sharper finishing. Midway through the first half Chalmers wheeled and clipped in the opening goal after Stirling and McCartney had made a neat incision on the right. Before the interval another Stirling cross eluded Lawson and allowed Booth to further improve Clyde's position. With four minutes to go and the score unchanged it can only have been professional pride and ingrained good habits which saw

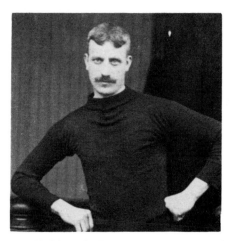

J Fraser, outside-left in the Dundee Cup-winning side of 1910

Hunter chase a loose ball into the Clyde area. The defenders, tormented by the imminence of glory, lost their nerve however and Robertson botched his clearance entirely. The ball rebounded off his colleague Blair and into the net. Some reports, with laudable charity, awarded the goal to Hunter but the Clyde skipper was adamant that an own goal had been scored.

For Clyde now the remaining minutes stretched and stretched, seeming to provide countless opportunities for their opponents. The equaliser had the simplicity of the inevitable as Langlands hit Bellamy's corner high into the net. Chalmers was then given one last chance to clinch the match for Clyde but all precision had been drained and he finished abysmally.

The contest extended beyond the final whistle as Lee of Dundee and McAndrew of Clyde struggled to take the ball as a souvenir. Footballers are traditionally superstitious and it may have been Lee's success in winning that lesser trophy through the eventual tossing of a coin which led him to announce later that he would eat the Tay Bridge if his side did not now go on to win the Cup.

After two hours play the following Saturday (extra-time for Final replays had now been introduced) Lee may have felt as if he had actually attempted to digest that epic structure. Both sides were reduced to utter exhaustion by a heroic struggle enacted amidst a great deal of weather, but there was no by-product in terms of goals. The Clyde youngster Jackson collapsed and his glaur-covered body was removed from the field some minutes before the end. Dundee stood up to the strains rather better than the Glasgow side and were clear favourites for the replay four days later. They had benefited by the introduction of Neal for Lawson (which brought the number of Englishmen in the side to four, the others being Lee, Dainty and Bellamy) and had in any case borne muscular development in mind when choosing their team. Comrie had been preferred to the more delicate Main and his presence mattered more and more as the Final lingered on. It was undoubtedly also of significance that the side was trained by Longair, their grim centre-half of the 1890s.

The fans had other resources to call on in recuperating from the two hours of football. One paper summarised the day: 'There was a first "hauf" and a second "hauf", and there was another "hauf" and another second "hauf", and after the game there were several final "haufs"'.

The third match at last separated the sides and once again Dundee demonstrated their persistence. They were a goal down after three minutes but a Bellamy header from a corner brought them parity by half-time. It was Hunter who at last gave the competition of 1910 its effective end. Defensive hesitancy by Robertson and McAteer allowed him to break clear and from what seemed an impossible angle he blasted the ball over the keeper's shoulder. With the aid of local subscriptions the club was able to pay a bonus of between £30 and £40 to each player. Given the amount of overtime worked, it was no more than their due.

Over the centuries philosophers have been concerned with the question of the existence of God but the Scottish Cup of 1911 leads one to suggest that they might profitably pay more attention to football, for Hamilton Academical's appearance in the Final can only be attributed to divine intervention.

They were to finish in sixteenth position in the League and a first round draw away to Third Lanark seemed likely to leave them with the sole responsibility of fending off relegation. Even when they received the unexpected bounty of an inexplicable penalty after twenty-five minutes they seemed loath to accept it. Davie blasted it at international goalkeeper Jimmy Brownlie and he inadvertently saved but was knocked over in doing so and the ball simply rolled back to the Hamilton player who despatched it with aplomb. In an unavailing attempt to redeem themselves Thirds threw everyone, including Brownlie, into the attack as the game drew near its finish.

A fortnight later Hamilton themselves were struggling with lesser opponents and Johnstone were only five minutes from a famous victory at Douglas Park when a penalty kick arrived like the Seventh Cavalry. The award, as so often, was conceded by a forward unable to cope with the requirements of defending and Hamilton accepted the gift in less intricate manner than at Cathkin. A fortnight later they comfortably disposed of Johnstone 3-1 and even provoked fisticuffs amongst the home side's supporters.

Clem Hampton of Motherwell ushered Hamilton through the next round by dropping the ball at the feet of Miller, a recent signing from Larkhall, when the scores were tied at 1-1. Dundee, conquerors of Rangers in an earlier round, seemed bent on cancelling Hamilton's appointment with destiny when they led 2-0 with two-thirds of the game gone. A goal from J H McLaughlin, the son of the Celtic legislator and playing in his first season of senior football, brought Hamilton onto their shoulder and the inevitable penalty, with 'Davie as shootist', saw all Dundee's previous superiority annulled. The game was decided by the type of goal which is almost mandatory in such encounters. From a corner-kick centre-half W McLaughlin leapt to plant a header in the Dundee net.

That semi-final was really the moment for Hamilton to break open the champagne, for little charity was to be expected from the side who would share Ibrox with them in the Final itself. Celtic's great run of League championship successes was at an end and their smooth, rhythmic attacking was no longer much seen but they still possessed some alarming virtues. They had reached the Final, for example, without committing the *faux pas* of losing a goal and in McNair and Dodds they possessed the finest full-back combination of the age. Centre-half Loney, it is true, had broken his arm in a tie with Clyde but Celtic were able to replace him with McAteer who had filled that position for the Shawfield side in the previous year's Final. Failure in front of goal was, then, more of an irritant than a true disability for Celtic.

Hamilton were perceptively marshalled by inside-right Waugh, who had spent an earlier part of his career at Tynecastle where he had faced the hopeless task of trying to win Walker's place, but he could bring little sustained pressure to bear on Celtic. There was hardly a semblance of a save never mind a goal and the fans did not even have the prospect of the captains fighting over the ball at full-time to look forward to. Davie had landed the first ball on the North stand and the replacement was provided by hosts Rangers who claimed it at the end.

A Miller (left) of Hamilton heads clear from McMenemy of Celtic in the first match of the 1911 Final. The Hamilton jersey was normally cerise and French grey hoops at this time.

The start of the replay was delayed by some impromptu pre-match entertainment. A rabbit ran on to the field of play and could not be taken into custody. Several players sacrificed dignity in tumbling over as they attempted to catch it and some minutes passed before Celtic forward Hamilton at last got a firm grasp of it. The omens for rabbits were not good and Celtic were not long in putting their opponents under equally sure control. Right-half Phil Watson, once a player at Parkhead, offered keen resistance for a time but every one of the 25,000 present knew a goal must come. It did so in typical fashion when a genteel run by McMenemy across and into the Hamilton area was crudely interrupted by Quinn racing in to part the ball from his colleague's boot by lashing it into the net. A young Hamilton team accepted the conclusion of a splendid run and conceded a clincher to McAteer.

Celtic again strode confidently to the Final in 1912 but at least Scottish football, as represented by Aberdeen, could credit itself with having reminded them that their defence was made of the same fragile clay as the rest of suffering humanity. Away to Aberdeen, the scoreline grew worse and worse for Celtic as their superiority became more and more evident. Aberdeen's first shot was a scorer, McAteer missed a penalty for the visitors, and Main skipped impudently round McNair to make the score 2-0 early in the second half. Celtic could not have been more astonished if the laws of gravity had been repealed but the universe resumed its normal character eventually and they added two goals to their own account. The replay saw them record a mundane victory.

The semi-finals of that year were the first to be played at neutral venues and Celtic were opposed at Ibrox by Hearts. The Edinburgh side had only Walker's *savoir faire* to place against a Celtic side which ran on a full tank of experience. Walker, to make matters worse, found himself directly opposed by Jimmy McMenemy, who had been switched from inside-right to inside-left. McMenemy demonstrated the range of skills which made the positional change possible by scoring two goals, one with either foot, in a 3-0 victory.

The re-jigging of the Celtic forward line had been required by the emergence of a uniquely talented inside-right. The magnitude of his talent only gradually became apparent and the press can be forgiven for devoting little attention to the man they referred to, at that time, as Pat Gallagher. As 'Patsy' he would dominate the dreams of his club's support in the years following the Great War.

Hearts' chances at Ibrox had been impaired by a current instalment in the grinding struggle for social change. The miners were on strike to rid themselves of the system whereby the individual's earnings were entirely related to the amount of coal he produced, even though some faces are manifestly more difficult to work than others. As coal stocks grew scarce the train network ground to a halt and Hearts brought no football specials with them. The true grit of the hardened supporter should not be underestimated, however, for a crowd of 127,000 had attained Hampden for the international with England the week before when the same difficulties applied. The strike, incidentally, led to the introduction of the Coal Mines (Minimum Wage) Act.

The Final was turned into a family affair by the success of Clyde, who were managed by Alec Maley, brother of Celtic manger Willie. The third brother, Tom, had a dazzling career as Manchester City manager disrupted when the FA banned him for making illicit payments to some of his players, thus taking their earnings above the prescribed maximum. The Clyde trainer, as in 1910, was William Struth, later to govern Rangers with an authority comparable to that of a feudal lord.

Lift-off for Clyde had come in a troubled victory over Rangers at Shawfield. Morrison, customarily a half-back, was pressed into service at centre-forward instead of the injured Cameron, and played with an exuberance which suggested that his heart's desire had been granted. Presumably the brace of goals he scored constituted the fulfilment of the other two of his three wishes. Clyde were leading 3-1 when a resounding challenge on Bennett gave the Rangers support the excuse to intervene on, as they saw it, their side's behalf.

That tackle, committed with seventeen minutes to go, concluded the game because several thousand of the 50,000 said, slightly improbably, to be present burst on to the field of play. One man attempted to punch Clyde's Gilligan and, although he was said to have missed, was later charged with both breach of the peace and assault. The sentence invited him to choose between a £5 fine and thirty days in prison. Rangers pre-empted the SFA's deliberations by conceding the tie.

Clyde were once again forced to improvise in team selection in their tie with Third Lanark in the semi-final. Thirds, in the early stages, exploited that

Gallagher turns away having scored his side's second in the 1912 Cup Final. Team-mate Brown lies on the turf while the Clyde keeper appears non-plussed.

instability and took the lead. Although managing to equalise, Clyde seemed to be in the midst of an identity crisis. Perhaps that was hardly surprising since they were wearing Queen's Park strips to avoid a colour clash. The board of the club, concerned by what they saw, left the stand at half-time to go and address the team. Whatever the reason, Clyde were renewed after the interval and Allan, who had been tossed into the fray because of the pre-match injury problems, scored twice.

With icy realism, Clyde concluded that the semi-final success was its own reward and did not include Allan in their Cup Final selection. Despite that, however, they could not field a team to match the Celtic expertise. When faced with the wind against them in the first half of the Final they impetuously tried to take the game to Celtic but succeeded only in exhausting themselves. Celtic held only a one goal lead at the interval — a McNair free-kick having been allowed to reach McMenemy — but faced spent opponents thereafter. Gallagher placed his first stroke on the canvas of his Cup Finals by scoring a second and securing his side's victory.

Falkirk warmed up for the contests of 1913 by pressing the self-destruct button. A run of League success which had seen them unbeaten for eighteen weeks was terminated by Clyde at Brockville. The event may be assumed to have raised the temperature within the club but Falkirk were still not quite back on the rails when they played Morton in their first tie. The replay, which followed a 2-2 draw, found them back in the old routine and winning 3-1.

The subsequent round, though, must have shackled them with recollections of the club's history in the Cup. It was the fourth time they had been drawn against Rangers and they had yet to notch a victory. Falkirk were less than bashful at Ibrox — early on Tom Logan bowled over his brother James, who played for Rangers — but nonetheless depended on factors beyond their control to break their duck. Goalkeeper Hempsey played as if his hands had become blunt instruments and conceded two sloppy goals. By half-time Falkirk led 3-0, yet they won only two corners in the match and the first of those came as late as the sixty-fifth minute. A single goal by Rangers was scant reflection of their dominance. Chief amongst their tormentors had been Croal and Rangers had to ponder the galling and perplexing fact that he had been an undistinguished full-back on their books three years before. Now he was a midfield overlord of international standard who had the courage to confront the physical hazards which are a normal part of Cup contests.

In the semi-final against Hearts his side played at a pace designed to limit the effectiveness of the more cerebral Walker, and Croal suffered the consequences stoically. Injured early on, he returned after treatment but was once again forced to leave the field. Falkirk started the second half without him but Croal, now making more farewell appearances than Dame Nellie Melba, returned to the ring once again. When he next left it he was accompanied by a posse of ambulancemen who ensured that his afternoon's sport was at an end. There was no novelty in this for Croal had been knocked unconscious and twice removed from the action in a League match with Celtic the week before. The sub-plot in the semi-final was Falkirk's 1-0 victory over Hearts.

It was a year when the Cup was ruled by exceptions and the fates managed to provide the 'Bairns' with opponents who could fairly be described as underdogs. Since their foundation in 1883 Raith Rovers had been the occasion of much civic pride in Kirkcaldy. From the usual obscure beginnings they had risen first to Junior status and had then been accepted into the Second Division. The winning of the Qualifying Cup and the attainment of First Division status had been the next rungs on the ladder. The Scottish Cup, though, seemed an unrealistic ambition and Raith Rovers' gallant attempt to bring it to the town becomes all the more remarkable when the condition of the club at that time is considered.

The ambitious directors reacted with something approaching revulsion when the club finished in fifteenth place in season 1911-12. Seven players (including Bill Morrison from the Clyde Cup team) were signed over the summer but Raith, still not content, sacked manager Peter Hodge in November. Cynics would point out that all the reconstruction led only to sixteenth position in 1912-13 but that would be to ignore the fact that the addition of some new elements to the equation had produced the answer to every provincial club's dreams — an appearance in the Cup Final.

Raith began their Cup run with a new trainer but without a manager and under the effective control of secretary James Todd, a plump gentleman with, paradoxically, the kind of saturnine appearance designed to motivate any team. Despite beating Broxburn 5-0 in their first tie the club saw clearly that a lack of firepower would soon bring the completion of their run unless a further signing was made. In February Englishman Fred Martin was signed from Sunderland and it was his goal in the semi-final replay against Clyde which purchased Raith Rovers their place at Celtic Park against Falkirk on 12 April.

The press were none too comfortable with the idea of the understudies taking over the Gala performance, a fact clearly announced by their decidedly

Logan, scorer of Falkirk's second, pushes past a Raith Rovers opponent in the 1913 Final

off-key prose. The *Scottish Referee* spoke of Raith as having 'set ablaze the noble Firth that laves the linoleum centre of Scotland'. The waters, it would seem, were left to proceed with that laving largely unsupervised by the local populace, for a creditable crowd of 45,000 turned up for the Final.

One of the first things they would have noticed when the teams took the field was that Falkirk had adopted an all-white strip to avoid a clash of colours. Their play was not equally pure but it was still too much for Raith. After twenty-five minutes Croal broke through and the keeper could only push his shot up into the air for Robertson to head home. After fifty minutes some 'peculiar play' by McNaught dumbfounded the defence and Tom Logan provided an orthodox finish to his eventual cross.

On their return to Falkirk the team could hardly make their way from their train carriage, so large was the crowd indulging in high density partying. The town's main street was closed as they made their triumphal journey towards the happy destination of the Empire bar, which was owned by the club's president.

But the era was Celtic's and it was fitting that it should end with their Cup victory of 1914. Hibs stood in their way in the Final but the Edinburgh club's principal boast was of stout defence and consistent team selection (the same eleven players represented them in all but one of their ties that season) and it was to be expected that they would do no more than obstruct Celtic. The suspicion that they were suffering from a bad case of anonymity is supported by the fact that the brake taking them to Ibrox was stopped by the police in Copeland Road. Fortunately manager McMichael was able to persuade them that it would be better if the occupants were allowed direct access to the stadium.

Nervousness in the Celtic ranks allowed Hibs some threatening moments. Notably, Hendren went clear and 'it seemed all Lombard Street to a china orange' that he would score until Dodds made a late intervention. In general, though, the game was consumed by blankness and no goals interfered with the tedium. Celtic were in a position to do something about such sterility and replaced the disappointing Owers with McColl for the replay. It was as if a dud fuse had been replaced and much heat and light resulted immediately. Both he and Browning scored twice while Hibs could only manage a single goal.

Anyone thumbing through the *Glasgow Herald* on the following morning in search of the match report would have found few signs that the world he knew was about to end. On page nine, however, it was briefly reported that concern had been expressed in Paris over the fact that a Berlin artist named Repner proposed to send a bust of the Kaiser to an international exhibition there. The tensions contained in that squabble would soon spread to cover not only the columns of the *Herald* but also the surface of Europe. When the Cup contest was restored in 1920 it would be watched by a changed audience in a changed world.

Commemorative plate for 1913-14, in which season Celtic won both League and Cup

Jinxes and giant-killers

LONG BEFORE the sirens sounded in the shipyards on the Clyde that afternoon early in 1920 there were workers downing tools and hurrying away. There was unfinished business to attend to for Rangers had chosen to schedule their first round replay with Dumbarton in midweek and, in the days before floodlighting, it started comparatively early. Football was the ruling passion and 20,000 attended at Ibrox.

The yearning for the game is easily explained since society had scarcely recovered from the most destructive war there had ever been. Past traumas were difficult to escape and the Sunday papers covering the first round of the Cup (it had been in cold storage since 1914) carried front page stories about the arraignment of war criminals, notably General von der Lancken who was charged with the killing of Nurse Edith Cavell.

Not everyone was sympathetic to the practice of foregoing an afternoon's wages in favour of a Cup-tie. The Shipbuilding Employers' Federation felt that Britain's fight to re-establish itself in the marketplaces of the world would be hindered by it and wrote to the SFA protesting over the playing of midweek matches. It is noteworthy, though, that they did not dare go so far as to sack their absent employees.

The Cup competition of 1920 suggested, falsely, that the post-war football scene was to have little connection with anything that had gone before. The game's giants seemed constantly to mistime their punches and, often enough, would miss altogether. There was a species of consolation for Celtic in knowing that they were simply not good enough but Rangers had to cope with the frequent failures of a side which was unquestionably the most gifted in Scotland. A journalist of the time places their gate receipts for the season at a massive £50,946 but they were not to number the Scottish Cup among their assets.

The quarter-final brought that hoariest but most gruelling of matches, an encounter with Celtic. Once the 80,000 crowd (who had begun to arrive with flasks, sandwiches and decks of cards some three hours before kick-off) had witnessed Rangers' 1-0 victory the future progress of the competition seemed clear. The Cup was 'practically won' said ex-Ranger Neilly Gibson and who could argue when their opponents in the last four were found to be Albion Rovers?

Only one national League operated in Scotland from 1915-16 to 1920-21 and Albion Rovers were playing their first season in it. Determined efforts were being made to ensure that they comported themselves in an impressive manner. Their new Cliftonhill ground was proudly pressed into service even though they had to endure, in consequence, the mild embarrassment of not having their stand ready in time for their quarter-final tie with Aberdeen (a 2-1 victory). The team, however, proved less effective at laying the foundations of League success and Albion Rovers were to finish the season in 22nd (last) position.

Their Cup side was composed of the kind of artisans who have made up the supporting cast on all the Saturdays of the game's history. Typically, they were an itinerant bunch; the backs had been with Motherwell while Kilmarnock, Queen's Park, Dumbarton, Celtic and Fulham had been some of the ports of call of the others. They had no hopes of glamorous careers but the passing seasons had still left them sufficient dreams to fuel one frantic assault on the big-time. Their struggle to defeat such as St Bernard's created the impression that they would be no match for Rangers in the semi-final at Celtic Park and the Ibrox side were probably grateful that the problems which saw them play the versatile Jimmy Gordon (normally a full-back or half-back) at centre-forward in place of the sick Andy Cunningham had not afflicted them at a more exacting time.

Rangers did take the lead but justice was done when Ribchester's penalty, following a handling offence, paved the way for a replay. The Glasgow side were unsettled by the fact that they had barely merited a second chance but seemed to decide that it could be ascribed to duff bio-rhythms. Jimmy Gordon commented, 'You get up five minutes late in the morning. The porridge is burnt, the ham and eggs are scorched, and the tea is boiled . . . well that was our position on Saturday. Even the ball seemed to be against us'.

If a 1-1 draw is the equivalent of a culinary foul-up then what followed can only be compared to the kitchen exploding. After a second draw (0-0) a crowd of 53,000 turned up expecting, for the most part, to see Albion Rovers given a refresher course in the footballing facts of life. Instead, roles seemed to have been reversed and Albion Rovers played as if they were favourites dealing capably with feisty, but ultimately inadequate, opposition. With only a quarter of an hour gone, Hillhouse cut in from the wing and guided a right-foot shot beyond Rangers' English keeper, Herbert Lock, and as half-time drew near Guy Watson hit a twenty-yarder of a ferocity which suggested he had been saving it up over the years. That was to be the culmination of Rovers' Cup history and there was a reward in sturdy, materialistic terms as well, for the gate receipts generated by the 120,000 who watched the three matches would doubtless have been adequate to purchase a few trimmings for their new ground.

The most significant, slightly less romantic, action had been taking place on other fields in other ties. Kilmarnock had the appropriate number of those who have clocked up sufficient mileage to judge correctly the balance between caution and optimism required by Cup-ties. Goalkeeper Blair, right-back Hamilton, and centre-half Shortt could claim a total of twenty-four years with the club. When dollops of frantic running were called for, the duty could safely be entrusted to newcomers Gibson and Bagan. The latter had won a Junior Cup-winners' medal with Rutherglen Glencairn the previous season and was now set on the same course in the senior equivalent. The feeling that the Gods had decreed that Kilmarnock and 1920 would, throughout the ages, be tied inseparably in the pages of Rothmans was prompted by the arrival in November 1919, from Battlefield Juniors, of J R Smith.

In the Cup-ties, he played like a man with a mission, even if, on at least one occasion, success for Kilmarnock was ensured only by the referee seeming to join him as a disciple. Having scored twice in a 4-1 defeat of Queen's Park he was faced by a more alarming tie in the last eight. Non-League Armadale, that season, were exactly the kind of team to induce paranoia and panic in more favoured rivals and had already accounted for Clyde, Hibs and Ayr.

Kilmarnock had little appetite for such an away tie and only when they had emerged on the smug side of a controversy were they able to deal with Armadale according to their merits. After twenty-eight minutes a Smith shot bounced down from the underside of the bar and was judged to have crossed the line before being cleared. Kilmarnock's 2-1 victory turned on that decision and the crowd were enraged to such an extent that only a police cordon and some percussive use of batons brought the referee to the pavilion.

1920. Kilmarnock (hoops) on the attack. Penman of Albion Rovers (centre) attempts to intervene. A massive crowd of 95,000 watched the first post-war Scottish Cup Final.

Kilmarnock, though, went on to provide an object lesson in dealing with adversity in their semi-final match with Morton. Two behind in the first half, the Ayrshire side hungrily exploited defensive weaknesses and equalised with goals from Malcolm McPhail (elder brother of the more famous Bob) and J R Smith. At that poised moment, the crucial action gathered itself once more around Smith. If it was unedifying for full-back Ferrier to stub the ground and sclaff his goal-kick to the centre, the aplomb with which Smith gathered the ball and compounded the defender's misery can only be admired.

The attendance at the Final shattered expectations and Scottish Cup records alike. The game was watched by 95,000 and the Kilmarnock man who claimed that only a dog had been left to guard the town might almost have been believed. Sadly, there was little stewarding and the crowding was so great at the upper reaches of the terracing that several people who tried to escape the crush at half-time were unable to get out. At the front there was considerably more space and parties of spectators were walked round the track and invited to climb in over the barricades.

In the papers that morning it was reported that a devolution bill had failed to secure a second reading but the attendance at 'the nearest thing to a National Assembly the Scots have' (as Bob Crampsey has described Hampden's big match occasions) testified that enthusiasm for the Scottish Cup and pride in Scottish identity were as great as they had ever been. The matter before the 'House' made for an enthralling afternoon. At first the game looked like being the happy ending to the Albion Rovers story for, after five minutes, Ribchester's cross was steered into the Kilmarnock goal by Watson but the Coatbridge side had been irreparably weakened before the Final and lacked the resources to camouflage it. Their Irish centre-half Duncan was unfit and inside-forward Black was unhappily converted to the position. Gamely though he struggled, Albion Rovers could not succeed, at any point, in extinguishing Kilmarnock's hopes of scoring. The equaliser came from inside-left Culley and the Ayrshire side took the lead when Shortt burst forward, as if in literal pursuit of the Cup, exchanged passes, and ran on to score. Albion Rovers, though, would not readily abandon their dreams and an uncharacteristic error by Hamilton allowed Hillhouse to level the match. The stage was set.

Throughout the season J R Smith had played with an innocence which, though effective, horrified the veterans. Reasoning that the shortest distance between two points is a straight line, he refused to be ushered wide and consistently ran the ball into the thick of the area. There are penalties for such recklessness and he paid an instalment on them in the Cup Final when, early in the second half, he collided with the Rovers keeper and left the field for treatment. He returned unabashed and responded to the invitation of a precise Culley flick by driving forward with a vigour that was not to be denied. Cup fortune had followed Smith that season and the finish he provided was definitive. For the first time in their history Kilmarnock had won the Cup.

Nor was that the end to this period of power sharing in Scottish football for 1921 saw another new name added to the Cup (or, to be precise, its plinth) but it was a long road for the team which eventually attained the position.

Despite spending the week prior to their tie with Hibs preparing at Skelmorlie, Partick Thistle could only draw 0-0. Indeed, Jimmy McMenemy, who had come from Celtic in 1920, blamed the performance on the lack of hard training and the number of salt baths indulged in at the retreat. The contest went a second replay before McFarlane, who had previously looked as if he was attempting to give goalscoring up as a bad habit, hit the first and only goal of the tie.

The impression that the 1921 Cup contest was a long-term project for Thistle, to be toyed with at their leisure, persisted, since the ties with Motherwell and Hearts occupied six games in all. In truth, though, the pace was hectic for they were twice behind in the first of those ties and their second equaliser, from McMenemy, was certainly in the avoidable category. Eventually, it was a McFarlane goal in the third match which eliminated Motherwell. Further appalling football marked the semi-final but, at the third time of asking, Blair and Kinloch recalled the purpose of the game sufficiently to score the goals which beat the Edinburgh side.

The prevalence of draws did not go unremarked and there were ill-humoured mutterings about results being fixed. The *Weekly Record* carried a jocular version of them — 'I also have it from a man who knew the charlady of the woman whose cousin heard a fellow who has *seen* them tell the story, that managers often conspire together before ties.'

Rangers displayed a more brusque manner in their ties and even the occasional slip, such as a 0-0 draw with Alloa, led to a 54,000 crowd for the replay. A club such as Rangers can never adequately revenge themselves upon lesser opposition but injured pride must have been slightly soothed by their 4-0 victory over Albion Rovers in the semi-final. The Rangers side had grown strong that season for although 'Doc' Paterson and Jimmy Gordon were gone they had experienced an extraordinary influx of new talent. Alan Morton had been signed from Queen's Park in the close season of 1920 while Billy McCandless and the gargantuan figure of Davie Meiklejohn had taken up permanent residence in the side. Partick Thistle were given little chance of beating them.

The Final, as an occasion, was largely spoiled by the actions of the SFA. They decided to play the game at Celtic Park and, in an attempt to keep the attendance at a manageable level, doubled the standard admission rate from 1s (5p) to 2s (10p). The *Daily Record and Mail* waged a campaign against the decision and had evidently made a sensitive assessment of the public mood. Something approaching a boycott took place and the lavish transport facilities laid on by the Corporation were largely wasted since only 28,294 troubled to attend.

Not only the crowd was depleted for Thistle too approached the Final in distressed condition. Centre-half Hamilton and left-half McMullan (the latter having been injured in Scotland's 3-0 victory over England the previous week) failed to recover in time. Crucially, however, McMenemy declared himself fit to play.

Some players, when past their best, find that the deterioration in their abilities stops, for a time, at a level which leaves them with a fair measure of their former excellence. McMenemy's intelligence allowed him to extend his career. If the body was slower, less supple, less responsive, astuteness and experience might ensure that the player positioned himself more perceptively and had less need of haste. With McMenemy's appearance it was guaranteed that there could be no easy victory for Rangers. He no longer played so much of a creative role but his orchestration of Thistle's defence ensured there was no early goal to calm the Ibrox side's nerves.

The match was played in the midst of a miners' strike and with a general strike feared to be in the offing. One report commented on the Final in the terms of that other dispute:

> Partick Thistle called to the conference. Refused to accept the terms offered from Ibrox. Go out for direct action. Blair joins in the strike.

More prosaically, Thistle endured some pressure and hit hard in the thirtieth minute while Bowie was off the field having an injury treated and a pair of shorts replaced. Borthwick played the ball to Blair on the right-hand corner of the area and the winger's speculative shot was handsomely rewarded when goalkeeper Robb failed to interrupt its progress. Thereafter Rangers could make nothing of the Thistle defence, in which the veteran Bulloch was outstanding, and the realisation soon grew that the Cup was destined for Firhill.

For McMenemy, the joy of winning, so late and so unexpectedly, was acute and he confirmed what many suspected by announcing that he valued the medal more than anything he had ever won. As a true professional, however, he also expressed sympathy for the Rangers players. Their failings were being loudly announced by the press — one report said their forwards were 'as slow on the ball as are tortoises at a water-melon breakfast' — but McMenemy readily acknowledged the extent to which success and failure are apportioned through nothing more than happenstance. The medal, he said, would be mounted on his wall with a horseshoe on either side.

By now, the annual appearance of the Cup competition must have held for Rangers all the charm the summer examinations have for the average schoolboy. In 1922, nothing happened to change that. Again they took up their place in the Final, having received extraordinary assistance when drawn to play Partick Thistle in the semi-finals. At the SFA meeting Celtic Park seemed on the point of being chosen as the venue when the Maryhill club's representative protested that there was no sense in two Glasgow clubs sacrificing revenue to a host. It was found that the regulations simply gave the SFA the right to fix the semi-final locations and did not stipulate that neutral grounds be used. The Thistle and Rangers representatives left the room to strike up a bargain and returned to propose that the match be played at Ibrox. This was carried by eight votes to six. 'We should keep our own fish guts to our own sea-maws,' the Thistle man had said (sea-maws=seagulls) and the move had indeed some financial sense but the Maryhill club's prospects had been sacrificed.

The 55,000 crowd watched Thistle slip hopelessly to a 2-0 defeat. Rangers had, however, displayed creditable grit when involved in a more trying contest with St Mirren in the quarter-finals. Duncan Walker was on the way to setting a club record of 45 League goals that season and he showed his accuracy also extended to the Cup by giving his side the lead at Ibrox. Rangers seemed to have nothing to offer in response but pushed on doggedly and eventually produced an equaliser out of sheer persistence. When Finlay pushed a pass-back wide of his keeper it seem that the worst St Mirren faced was a corner-kick against them but the Rangers centre, Henderson, launched a desperate pursuit, managed to keep the ball in play and squeezed it across and into the goals. There was no mistake in the replay at Love Street.

The defeat of Celtic at home by Hamilton Academical (their first loss at Celtic Park that season) had set hopes of a Cup Final appearance rising in many clubs throughout the land but it was Morton who claimed the prize. The crucial factor in their rise was the punishing form of their centre-forward, George French, who had previously been linked with bigger clubs, including Rangers. He caught the eye with a hat-trick against Vale of Leithen in the first round and his menace was no blunter four rounds later, in the semi-final, against Aberdeen at Dens Park. He had given his side a 2-0 lead by half-time, displaying on each occasion a blinding simplicity which left the defence floundering. A through ball from McKay was snapped in as it came to him and he followed that feat with another controlled explosion when he rounded Hutton and shot past Blackwell. French confined himself to simply creating Morton's third, from McNab, in a 3-1 victory.

Dundee trainer, Bill Longair presented the Greenock side with a policeman's helmet to mark their feat but although they took it to Hampden as a lucky mascot its worth in that capacity seemed at first to be doubtful.

Morton were thrown into despondency on the day of the Final when they learned that French was not fit enough to take his place in the side. The team had a comforting look with its dependable backs (both of whom had been with Rangers) and men like Gourlay and Wright who could be trusted to impose themselves on the afternoon. The inside-forwards, McKay and A Brown ('The Twins'), were in their first season of senior football and seemed to hold the promise of much creative vigour in the years ahead. But without French, how were Morton to win that afternoon?

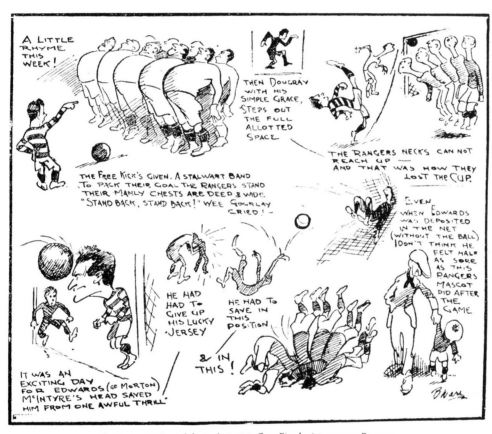

Cartoon report on Morton's 1922 Cup Final victory over Rangers.
Some impression of Gourlay's goal is conveyed.

Endurance and good fortune had much to do with it. Goalkeeper Edwards was forced to exchange his blue jersey for a grey one before the start but when the game finally began Rangers could not long be held off. Within seconds Alan Morton had hit a post but the team which shared his name accepted that piece of luck and remained calm. After twelve minutes it was Rangers who cracked. Billy McCandless left a pass-back short and Robb, in an attempt to rectify matters, handled the ball just outside his area. The Rangers' wall at first refused to go back the ten yards but Jimmy Gourlay, who had first signed for Morton in 1913, was not to be rushed and waited till the referee marched them back. Then, when the whistle blew, he hit the shot of his life. It curled over the end of the wall and precisely entered the keeper's top right-hand corner. As in the year before, one goal was enough. Late on, Alan Morton rounded the keeper but found Gourlay, almost demoniacally, back to kick his shot off the line.

Rangers deserve some sympathy for they had been reduced to ten men after twenty minutes when their captain, Andy Cunningham, left the field and was taken to the Victoria Infirmary with a fractured jaw. Morton could point, though, to their ill-fortune in losing French and to the fact that four of their players had required treatment in the match. At one point it had not been clear if Jacky Wright would even be able to play on.

The game was surrounded by numerous peculiarities. Neither manager, for example, saw much of the action. Bill Struth, who had become manager in 1920, belied his reputation for callousness by accompanying Cunningham to hospital while Bob Cochrane, of Morton, sat in the dressing room assessing the progress of the match through the medium of the ebb and flow of the crowd's roars. This was his normal practice for he found the tensions of a game almost intolerable. Happily, he was tempted out long enough to observe Gourlay's goal.

Those who ran the club do not seem to have had much enthusiasm for the Final either and had brought no champagne to Hampden. The success was celebrated with supplies borrowed from Rangers, whose goodwill must have been sorely tried, and, what is more, those revels were cut short. Within an hour of the game ending Morton caught a train at Mount Florida and headed South for their Easter holiday match with Hartlepools United. It was the following Wednesday before the team returned to Greenock. Most likely, though, the Morton players were impervious to such irritations and perhaps Jimmy Gourlay was even allowed to run through his programme of Burns songs as the train rattled them away from the scene of their triumph.

Speaking on behalf of Rangers after the match, John Ure Primrose was said to resemble 'a man reading his own burial service' but for football in general it was a time of teeming life. The Final had been watched by 75,000 (mostly paying the restored 1s (5p) rate) and, in the fifty years which followed, the attendance at Cup Finals only twice dropped below that figure.

Celts, Diamonds and Saints

SHOWBIZ AND Scottish football have had a mercifully slight acquaintance. The average fan views the entertainment industry as a form of sedative to be taken when concern for the fortunes of the local team threatens total derangement. The 1923 Scottish Cup competition, however, contained one occasion on which the game flirted with such distant glamour. Queen's Park's second round tie with Bathgate at Hampden featured a kick-off by HRH Prince Albert, the Duke of York (later King George VI), who was on an official visit to Glasgow at the time. Whether in gentle mockery of the host club's traditional image or out of habit, he sported a bowler hat and carried a rolled umbrella as he regally knocked the ball off the spot. The astounding crowd of 50,000 drawn by the royal presence obtained no closer view of him for, as a newspaper of that day put it, 'the suggested joy-ride round the track has been declared napoo'.

A fortnight earlier, a sprinkling of stardust also settled on the shoulders of the Lochgelly and Celtic players contesting a first round tie. The game is one of the earliest in Scotland to survive on film but viewing it today is a less satisfactory experience than might be supposed. It was made by a local cinema owner and more attention is paid to faces on the terracing than feet on the park. This is forgivable since the people of Lochgelly no doubt shared in the normal human desire to see themselves on screen and could rightly be expected to flock to the cinema for that purpose but it remains galling that the chance to record a player such as Patsy Gallagher was lost.

Celtic scraped through by three goals to two in the unfamiliar setting but thereafter displayed an assurance which had previously been lacking in their League performances. Celtic certainly had the flair to accomplish Cup success once other areas of the team had been persuaded to provide the application which gives such skill its focus. Apart from the unaccountable wiles of Patsy Gallagher, there were also the more orthodox but nonetheless subtle promptings of Adam McLean in the forward line. Attentive to their instruction and further profiting from the service of a direct, tearaway right-winger named Paddy Connolly, centre-forward Joe Cassidy breenged happily through the competition. In the first three ties he scored nine goals and did not falter in the later stages either.

The brake was only applied once, and that by Dave Morris of Raith Rovers who was playing with all the relish of a man about to win his first cap. Despite the presence in the side of Alex James, who would be recognised with Preston and Arsenal as one of the game's greatest inside-forwards, Rovers were forced into a holding operation at Celtic Park and the quarter-final was lost when a solitary defensive blemish allowed McLean to usurp Cassidy's normal duties.

Celtic themselves knew something about defence and demonstrated the fact in their semi-final against Motherwell. In 1925, the laws of the game were changed so that only two, instead of three, defenders were required to play a forward on-side and it is rightly said that this new dispensation forced clubs to give their centre-halves a more purely defensive role. Even before that, however, defensive considerations were receiving more attention.

Celtic had much to fear from centre-forward Hugh Ferguson (who notched 283 League goals with Motherwell as well as scoring the goal which brought the FA Cup to Cardiff in 1927) and it was widely noted that Celtic's centre-half, Willie Cringan, dogged his footsteps throughout his side's 2-0 victory. Cringan's success was achieved, incidentally, despite the words of his wife that morning, who had wished him well but told him she thought Celtic would lose (his four-year-old son had said otherwise and even predicted the scoreline).

Dynastic conflict was once more imminent for the other Finalists were Hibs, who were then managed by Alec Maley. For the second time — the first had been in 1912 — he was in direct opposition to his brother Willie in the Cup Final. A further link was provided by Jimmy McColl of Hibs, who had played for Celtic in their 1914 Final replay. The occasion was bound to be a stern one, for Hibs had not lost a goal in that season's competition while Celtic, for their part, could ally to Cringan the beefy presence of the McStay brothers. Hampden's atmosphere was also dampened by a new regulation. An announcement in the morning's *Daily Record and Mail* read, 'No person carrying Bugles, Ricketties, Flags etc., etc., will be admitted to Hampden Park to-day. By order of the Queen's Park FC.'

One error was enough to decide this sepulchral Final and it was made by Hibs' international keeper Willie Harper. He misjudged the bounce of a long punt into the area and Cassidy was in attendance to score the game's only goal and his eleventh of the tournament.

Unprepossessing though that particular scrap may have been, the public's taste for Cup football showed no signs of slacking. A quarter of a million people watched the sixteen second round ties in 1924, a total bolstered by the 40,291 who saw Rangers eliminate St Mirren at Love Street.

On the same day, Airdrie were carrying out the chore of beating St Johnstone 4-0. The ease of that performance might have been expected to distinguish Airdrie's performances in the early stages of the Cup for the club was in the midst of a Golden Age which not even the most grossly optimistic would have predicted. By the end of the season the number of internationalists at the club had risen to four, while three others would later gain the same honour. In the latter category was a youngster named Bob McPhail, then in his first season of senior football, who would go on to gather all the game's prizes in the years ahead. One of the internationalists, goalkeeper Jock Ewart, bravely remarked that the side had men destined to win 'a niche in the football hall of fame'. Time proved him guilty of understatement. Only an entire museum would suffice to record the feats of centre-forward Hughie Gallacher.

He had come to Airdrie from Queen of the South with, inexplicably, no money changing hands. Almost immediately, the little forward began to reveal the dizzying depth of his talent. Despite his size, he led his line with unflagging aggression, but that physical devotion to goalscoring never prevented him from displaying the deftest of touch in possession. When he chose to hold the ball up and wait for reinforcements he was almost impossible to dispossess. His talent was beyond question and almost beyond price — more than once he was the subject of sensational transfers. Tragically, his temperament was as volatile as his skill and a sad personal life became more apparent in the later years of his career. He was to die comparatively young.

1923. Shaw of Hibs clears from Patsy Gallagher. Note the referee's thoroughly sedentary style of dress.

Despite the emergence of such stars as Gallacher and McPhail, there were moments when Airdrie's quality seemed to be of as much relevance as a ballroom dance certificate in an abattoir. For most of their first round match with Morton they were one down and the last minute winner drove the Greenock side to near-frenzy. Gallacher hurled himself at a cross, missed it altogether, landed in the net, and in doing so distracted the keeper sufficiently to allow Russell to score. Morton naturally felt cheated and claimed off-side against Gallagher but the referee ruled that the centre, lying amidst the rigging, was not on the field.

After the relaxation of a 5-0 victory at Motherwell, Airdrie once more revealed a worrying tendency to embroil themselves in the most ludicrous of difficulties. With the score at 1-1 Ewart came very close to presenting Ayr United with a place in the semi-final. In his eagerness to push his colleagues onwards, he raced after a ball which was running behind, grabbed it, and hurled it wildly at an Ayr player. The ball was played wide and a goal scored from the cross. Astonishingly, however, the referee redeemed Ewart's error by judging the Ayr winger to have been off-side.

Four days later, a blitzkrieg at Somerset Park gave Ewart the chance to re-habilitate himself and he seized it by keeping the score at 0-0 throughout the two hours of the match. Another week, and the two sides were again playing out an extended deadlock, 1-1 after extra-time at Ibrox, and the congestion of the fixture list meant that they were forced to meet again twenty-four hours later. With weariness and injury effectively reducing Ayr to nine men, Airdrie had sufficient edge to retain the one goal lead presented to them by a goalkeeping error.

Two more days, and Airdrie were playing Falkirk in the Scottish Cup semi-final at Celtic Park — it was their sixth match in fifteen days. For an hour they were able to play with verve but the football variety of jet-lag then began to tug at their sinews, breaking their hold on the match. Fortunately, Falkirk had by that stage given them a lead capable of defence. At 1-0 their right-back had clumsily collided with his own keeper, knocking the ball loose to Sommerville in front of the unattended goal. Falkirk were not disheartened though and Puddefoot (to become an English intenationalist while with Blackburn Rovers) pulled one back with all of eighteen minutes remaining and seemed likely to level the match when he went clear in the dying minutes. It was then that Ewart claimed his team's place in the Final by hurling himself at the forward's feet. He blocked the shot sufficiently for a team-mate to clear but was concussed in doing so and had to be carried off. With right-back Dick in goals Airdrie held out.

The team to share Ibrox with Airdrie, in what was the last Final to be played away from Hampden, must have been almost as weary. In the twelve weeks before the Final, one paper reckoned, Hibs had played twenty-two matches. Team selection naturally troubled both clubs. Both gambled, but with widely differing results. Hibs picked 'Ginger' Dunn at inside-right, even though his fitness was in doubt, and experienced the chagrin of seeing him go lame early in the game. Airdrie, for their part, chose James Reid, who was going on thirty-four, at outside-right instead of Murdoch, in the hope that his experience would lend stability. It did.

The entire Hibs team had played in the previous year's Final but it was Airdrie who seemed at peace with the occasion. There was sureness throughout the team and it was their energetic left-half, Bobby Bennie, then among the uncapped contingent, who dominated the play. The actual goals, however, were provided by one of the star names, inside-right Willie Russell. After two and a half minutes Bob McPhail flicked a corner on and Russell stooped to conquer, heading past Harper. Seven minutes from the interval he was astutely positioned to send Bennie's high, drooping cross into the net.

Russell of Airdrie (left) turns away, having beaten Hibs' keeper Harper with a header and putting his side one up. The defenders are (left to right) Dornan, Shaw, Dunn, Miller and McGinnigle.

It was Airdrie's composure, too, which saw them through a second half moment of crisis. McColl of Hibs went down near the bye-line and the unsighted referee looked to his linesman, who appeared to be pointing his flag towards the spot. A penalty was awarded but Ewart remained convinced the referee had misinterpreted the signal and asked him to go and speak to his linesman. This the official did, to be told a goal-kick was being indicated. Airdrie's two-goal lead was preserved and the Cup went to Broomfield for the first and, so far, only time.

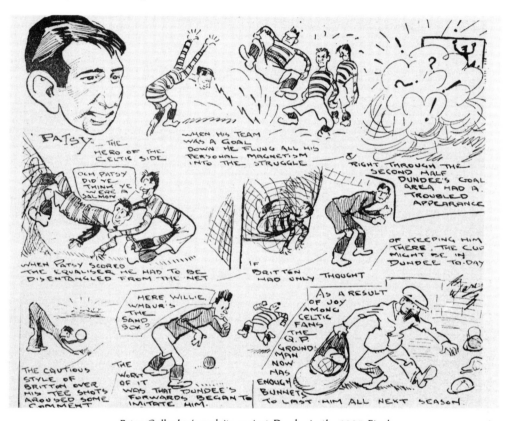

Patsy Gallagher's exploits against Dundee in the 1925 Final

The story, of course, has a dispiriting epilogue. The goalscorer went to Preston in August 1925 (the £3650 gained was spent on a new stand which was referred to, with lugubrious humour, as the 'Willie Russell Stand') and Gallacher moved to Newcastle four months later. McPhail at least joined a Scottish club, going to Ibrox in 1927.

The season after Airdrie's breakthrough it was once again the turn of football's larger predators. An eclipse threatened Celtic in their first round tie with Third Lanark but the phenomenon was purely astronomical (the period of darkness coming just after half-time) and it was their opponents who were overshadowed in the sporting sense. Jimmy McGrory, Celtic's very own force of nature who had newly established himself, scored four times in a 5-1 victory.

Celtic were playing with much resolve and the demands made of their players were immense. At the quarter-final stage Celtic became enmeshed

Hampden, big match, c. 1926

with St Mirren and required three games to unpick themselves. In the last of these Hugh Hilley broke his nose (a mishap he had already suffered more than once that season) but was informed by his manager that there was no significant damage and told to play on. The moment of truth arrived at half-time when it became clear that Hilley could not be allowed to take his ease in the dressing room lest he pass out. As the players came in from the cold, Maley turned them round and sent them back out again. Hilley retained consciousness for a further forty-five minutes and Celtic won 1-0. The reward for this stoicism was great for the semi-final turned into a jamboree in which Celtic took five goals off a thoroughly befuddled Rangers side.

The Final of 1925 was to allow Patsy Gallagher to bid farewell to the Celtic big-time in the most astonishing and, for him, fitting manner. The following

1926. Morrison of St Mirren punches clear from McGrory. The other players are (left to right), Summers, Morrison and Finlay. Celtic wore white jerseys with a shamrock crest in this Final.

season, injury problems slipped him away from the first team and, eventually, off to a productive spell with Falkirk. The players of Dundee constituted the props for the Irish conjurer's last bravura Celtic performance but at first they displayed disturbing signs of having designs on the Cup themselves. Davie McLean, who had been with Celtic all of nineteen years before, gave them the lead.

It was in the second half that Gallagher began to build towards his final by urging, prompting and inspiring his team-mates towards the Dundee goal. Appropriately, it was he who turned all his team's strivings into a moment of untarnishable glory. The goal in question has almost become lost in the extravagant and slightly fanciful recollections of it which were penned decades later but the truth, as recorded in contemporary reports, is remarkable enough. A Connolly free-kick was flighted in to Gallagher in the thick of the dark blue jerseys. The little Irishman somehow twisted, tricked and squeezed his way through, adding the final flourish of catapulting himself over the line with the ball wedged between his feet. Indeed, his boots were caught up in the netting and he lay there, like some bizarre but glorious catch from the sea depths, until the other players freed him. The rest of the game was simply a matter of awaiting the Celtic winner and McGrory duly provided it.

The day was Gallagher's but Celtic, looking to the future, gave McGrory the Cup to hold as the team carriage led a procession of brake clubs back into town. McGrory had shown a wonderful appetite for the whole Cup occasion, even being relaxed enough to briefly don a straw boater handed to him by a supporter as the teams ran out. In his own way, he would become as great a figure as Gallagher himself.

It is hilarious, if also slightly sad, to note that J J Lang, who had played in the 1874 Final, reported of the now celebrated Final of 1925 that the players involved did not measure up to those of his own day . . .

Celtic won the League only twice in the 1920s, a fact which indicates that there was nothing inevitable about their Cup triumphs and, as the Final of 1926 showed, their weaknesses could not always pass unexploited. For one thing, they could sometimes seem to be hypnotised by the delicacy of their attacking patterns and forget the purpose of the game. The St Mirren half-back line in that Final was not inclined to accept the role of adoring spectators with ringside seats. Instead, they harried and tackled incessantly, making Celtic's studied approach seem like mere fecklessness. It was said of Morrison, Summers and McDonald that given a bag of salt they would devour any forward line. Certainly, they approached Celtic with a healthy appetite.

As so often, though, an authoritative performance in the Final was prefaced by periods of self-doubt in earlier rounds which were only overcome through good fortune. A tetchy third round win over Partick Thistle was a case in point. With the score tied at one apiece the Thistle right-back, O'Hare, had to be carried off following an accident but the Glasgow side found that this blow was only the fates' way of limbering up for a truly punishing swipe. The bounce ball following the injury broke directly to Morgan who wasted no time on sympathy and slammed in the winning goal.

1927. Wood's header beats Thomson to put East Fife one up. Celtic swiftly redeemed the situation.

The team from Paisley took heart and readied themselves for the Final by giving their very best impersonation of redoubtable pros in the penultimate round against Rangers. Although the Ibrox side were reckoned to command the greater attacking force they found it almost impossible to bring it tellingly to bear and eventually lost 1-0.

St Mirren were certainly not expansive performers in opposing penalty areas but what they did gain they were well qualified to keep and in Davie McCrae they had a nimble centre who would have made space for himself in a matchbox. It was clear, therefore, that they were not the team to concede an advantage to, but Celtic, foolishly prodigal, did just that.

Before those events, though, there was joy for the men who had nurtured the game when a crowd verging on 100,000 gathered at Hampden. A more dismal consequence of that congestion was a disruption of train services on the Cathcart Circle which prevented many fans from reaching the ground till well after kick-off. This was particularly regrettable for those who had come from Paisley.

From that kick-off, St Mirren flowed forward with an urgency which might eventually have been revealed as bluff had it not immediately brought them the most concrete of gains. A Howieson shot was cleared behind by the Celtic defenders, leaving goalkeeper Shevlin to deal with a corner before he had even had time to calm his nerves. He flapped at the cross as it flew over and McCrae, finding himself in a rare moment when dream and reality fuse, headed his side into the lead.

Neither Celtic in general nor Shevlin in particular ever recovered from the reverse. Before the game had quite filled a half hour Howieson hit a shot which suggested he thought it a day for pushing his luck. His half-shot, half-lob caught Shevlin, seemingly, half-awake, and a St Mirren victory was sealed. With neither Patsy Gallagher nor Adam McLean to plot a path through such troubles, and with McGrory's aggression for once parried, Celtic's hopes were

An early attempt at crowd control. Hampden c. 1927.

extinguished. Sixty untroubled minutes later St Mirren were heading for the Cup presentation, the dressing room, and the case of whisky put up for the winners by Messrs Whyte and Mackay. A good piece of advertising this, since one of those bottles cropped up in the club's story, and in the press and television, all of thirty-three years later.

The simple monetary rewards were scant and a small bonus of £8 — only slightly more than would have been earned as a weekly wage by one of the game's better players — entered the pockets of Paisley's heroes. Others, though, knew how football might be turned to profit. The local MP, Mr Rosslyn Mitchell, earnestly joked that the club's improvement could be traced to his General Election victory of 1924 and maintained his high profile with the press by proclaiming the post-match celebrations as 'a real communion of saints'.

The strong joy which St Mirren and Paisley experienced was perhaps no longer available to Celtic, for whom success was a duty, but the Glasgow club would have allowed themselves at least a sigh of satisfaction when they regained the Cup in 1927 by defeating, of all people, East Fife, then a middling Second Division side.

The men from Methil recorded some remarkable victories, notably when they won a second round replay at Aberdeen, but their real worth was painfully revealed when only the two First Division players on loan to them — Gilfillan and Edgar of Hearts — seemed to belong at Hampden. Gilfillan was Hearts' regular keeper in the later part of the season and played in the Edinburgh club's League games between East Fife's semi-final and Final appearances. It is nonetheless the case that the players began the Final as if reading from the script of an entirely different play. The rag-tag side, in which only inside-right Paterson had cost money, went into the lead in the seventh minute through a goal from the prolific Jock Wood.

Almost immediately, though, Celtic got down to the serious business of the day. East Fife's Robertson conceded a foul on the right and already, no doubt, a bundle of nerves was further upset when McLean made a threatening gesture at him. When the ball was fired into the goals the unsettled full-back stabbed it past his own keeper. From then on East Fife's stature dwindled back to its true proportions and further goals by McLean and Connolly saw Celtic's supporters celebrating long before the finish. They could do so sure in the knowledge that any break-outs by the Second Division side would be inadequate to defeat a brilliant young goalkeeper named John Thomson.

For some in the Celtic ranks the Final turned into a rare chance to clown in front of more than 80,000. Tommy McInally, then in his second spell with Celtic after some seasons with Third Lanark where he was the subject of transfer interest from Rangers, delighted in hitting preposterous shots which soared high, wide, and ugly.

Two days after the Final, Celtic played an Old Firm match at Parkhead and paraded the trophy. At that moment a Rangers fan collapsed and it was conjectured that he had fainted at the sight of the Cup. Observations concerning the club's estrangement from that particular piece of silverware, however, were about to be dropped from the repertoires of the comedians who basked in the limelight of Glasgow's Music Halls. Rangers won the League match 1-0 and the ability that displayed was about to force an entry into the game's premier competition.

Exits and Entrances

IF YOU HAD been at the Cup Final that day and were in need of a little mollification following Celtic's unexpectedly heavy defeat then the artistic stimulation as provided by George West in the Princess Theatre's production of 'King o' the clubs' was probably suspected of being the very thing to bring you out of yourself. The chances were, however, that you left the auditorium early that night of 14 April 1928 with a view of the popular stage not dissimilar to that of Mrs Lincoln after John Wilkes Booth had totally spoiled both her night out and, especially, that of her husband.

As if losing to Rangers by four goals to nothing was not bad enough, the end to an imperfect day came with the Scottish Cup itself being displayed to a response from the audience in excess of any level Mr West and his troupe had ever before elicited in all their years of treading the boards.

The very idea of Rangers submitting nowadays to such a weakness as flaunting their success in a place of public entertainment would be a non-starter but their triumph of the late twenties was no ordinary event. In fact, this Scottish Cup victory was the light at the end of a long, dark tunnel, bringing to a close a record of failure which, had it occurred in subsequent years, would possibly have brought forward calls for an enquiry by the Secretary of State for Scotland. By 1928, fifty-six years after they had been brought into being, Rangers had won the Scottish Cup a total of four times, the last of which had been a quarter of a century earlier. While these achievements might have been the cause for a quartet of civic receptions in other quarters, for those to whom the club represented a way of life it was a source of unremitting anguish that, unless you were approaching forty or had almost total recall, you had never known what it was like to leave Hampden with a smile on your face. And there was even worse.

Celtic, already thought of as Rangers' historic rivals even though they had a lifespan which was fifteen years shorter, had by that time won the Scottish Cup twelve times since first competing in season 1888-89, then a record. It would be equally incomprehensible to those looking aghast at those figures now that one reason put forward for this strange omission on Rangers' part lay in a certain unwillingness for the fray when the post-Victorian chips were down.

Tacit agreement with that assessment came with the signing of Bob McPhail, an inside-forward, from Airdrie at the outset of that 1927-28 season. A man of indomitable spirit both on and off the field, who works to this day in the office of the electrical firm he started in Glasgow, McPhail ultimately went on to become the club's highest ever goalscorer with 281 to his credit. He was as hard as bell metal and also went down in the gossip pages of the club's history for being the man who almost single-handedly did away with the Ibrox practice of players receiving payment in kind for matches. He had the audacity to tell the legendary figure of Rangers manager Bill Struth that canteens of cutlery were no use if you did not have 'enough money to buy a steak'. When it was expected that a seismologist could have taken a reading in the Rangers dressing room that day, prior to Rangers playing Arsenal in what was to become an annual friendly, and before the words had been fully uttered at that, Struth said nothing in reply. Cutlery as currency in place of a win bonus payment was forgotten about thereafter.

McPhail had been part of an Airdrie team which had won the Scottish Cup in his first season as a professional four years earlier and one which had not known a defeat from Rangers since the 1922-23 season, re-emphasising the peculiar lack of a hard core within the teams coming out of Ibrox. The arrival of McPhail was seen also as a way of ensuring the maximum output from the man who had been Struth's first signing for the club in 1920 — Alan Morton. The most revered Rangers player of all time, Morton was a rare talent and his portrait hangs inside the awe-inspiring foyer at Ibrox, to be seen by those whose inclination it is to lift their eyes above ground level and show a refusal to be intimidated by their surroundings. In the days when the ball was still laced up and swelled to a barely moveable weight at the sight of rain, and when players' legs almost buckled under the combined pressure of cumbersome boots, the tongues of which screeched to a halt at the base of those protective pads made from leather, cane and foam rubber known as shin-guards, Morton, standing 5 feet 4½ inches and weighing 9½ stones, was respected as the finest product of the domestic and indeed the British game.

Incongruously, though, Morton's time at Ibrox took in periods of remarkable sterility for the club. One year before he and McPhail were paired together on the left wing, for example, Rangers had finished the season sixth in the League, their lowest ever placing, and had won nothing at all. So it was that the public interest in seeing if the club could at once break its long standing curse where the Scottish Cup was concerned, and instigate a more general revival for itself, reached then uncharted heights.

The crowd of 118,115 at Hampden was a record for a domestic football match in Scotland. It was also the first time that the Glasgow constabulary had been used as the sole means of crowd control. This was a puzzling milestone since almost twenty years earlier a Rangers-Celtic Scottish Cup Final had ended in a riot and the retention of the trophy by the SFA, suggesting only that this deployment of the police was a tardy attempt at getting to grips with the matter of public order, although there would be plenty of practice in the years which followed.

It mattered not to the attendant and well-behaved throng on that day, however, that David Lloyd-George was in Glasgow on matters of state, or that news had filtered through of the first ever East to West crossing of the Atlantic, by Commandant Fitzmaurice, Air Chief of the Irish Free State. After all, a sense of perspective must be maintained. By half-time not a goal had been scored but the save from the Rangers goalkeeper Tom Hamilton from Paddy Connolly's shot had struck those who wanted to believe that it was, and the others who feared to contemplate the possibility, as a turning point in the game.

At one minute past four the messages received were lucidly translated when Rangers were granted an indisputable penalty-kick from which Davie Meiklejohn scored. Three more goals were added in the time which remained before Rangers made their unheralded appearance at the Princess Theatre for an extra curtain call. Not only because of that victory was the year to be one which would be underlined when the game's history was set down. Two weeks

Thomson, J McStay and Fleming tangle as a corner comes over. From this situation Bob McPhail scored Rangers' second in the 1928 Final.

Rae of Partick Thistle punches clear from Fleming of Rangers in the 1930 Final replay. He was, however, beaten twice in the course of the match.

before the Cup Final the 'Wembley Wizards' were enshrined for the feat of defeating England by five goals to one, a game which also gave even wider currency to the nickname 'The Wee Blue Devil' whenever Alan Morton's name was mentioned. Inside Ibrox, though, he was known as the 'Wee Society Man', a reference to Morton's penchant for going to his everyday place of work as a mining engineer wearing a bowler hat, lightweight overcoat, and carrying a rolled umbrella — the sartorial style of those who carried out the less exerting function of dealing with penny policies and the like as collectors of insurance money.

It was an odd feature of Morton's career with Rangers that he never trained with his peers, coming to Ibrox in the evenings from the pit in Lanarkshire to perfect his art. That no one would have noticed as much on a Saturday would be ascribed later by his partner McPhail to the fact that football was always easier when you had good team players as opposed to a team of good players. Morton was a purist and occasionally impatient with those he believed to have let their standards drop. Once he allowed a pass from McPhail which was, in the case of the diminutive winger, above head height to go out for a throw in. Vaguely abusive enquiries for an explanation were answered in semaphore pointing out that football implied what it said and that the head was only to be used *in extremis*.

While having a fair conceit of himself, it was also not unknown for Morton to lose the place with those less gifted than himself, whose role in life was to deny such as he self-expression. On one occasion Bram Stoker's copyright was infringed in memorable fashion when he removed a corner flag at Stark's Park, Kirkcaldy, and threatened to use it as a stake on an over-enthusiastic Raith Rovers full-back who had shown scant regard for reputation.

Nevertheless Morton is remembered best for that balance which came as a result of his uniquely prepared boots. He wore only three studs, one at the toe and the other two under the ball of the foot, thereby enabling him to pivot more quickly and complete the entrancement of a full-back still coming to terms with an outside-left who was naturally right-footed and crossed the ball in that cock-eyed way. The cross which hung in the air longer than the aroma of a cheap cigar was Morton's trademark but it was entirely typical of the team who had this exceptional weapon on their side that they should return to their days of nervous disability in the following season when confronted by Scottish Cup Final opponents who ought to have broken up inside Hampden's bowl like soluble aspirin.

Kilmarnock were a team without a manager, the title only later being accorded secretary Hugh Spence, and chosen by a selection committee who approached Hampden with the full set of drawbacks. They were in every way in a state of reduced circumstances, limited by injury to the extent of being without four key players, deflated after an indifferent season in the League, in which they were to finish tenth, and burdened by financial worries. It had even been necessary to go to Aberdeen and ask for Hugh McLaren on loan for the semi-final, in which they had contrived to beat Celtic by the only goal, and the Final itself — something which was permissable under the rules as they stood. The decision of all the players to have their hair cut on the day before the Final, however, resembled only a commendable wish to look smart for their own funeral.

It was a well-attended service, too, with 114,708 possibly moving the Kilmarnock treasurer to think that the score was an irrelevance, anyway, since financial ruination would be avoided by the kindest cut of all, their share of the gate. The burial seemed timed to begin at seventeen minutes past three when Rangers were awarded a penalty to give them the chance of demoralising the opposition in the same manner as they had Celtic the year before. Tom 'Tully' Craig, so called because he came from Tullibody and one of those rarities, the player who has been with both Celtic and Rangers, stepped forward to take an award which had first been rejected after consultation between the referee and one linesman but given after a second opinion was sought from the other, a bout of indecision which took a full three minutes to be brought under control.

Kilmarnock's goalkeeper was Sam Clemie, a man of few words and all of them simple, as he would demonstrate later in the day. His save from Craig appeared to interfere with the concentration of the Rangers players and when half-time was reached without a goal being scored Kilmarnock began to entertain irrational thoughts of visiting the town's Grand Hall for something other than a wake. Two goals, one each from Aitken and Williamson, offered conclusive proof that they were correct, but this extraordinary game was still to provide another epoch-making moment. Possibly stricken by an overwhelming desire to take a Cup-winners' medal at all costs, the Kilmarnock forward 'Peerie' Cunningham resorted to chicanery and the frustrating tactic of deliberately running off-side and so conceding free-kicks which wasted time as the game's closing minutes passed like days. This blatant contravention of the spirit of the game so incensed Rangers' Jock Buchanan that he harangued the referee, Tom Dougray from Belshill, to the extent that the player was sent from the field for dissent. This made Buchanan the first-ever player to be sent off in a Scottish Cup Final and it would be fifty-five years before the next offender suffered the ignominy of the maximum penalty being enforced.

If Buchanan was the villain of the piece then Clemie, the Kilmarnock goalkeeper who had changed the course of the game, was the hero of the hour, if somewhat short on the powers of valediction to sum up his contribution. Escorted to the Grand Hall by a fire engine, possibly dialled on the emergency service since no one could have been expecting the need for its assistance, the team were prevailed upon before leaving to make individual speeches on the subject of this historic occasion. Clemie, from Lugar, moved forward unsteadily to utter the immortal words, 'I can save penalties, but I canna' speak'. His peroration was matched only by the observation of the club's treasurer who, in reply to the thanks proferred publicly by his President, Andrew McCulloch, for executing the fiscal matters of the team with such probity, said it was easy to be honest 'when the purse is empty'.

It would have been less than truthful, though, to suggest that the occasion of their defeat emptied the new stand Rangers had opened at Ibrox shortly before. In the season which followed they were, as McPhail would recall many years later, still looked upon as 'tin gods', even if he had the sneaking suspicion that his occasional travelling companion on the train from Barrhead to Glasgow, the National Chairman of the Independent Labour Party and the honourable member for Bridgeton, Jimmy Maxton, had no idea who he was. The MP would have been unimpressed anyway by a footballer receiving double the national average wage while he was engaged in fighting for the creation of a new social order.

The masses, though, would have been rather more taken with the idea of sharing McPhail's compartment. The home-based players' stock remained high following yet another win over England, this time at Hampden and in sudden and dramatic circumstances rather than with the sustained brilliance which had characterised the previous year's spectacle. Alec Cheyne, a youngster from Aberdeen who had been called in for his first cap as a replacement for Muirhead of Rangers only forty-eight hours before the international, scored from a corner-kick in the last minute, thereby substantiating a theory held later by Alan Morton that in the years between the Great Wars Scotland spawned sufficient players of quality to provide several international sides.

If the theory had been accepted with the proviso that Morton make himself

Fleming of Rangers beats Clemie but McEwan is on hand to clear. Such heroics helped bring Kilmarnock the Cup in 1929.

available for the first eleven chosen no matter what, it did not necessarily follow that without him Rangers were rendered incapable of achieving anything substantial. The last word in elusiveness he may have been, but irreplaceable he was not as his club proved when winning the Scottish Cup again in 1930. They had progressed there to a meeting with Partick Thistle with only one reminder of their sordid past, when they were taken to a replay at Central Park after Cowdenbeath had shared four goals with them in the first match of their second round tie at Ibrox.

Almost one hundred thousand people had watched their semi-final with Hearts at Hampden amid a growing campaign to have both penultimate rounds played on a staggered basis so that the paying public could witness all four teams in action. But money and inconvenience were no object to the likes of those who formed the crowd of 103,686 for the Final replay held at six o'clock on 16 April 1930, following a goal-less draw the previous Saturday. There was, incidentally, a mutual agreement that both clubs should change their colours for the return game and that blue, interestingly enough, was to be banned, although there appears to be no logical reason for this decision.

The replay was Alan Morton's first game since injuring himself eleven days earlier while playing for Scotland at Wembley in a match lost by five goals to two. A recurrence of the trouble left him lame with only fifteen minutes gone. He played no significant part in the game thereafter and, in the days before substitutes were allowed, eventually departed the scene altogether to leave Rangers with only ten men. Morton was nearing the end of his time with Rangers in any case and within three years would retire and take up a seat on the board of directors at Ibrox, where he remained until his death in 1971.

On the night Morton's ineffectiveness was compensated for and, although Torbet equalised Marshall's opening goal for Rangers, 'Tully' Craig, in the best traditions of Scottish Cup coincidence, was able to get the winner for the Ibrox club twelve months after his mistake had cost them the trophy.

Rangers, their pride reinforced by taking the Cup twice in three years, were headed for a period of spectacular dominance where the Scottish Cup was concerned. In 1930 almost half a million people had watched them play a total of seven ties, underlining their growing drawing power and the burgeoning appeal of the Scottish Cup itself. The best years of the Struth era were at hand and the manager had summed up the defeat of Partick Thistle by praising his vanquished opponents in the bellicose terms which tripped most readily off his tongue. They had, he said, 'died gamely'.

Ten days after the Final replay, Rangers, due to play Cowdenbeath at Central Park in a League match, refused a request to bring the Scottish Cup to Fife so that the big crowd might gaze upon it. The trophy, free enough with its favours even to make sure the biggest club in the country had no monopoly on it, was not to spread itself so thin that it was ever likely to be seen at close quarters in Cowdenbeath by means other than public exposition.

But Rangers, who had been happy enough two years earlier to depart from their traditionally circumspect ways and let the silverware adorn the Saturday night stage of the Princess Theatre in Glasgow, were now becoming too big to 'trot the pot around', as they put it. Just how big they were to become in terms of what was still regarded as the most prestigious competition in the domestic game would become apparent in a very short time when the pot found extreme difficulty trotting any further than Govan.

Steeltown blues

THERE WERE countless new sights (and, a little later, sounds) to wonder at. In every High Street in the country the curtains were drawn from a window which looked onto the entire world. In the Scotland of the 1920s cinema had boomed. Glasgow, in that period, possessed more picture houses than any city in Europe and the arrival of the first 'talkie' there in 1929 honed the enthusiasm of that vast audience still sharper. Even when the programme was dull, though, the hall itself might provide ample diversion. The Kelvin in Glasgow had a large and intricate model of a mosque beside the stage as part of its extravagant décor.

The new entertainment business wisely paid tribute to the traditional pastime when, in 1931, the first of those talkies to feature football as an essential element of its plot, *The Great Game*, was shown in Scotland. The real thing, its pulse live and not recorded, retained its distinctive appeal even if the 1931 Scottish Cup competition had the kind of emotional and dramatic conclusion which suggested that something had been learned from such celluloid escapades as *The Perils of Pauline*.

The world was a colourful, if occasionally frightening, place as Celtic and Motherwell took their first steps on the road to Hampden and a new style was emerging as the newspaper business sought to reflect the fact. The *Daily Express* had broken new ground in the trade as it applied a clear lay-out, a direct prose style, and an enthusiasm for opinionated feature writing (rather than plodding reporting) to the business of telling its readers of the doings of such as Al Capone. Towards the end of January it revealed that he was trying to take over control of Hollywood's speakeasies (America squirmed beneath prohibition) and the *Express* swiftly compared him with another, eventually more lethal, trader in extortion — a 'Gangland Musceleini' it called Capone.

Football made for good copy as well and the same paper could speculate on which of the three second round ties (Rangers *v* Dundee, Clyde *v* St Mirren and Kilmarnock *v* Hearts) the 'growing army' of neutral fans should go to. Those pacifists, if many such there really were, would have seen an upset at Ibrox where the dour Dundee team won 2-1. Before the match, however, many of the previews had expressed doubts about a Rangers side still considered a little brittle in the Cup. Indeed, so many of the reporters had 'hunches' about the outcome that the gentlemen of the fourth estate must have resembled a pack of actors auditioning for the part of Quasimodo.

Motherwell's victims in the second round were Albion Rovers and the progress of the match offers its own account of the style of the side. Although the Coatbridge team took the lead Motherwell were able to apply an attacking force which swept that goal from the reckoning as if it were a puff of cigarette smoke in a hurricane and eventually won 4-1. Their forward line was a glittering combination which has continued to play extra-time ever since in the minds of those fortunate enough to have seen them.

The right-winger, John Murdoch, had been overlooked in favour of James Reid when Airdrie chose their side for the 1924 Final but, following his move to Motherwell in 1928, he had developed impressively. Early in 1931 he had been capped against Northern Ireland, recognition granted because of his impressive goal-scoring feats. By the time of the Final he was the club's top scorer with 20 and although his colleagues mocked the fact that he invariably claimed them from close in, promising to present him with a silver medal should he score from a respectable distance, their humour stemmed from a deep gladness that he had such a knack.

Inside from him was John McMenemy who had won a Cup-winners' medal with Celtic in 1927 but who had never quite hit it off with Willie Maley. Since joining Motherwell in 1928 he had gained a measure of strength to add to his clever ball-play and controlled passing.

The centre-forward was a goal-scoring prodigy named Willie McFadyen. Strong, direct and good in the air, he was the perfect foil to the more artistic performers and he would, in the following season, create a surely unbeatable record of 52 League goals as his side took the championship.

The left-wing pairing, however, are names which can almost be thought of as the Rolls and Royce of the Scottish game. Stevenson and Ferrier were a species of perfection which captivated the eyes, and transfixed the full-backs, of a generation. Both the verve and hunger of Ferrier and the inspired prompting of Stevenson have their memorial in the scoring record of the former. In 626 League matches he scored all of 256 goals. The only criticism one can essay is that Ferrier had permitted himself to be born on the wrong side of the border, so, under the regulations of the day, denying the Scottish international side his presence.

Celtic had some impressive players, stern defenders like Willie McGonagle and Jimmy McStay, a midfield range which encompassed the stylish Wilson and the gritty Scarff, and even master illusionists in the attack like Alec Thomson and Charlié Napier. Realistically, though, with Motherwell approaching a peak it should not have been quite enough. Only the presence of Jimmy McGrory at centre left the outcome in a measure of doubt.

Added spice was given the encounter by the fact that it had been representatives of either side — Stevenson and McGrory — who had scored the goals in Scotland's defeat of England a fortnight before but it should not be thought that the era was uniformly in awe of its stars. James Crapnell, then of Airdrie, had originally been chosen for the side but when injury forced him to call off he seems to have been ignored altogether. He was not even given a ticket for the international and eventually paid his own way into the throng of 129,810.

Everyone naturally wanted Motherwell to win — they were the smaller club, they had never won the Cup, they had bravely hung on to their stars despite surprisingly poor gates — and it seemed at first as if that sentiment was to be satisfied. The crowd of 105,000, brought by 40 special trains and by the 237 tramcars and 79 buses which arrived at Hampden each hour before the match, saw a first half profitably dominated by the Lanarkshire side.

After only eight minutes a curling grounder from George Stevenson, having taken a kick off Jimmy McStay, scraped past John Thomson. Twelve minutes later another deflection off the luckless Celtic centre-back gave John McMenemy a goal and Motherwell a comfortable lead. Motherwell's serviceable defenders adeptly frustrated the Glasgow side, who grew more and more inclined to simply toss the ball towards McGrory.

The closest Celtic came to a goal in the first half was when they made two

McClory gathers as McGrory rushes in. The replay of the 1931 Final.

frenzied claims for penalties. On one of those Scarff and Bertie Thomson seemed to chase referee Craigmyle behind a goal. Craigmyle himself was to claim that he was simply moving to take up position for the corner which had been awarded but he had rather given the game away by admitting in an interview published on the morning of the match that he had once run from Celtic keeper Charlie Shaw in a similar situation.

There was little else to excite the Celtic support and the club's players dolefully noted the minutes being ticked off on the clock which stood on the stand (it was destroyed by fire in 1945). With seven minutes to go Celtic were awarded a free-kick twenty yards from the Motherwell goal. As Charlie 'Happy Feet' Napier (the nickname from an erratic running style) prepared to take it Motherwell over-reacted to the threat he posed. Aware that he had scored a crucial goal from such a position in a previous tie with Dundee United, they drafted too many men into their defensive wall. The cunning Napier then rolled the ball wide of that labour-intensive structure and through to McGrory who stepped forward and scored.

Still it seemed that Motherwell might stay ahead for they checked Celtic's first frantic surges for the equaliser and the Lanarkshire side's support began to hope. Some went further. They had brought with them large boards with the letters of their club's name on them and as the end of the game approached they began to hold them aloft. They had got as far as M-O-T-H-E-R-W-E when an on-field event cruelly disrupted their spelling-bee.

In the eighty-ninth minute Bertie Thomson burst down the right but found himself still covered. He turned back, putting the ball onto his left foot and curling it in towards the centre of the goals. Hurtling in to meet it was Allan Craig, the mainstay of the Motherwell defence. He was regarded as the last word in dependability and the club's manager, the former Dundee player John 'Sailor' Hunter, had ascribed the loss of a point to Partick Thistle the previous week to his absence.

As the ball curled in to the goal and away from him he stretched forward and the ball glanced against his head and past his keeper into the top of the net. Then he was lying prone on the ground, inconsolable, beating his fists on the turf. There was scarcely time for the game to re-start.

How much more painful it must even have become when Bertie Thomson was later reported as saying of his fateful cross, 'I thought it was all over. I was waiting for the whistle. I was hanging on to the ball to keep it as a souvenir, but found I couldn't play out time so I just slammed the ball anywhere towards the goal'.

Celtic's supporters were in little doubt as to the root cause of the goal. They reckoned that Craig had been panicked by the thought that McGrory might be lurking behind him (he was not). With this in mind a section of the Celtic support went to Willie Maley's Bank Restaurant in Queen Street seeking an audience with the great player. The Celtic manager would not hear of it and told them to 'clear off'. The denizens of the terracing, still high on their

Sam English (right, facing camera) has just scored his side's third in the 1932 Final replay

feelings of relief, did so, but only after dancing an eightsome reel in the street.

Motherwell were doomed in the replay. Celtic spread their play across the whole of their front line and McGrory was accordingly given a little more room. Hard though the Lanarkshire side fought they could not make good the losses of their goalkeeper McClory. His poor judgement played a part in all four Celtic goals (a brace for both Bertie Thomson and McGrory) and Motherwell could only produce two of their own.

Celtic celebrated the good fortune which had seen them through. As the team bus was briefly stopped in Cathcart Road a flapper (fashionable girl of the time) ran up. One of the players reached out of the window, picked her up and kissed her.

If that was the world of Mills and Boon it was back to the steady rhythms of the authorised timetable the following season. The lavishly gifted Rangers team arrived at Hampden with the minimum of fuss. The season was shadowed for them by the fact that their centre-forward Sam English had been involved in a tragic accident which led to Celtic keeper John Thomson's death in the Old Firm match the previous September. The event seemed to destroy English's career in the long term but in that season he remained professional enough to continue about his business and he set up the club's League scoring record. In the first round of the Cup he scored three of his side's eight against Brechin.

A sprightly Kilmarnock were advancing through a fairly kindly draw to meet them at Hampden. Although the Ayrshire side had won the Cup only three years previously there had been a number of changes. Kilmarnock, by playing Bell in goal and resisting the temptation to recall the experienced Sam Clemie, demonstrated their faith in the youth policy.

Rangers were the team of real stature, a fact palpably revealed when Bob McPhail's car was stolen after his side's 5-2 semi-final victory over Hamilton Accies. The police reacted as if they had been formed to cope with just this emergency. According to one report, 'policemen in speed motors scoured the city' until it was found the following day. The fact that McPhail owned a car also says much about the gradually improving status of the professional footballer.

The Kilmarnock side were connected in the public mind with a more bucolic image, a sheep to be precise. The animal was the club's mascot and the players were photographed with it in the press. Rangers, however, might have complained that it was a misleading symbol for the Ayrshire men contested the Final in a decidedly vulpine manner.

Cartoon record of the competition's 1933 conclusion. Note the mis-spelling of McGrory's name. It would appear that Celtic received coats as part of their prize.

Their eager and sharp half-back line allowed Rangers no time in possession and the Glasgow side fell prey to their own nerves, conceding a goal to 'Bud' Maxwell who had been something of a Cup hero that season. The youthful energy of the side distressed Rangers but it was that very quality (or, to be more precise, its attendant drawbacks) which lost them the advantage it had earlier gained. Bell, while doing nothing very wrong, had looked distinctly uneasy from the start and his nerves were apparent at the equaliser. The goal from thirty yards was not Bob McPhail's trademark, he was normally associated with the whiplash header at the far post, but it was precisely such an effort which defeated the sluggish-looking Bell.

So to a replay, and to a vital change in the Rangers ranks. Alan Morton had to drop out through injury but his career was ending and the side gained by the appearance of the very pacy Jimmy Fleming. Kilmarnock could not so easily contain the forward line and the veteran Sandy Archibald found it possible to apply his deadly skills. Fleming, McPhail and English all scored and Kilmarnock had nothing to offer in response.

In the early thirties, though, it is the Motherwell side and its Cup failures which continue to fascinate. 1933, it seemed, might well be their year. The team was considered to have been improved from two years before for as well as having the same attack they now fielded an international full-back pairing. Crapnell had joined them from Airdrie and Ben Ellis was a Welsh international-alist.

The most remarkable figure of the Cup run, though, was undoubtedly Willie McFadyen. He had set the League scoring record the previous season and his tally for the Cup competition of 1933 may also be a record. Details of John McDougall's goal-scoring for Vale of Leven in the 1878-79 competition are incomplete but McFadyen's performance might be thought superior in any case since far fewer ties are played by the major teams in the twentieth century structuring of the tournament. Aided by five against Montrose and four against Kilmarnock in a quarter-final replay, he scored fifteen goals prior to the Final. He also scored in every match his team played in the tournament before the big occasion at Hampden.

Sadly for Motherwell his feat remains a statistical curio for he could not add to his total in the Final against Celtic. Motherwell gave a shambolic display and McFadyen was left to make what he could, which was little, of the appalling service and support of team-mates and the tight marking of Jimmy McStay.

The centre-forward who mattered was Jimmy McGrory even if his goal was less than memorable. Mackenzie managed to dispossess Bertie Thomson but crashed his clearance against right-back Crapnell and the ball rebounded to lie in the goalmouth, almost immediately to receive the decisive attentions of McGrory.

The Celtic centre had scored the two goals which were the bedrock of Scotland's victory over England a fortnight before but it seems clear that it was his club who commanded his greatest loyalty. Certainly, his country never valued him as he deserved.

In the opening minute of the Final one of his teeth had been knocked out and he played the first half hour in a dazed state. He left the pitch at full-time with his right thumb staved, his ankle swollen, and his knee painfully injured. He would have thought little of it. 'Jimmy McGrory', recalled a team-mate four decades later, 'played as if he was Celtic'.

Back-handers and Front-runners

THERE WAS nothing answering to the description of the Scottish League Championship's predictability to be found where the Scottish Cup was concerned, even after it had passed its sixtieth birthday, when being set in your ways could have been excused as a condition which came with age. Up to the mid-thirties, only Queen's Park and Vale of Leven could claim the distinction of having won the trophy three times in succession, and they were two of only three clubs, Celtic being the other, ever to have played in that number of Finals consecutively.

Contrast that with the First Division title, still looked upon as the lesser of the two tournaments, which had already become the duopoly of the Old Firm with Celtic having won the prize seventeen times to Rangers' twenty-one prior to the 1934-35 season. Without wishing to detract too much from Vale of Leven or Queen's Park's achievements, it is a fact that the amateurs' entry into the history books was recorded in the pre-professional times which bore no comparison to the conditions which confronted the teams whose participation in one of the Cup's most colourful periods distracted attention from the events of the day.

In 1934 Adolf Hitler assumed dictatorial power as 'Fuhrer and Reich-Chancellor' arousing understandable suspicion in neighbouring Austria, political strife hinted at a violent future in Spain, and Italy and Abyssinia squared up to each other in a border incident; all of this causing the prevailing atmosphere to be likened to thunder rolling across Europe. More parochially, a smaller peal, but a significant bang nevertheless, shook the Scottish League in season 1934-35 with the case, unprecedented at managerial level before or since, of William Orr. A Scottish internationalist when he had been a full-back with Celtic, Orr had managed the Airdrie team which won the Scottish Cup from Hibs in 1924. His hitherto unblemished career was tarnished beyond repair, though, when Orr was found guilty after a League enquiry of having, as Falkirk manager, paid a bribe to an Ayr United player, Robert Russell.

A full-back who had come from Clyde and who was obviously suspected of wielding great influence, Russell was called surreptitiously to Brockville over a period of days for nefarious discussions and eventually paid the princely sum of three pounds to feign injury and absent himself from the match between Falkirk and Ayr which would have a decided bearing on which of those two clubs would be relegated to the lower orders. Every man has his price but Russell (who had once been a player at Brockville) seems to have come cheaper than most although he turned out to be a wise choice, if that is the apposite word, since Falkirk duly won both points.

Orr's deceitfulness was subsequently brought to light, however, and the manager suspended for life. His club, found not to have been a knowing party to his plan but ruled to be responsible for his actions nevertheless, was fined twenty-five pounds. In delivering sentence, the match was ordered to be replayed and Ayr reversed the result in front of an official League observer and ten thousand of the curious, thereby assisting in relegating Falkirk for the first time in the club's history. The committee of enquiry observed that the salutory lesson to be learned for the common good was that 'the confidence of the public must never be abused'.

With the aid of the Scottish Cup the 'People's Game' was able to retain its vainglorious title by more honest endeavours, as Rangers' first successful treble in the competition proved between 1934 and 1936. In reaching the Final, St Mirren, Hamilton Academical and Third Lanark, an unlikely trio even to their adherents in Paisley, Lanarkshire and the South side of Glasgow, helped re-affirm belief in the game being occasionally poor but always scrupulously honest.

The Scottish Cup still had its eccentric side, as in the case of Dalbeattie Star, the club who leased their ground from a farmer in Dumfries and who irked the bigger teams drawn against them by having their supporters pay admission money at the gate leading up to the property in question, possibly giving birth to the phrase 'gate receipts'.

In refusing to sell out their ground rights, a still common practice in those days, Dalbeattie's agricultural policy at least guaranteed the integrity of the competing teams, no matter how humble, in being in the Cup for prestige as well as profit. Rangers began their triumphal procession against another of the breed, Blairgowrie, in January of 1934 by scoring fourteen times at Ibrox and conceding only two, both presumably having been given away out of boredom. In doing so the Glasgow club equalled their scoring record for one match in the competition. James Fleming scored no fewer than nine of them in a remarkable match which began with a home goal after thirty seconds and ended with all those after Rangers' tenth coming in the last four minutes.

It was, as might have been suspected, a heady time in Rangers' life. Shortly before that season's Scottish Cup got underway the club had lost to Kilmarnock, but that was their first League defeat at Ibrox for three years and they had a team possessed of an awesome blend of youth and experience buttressed by a depth of reserve strength unsurpassed anywhere else in the country.

Some positions in the side, though, were regarded as being too important to be entrusted to those still with an air of untried vulnerability about them. The considerable talents of Bob McPhail at inside-forward, for example, were estimated as being of paramount importance for the Scottish Cup Final against St Mirren, even though the player had to take part with a mummified midriff to protect a groin injury. Observing the extravagant bandaging swaddled around his middle, McPhail remarked to the Rangers manager Bill Struth that he would not be able to lift his leg very high. 'St Mirren won't know that', was all he was told by way of consolation from a man with a low tolerance threshold whenever malingering was suspected. Only actual cessation of breathing, one is left to imagine, would have merited sick leave from Hampden.

Few others in a crowd of 113,403 would have known there was anything wrong with McPhail either, though, as he scored one of Rangers' five goals without reply against a team who reached the Final in spite of being in collective state of disrepair and who were relegated the following season as conclusive proof of their decline.

If McPhail had yet more damage to inflict on the unsuspecting in future Scottish Cups, the win over St Mirren was to be the high water mark in the

1934. Tom Hamilton punches clear from McGregor of St Mirren. Hamilton kept a clean sheet and Rangers scored five.

career of one of his team-mates, Doctor James Marshall, who up until then had combined his sporting activities with a place in the research department of Glasgow's Royal Infirmary. Continued inhalation of success had had a detrimental effect, in Bill Struth's diagnosis, on the good doctor's commitment to the cause and the player was transferred to Arsenal in time for the following season, so taking his medicine for the sickness of performing only when the notion took him, a terminal condition in the Ibrox set-up of that time.

Before taking his enforced leave of the scene, Doctor Marshall played one more match for Rangers when the team, who had already completed the Cup and Championship double at any rate, returned to Hampden four days later for their final League game of the season against Queen's Park. Scoring more than two goals would have enabled Rangers to surpass Motherwell's record of 119 goals in the League but a one-all draw meant that it was a case of what the good sward giveth the good sward taketh away.

As one door closed another seemed always ready to open at Ibrox, however, and the way was made clear after Doctor Marshall for the emergence of 'Torry' Gillick, a precociously gifted teenager who played outside-left and perfectly suited the aerodynamic theory popularly held within Ibrox to explain the construction of Struth's Rangers teams. The side was thought of as an aeroplane and aircraft could not reach for the heights without proper wings.

That Hamilton Academical should be their next Scottish Cup Final opponents flew in the face of all logic. Hamilton, however, had gamely refused all financial blandishments which came their provincial way and persisted in their avowed intention of winning the big pot. Their 1934-35 season had begun with the Douglas Park chairman Jimmy Lyon rejecting offers totalling thirteen thousand pounds from English clubs for two of his players, a gesture which would have caused the directors of both Hearts and Dundee United to blanche.

At that time the Edinburgh club's board had been physically attacked in the city's Free Gardeners' Hall for their inability to explain how, with travelling expenses for the previous season of only £1861 and total revenue of £17,000, the club had capital of just £2000 and was unable to pay out any dividend. Meanwhile at Tannadice, lack of income at the gates was said to be endangering the existence of the club.

If both stories offered proof of how some things never change, Hamilton must have had a premonition that this was to be their best and last chance to bask in the Scottish Cup's reflected glory. The not insubstantial sum of £300 was offered to Brechin City first of all to give up their ground rights for the first round at Glebe Park. Their refusal enabled Hamilton to save their money yet still negotiate a path through to meet Clyde in the next round. From being two goals down at half-time Hamilton eventually gained a three-all draw and won by six goals to three in the replay.

All their efforts, including the defeat of Aberdeen in the semi-final, drew scant reward when Hamilton's goalkeeper Peter Shevlin, a Cup Final winner with Celtic ten years earlier, was injured so badly he could not play against Rangers. He had, until then, been ever-present in the side that season. Hamilton refused to bow to any conspiracy of the fates and made one last grand gesture to contribute towards what they thought was their destiny. An audacious approach was made to Chelsea to procure the services on loan for the day of John Jackson, who was at that time the goalkeeper of the Scotland international side. Permission from London was refused, unfortunately, and the club took part in only their second Scottish Cup Final ever with a teenage reserve, Peter Morgan, in Shevlin's place.

It was not altogether the mismatch it might have looked however. By the

1935. One of Morgan's great saves for Hamilton. The forward on this occasion is Smith. Two goals from Smith, however, brought Rangers the trophy.

day of the Final Hamilton had finished fourth in the First Division and had scored a total of twenty goals on their way to Hampden. Strangely, although Rangers approached the ground from the opposite direction having retained the League championship, Struth's side still did not meet with universal approval, either. The main thrust of the criticisms made against them was that Rangers were dull and frequently afflicted by a 'sleepy sickness' as one hyper-critical journalistic observer of the time vitriolically described the side's malady in his copy. The mind may boggle at what it took to be considered a wide awake success then, or how the owner of the same *nom de plume* would have reacted to some of the dramatic misfortunes which were to befall the club in later decades, but no matter.

William Struth, Rangers manager from 1920 to 1954. The drawing was made in 1936.

Rangers had temporarily lost the services of their redoubtable wing-half Davie Meiklejohn, who had played in the Final of the season before, through injury, but in defence they were still as yielding as reinforced concrete. The soon to be fabled Jerry Dawson had taken over in goal and Jimmy Simpson, whose son, Ronnie, was to write a colourful passage of his own in the family history some thirty years later by contributing largely to Celtic's finest hour, took on a monolithic look at centre-half. The introduction of Alex Venters and 'Torry' Gillick beside the vast wealth of experience in the forward line hardly intimated imminent collapse, either. A discerning public appeared to have decided that the outcome was a formality at any rate with the Final attracting a comparatively low crowd of 87,286.

Low because this was the beginning of the game's major growth period at the turnstiles, after all. Earlier that season it had been stated that from the following year all top matches at Hampden would be all-ticket, a proposal which was shown to be totally justified when, the week before Rangers and Hamilton met, more than fifty thousand potential customers had to be turned away from the ground, leaving a more fortunate, and punctual, throng of

129,693 to watch Scotland defeat England by two goals to nil. Another two seasons would pass, however, before the all-ticket policy was properly implemented.

That same season a crowd of twenty-seven thousand had witnessed the semi-final of the Scottish Junior Cup between Petershill and Shawfield. In the end the Scottish Cup Final's outcome was predictable but not in the manner of its achievement for Rangers. An outstanding display of goalkeeping from the youngster Morgan, the highlight of which was a penalty save from McPhail, kept the score down to a narrow 2-1 win in the Ibrox club's favour. This still ensured that they would have the chance in the coming season to amend their own club record by becoming the first side in the twentieth century to win the Scottish Cup three times in a row, something they would contemplate on a Summer tour of the United States after they had completed what must have seemed like the altogether less daunting task of obtaining the necessary visas to enter that country.

Questions like: Are you an anarchist?; Are you a polygamist?; and Have you ever been in an alms house?, had obviously been compiled by the American immigration authorities without prior knowledge of the tight ship Bill Struth commanded from the bridge at Ibrox.

'Torry' Gillick could have offered sound testimony there, for he became the next player unceremoniously shipped out from Ibrox to England for insubordination in the form of laziness, the charge having been levelled against him by a remorselessly demanding manager.

Gillick had already gone to Everton by the time Rangers set out in pursuit of their target, one more instance of the club's refusal to let anything or anyone stand in the way of their grand design. Rangers, with commendable foresight, knew exactly in which direction they were headed and how many they wanted to come with them. Planning permission was sought, and granted, to extend their ground's capacity and there was a single-minded ruthlessness in operation on the playing side, too, on the way to meeting Third Lanark in the Final of 1936.

It was a peculiarity of Bob McPhail's otherwise outstanding career that in spite of representing his country against England on numerous occasions he had never played in the bi-annual meeting at Wembley. No particularly brilliant powers of deduction were required on the part of those with a cynical caste to their mind to see that the close proximity of this fixture and any Scottish Cup Final in which Rangers were due to take part offered the soundest explanation for this strange omission from his list of accomplishments.

No amount of persuasion will, to this day, coerce McPhail into admitting that this was indeed the case but his refusal to emphatically deny the theory may be considered admissable evidence that the Scottish Cup was held in even higher esteem on his part than participation in these historic confrontations.

How else could his absence from the legendary match in 1936 be explained. It was, if not because of a tactical withdrawal, as incongruous as the story of Tommy Walker, the then twenty-year-old forward of revered memory from Hearts, who scored the Scottish equaliser with thirteen minutes to go from a penalty kick delayed agonisingly when he thrice had to place the ball on the spot after the wind had done its damnedest to blow it, and Walker's concentration, off the mark. Walker, who thus became, temporarily, the most

1936. Bob McPhail in action in the Final which brought him his seventh and last winners' medal.

popular man in Scotland refused to become a passenger on the train taking the relieved team home to Glasgow. Instead he journeyed alone to Livingstone on the grounds that he did not like big crowds. This frame of mind obviously had no effect on his mental fortitude in front of tens of thousands who had held their breath for fear of adding to the wind velocity he overcame to attain storybook status that day.

One week later McPhail, the man for whom injury was a moveable feast, had been granted another miraculous recovery and took part in what was to be his eighth and last Scottish Cup Final.

His side's opponents showed even then the inclination towards living on life's razor edge which saw that they would, one day, be universally thought of as the much-loved but ill-fated Third Lanark. They had only gained promotion from the other ranks at the beginning of that season and their place in the Final at Hampden was all the more surprising because they were to finish only ninth in the League, never playing as well as some of their talented complement, like Jimmy Carabine, promised they might.

Internally, the beginnings of the malignant disorder which would see to it that the club had just over thirty years left in existence also showed up. There were serious misgivings expressed, for example, over the accuracy of the returns, both size of gate and receipts, from the first round win over Hearts, a forerunner of many such tales about the club which was reduced to paying out match officials from the takings of its one-arm bandit before the sorry end eventually came in 1967.

There was no doubt about their right to be at Hampden, however, following a convincing 3-1 win over Falkirk in the semi-final. The Brockville club, it may be noted, had cleaned up their business considerably following the bribe scandal and won promotion back to the First Division under the managership of Tom 'Tully' Craig, who had left Rangers to perform this restoration work on the club's image and standing.

Added piquancy was given to the story of that sordid episode, too, by the fact that on the day of the Scottish Cup Final Falkirk's disappointment at not being there may have been lessened by the 6-0 defeat of Ayr United at Celtic Park, a result which won the home team the championship and consigned the side involved with Falkirk to the dark place they themselves had recently left.

The Final was less remarkable, other than for the fact that Bob McPhail was allowed to end his Cup Final career in tidy and distinctive fashion. After only two minutes of play he took advantage of an uncharacteristic slip by the Third Lanark centre-half Denmark and scored what was to be the only goal of the game. Thus Rangers had won their treble and McPhail bowed out with a share of the record haul in this century of seven Scottish Cup-winners' medals, (Jimmy McMenemy and Billy McNeill reached the same total), six with Rangers and one with Airdrie.* For over forty-five years these medals nestled in a bank vault in Glasgow until an approach was made to their owner by Rangers last season.

They have since been transferred to the trophy room at Ibrox where they are on permanent display. At Bob McPhail's behest they will remain there until he dies, whereupon their future will be decided by his son.

To those who stop to admire them, McPhail's medals will be a fragrant reminder of one of the club's greatest players from a time when Rangers were busily establishing their foothold on the consciousness of the community at large.

The man himself is less sentimental about the period, observing drily that he has hundreds of other 'rewards' on his legs which no-one can see as a keepsake of those days. At the same time as McPhail drifted out of the big-time, Davie Meiklejohn, another inspirational figure at Ibrox, retired to count his haul of five Scottish Cup-winners' medals. One more of Struth's Rangers teams was breaking up and where the Cup was concerned a twelve year sabbatical, during which World War Two provided an ample diversion for half that time, would be necessary before normal service could be resumed.

It did not take anything like that long, though, to unearth some of those who would follow in the illustrious footsteps of their predecessors at Ibrox. After defeating Third Lanark, Struth led his side to Falkirk to provide the opposition in a benefit match for Brockville full-back Hugh Hamill. The occasion marked the debut of a teenager from Winchburgh whose exploits also became the stuff of Scottish Cup legend — Willie Thornton. The story continued to flow.

*Bobby Lennox of Celtic has eight winners' medals but three were gained as substitute and on two of those occasions he played no part in the game itself.

End of the beginning

THERE IS nothing which can be lost so irretrieveably as innocence. The Second World War was a prolonged violation of civil liberties which changed a nation's perception of itself. The conclusion of hostilities after six years brought up the dawn of a brand new, if not everyone's idea of a brave new world.

If the game of professional football remained entrenched as a sub-culture to which the populace turned as a morale boosting means of diversion, it too had misplaced for ever the traditional values with which it had taken its leave in a properly organised sense in 1939. To borrow from, and apply to the game, a phrase coined by Winston Churchill at the time, the outbreak of war was the 'beginning of the end' for the slightly eccentric behavioural patterns it was still possible to detect then. The end of the beginning of life in a more hard-bitten world came with the advent of peace time, when to play to win was not only acceptable but advisable in the pursuit of self-preservation.

The game brought officially into being in Scotland in 1873 had gone through the seven ages by the time the lights went out all over Europe and an impetuous new arrival had to be adjusted to when they went back on again. Before time was up on world peace the unthinkable was still capable of taking place, however, even in front of 93,000 people at Ibrox for the traditional New Year's Day fixture with Celtic in 1937.

Believing that the National Anthem was to played on the signal of the referee's whistle and prior to the kick off, the Rangers players stood rigidly to attention while the seemingly irreverent McGrory of Celtic centred the ball to Delaney. He took off unimpeded like a runaway piece from a fair ground football game and was only halted when McDonald of Rangers, who emerged from his trance-like state after noticing that the Govan Burgh Band were packing up their instruments and steadfastly ignoring the possibility of playing the National Anthem, tackled him and gave away a corner.

If they were overlooked that day because of some confusion, the proprieties were nearly always observed at any other time. When Rangers went out of the Scottish Cup in ignominious fashion to Queen of the South at Dumfries soon after, for example, taking away only a cheque for £240, which would not have covered their running costs at Ibrox for a week, there was never any hint of ill-mannered behaviour in spite of the crushing disappointment.

Unable to perform the then traditional act of congratulating their victorious opponents by shaking each one vigorously by the hand, because of a field invasion by ecstatic locals, the Rangers players to a man visited Queen of the South's dressing room afterwards and responded like gentlemen. To put the result before the spirit of the game was still thought reprehensible, and so Hearts were looked down upon for being so unfeeling as to break King's Park into little bits by scoring a dastardly fifteen goals, with none in reply, in the second round.

Just before half-time in the 1937 Final. The gates were closed after 147,365 had been admitted but many of those excluded lingered on.

One knew instinctively how one should act in any given situation in those morally incorruptible times. When the Scottish internationalist full-back George Cummings of Aston Villa was taken into protective custody for being the worse of strong drink at the wheel of his car, he found himself a former employee of the club within one hour of being convicted by the courts for that offence.

If such strict adherence to the moral code was still in vogue to this day, it may be thought, the unemployment figures would show a sharp seasonal increase. In Cummings' case, however, clemency was eventually shown and he resumed his career with the Birmingham club.

Hearts' punishment for breaching the unwritten code of ethics with regard to the actual playing of the game itself was to suffer dismissal at the unexpected hands of Hamilton Accies in the next round of the Scottish Cup. The less charitable and more aggressively nationalistic might have said this was no more than they deserved for becoming the first Scottish club to appoint an English manager, the former Arsenal and England goalkeeper Frank Moss.

He took over the day before the game and his wife, who knew as much about the Scottish scene as he did then, added one last, ironic touch by turning up at the match with good intentions and her old Arsenal scarf, the red and white colours of which were identical to those worn by the Accies players.

The Final itself that year, which was to be contested by Celtic and Aberdeen, was to be the last major occasion at Hampden which the SFA would allow to take place without a pre-determined number of tickets being sold first of all. If this was not an idea which met with universal approval, there had also been loudly voiced rumblings about the prices being doubled for the day, as well.

What actually happened, though, was that a crowd, which will now never be bettered for a European club match, of 147,365, with an estimated twenty to thirty thousand locked outside, turned up at Hampden. Even amid a prevailing atmosphere which might have been thought to be adjacent to the madhouse, a sense of order and occasion was still important.

These were the days of the white-suited figure of Eliot Dobie, noted radio and concert artiste, taking the podium and leading the multitude in community singing with instrumental accompaniment provided by the ubiquitous Govan Burgh Band.

The words of the songs were printed for the enjoyment of all in a special programme listing the pre-match entertainment. A practice which, had it not been discontinued naturally through a change in public taste, would certainly have fallen into disrepute in the decades which came after, when various lyrics would have been unable even to leave the printers for fear of infringing various laws concerned with public order and decency.

Suitably mellowed by the clearing of their throats on inoffensive material, the Celtic support in particular were encouraged to start up again after only eleven minutes when Johnny Crum lay handily placed to sweep in a rebound off a shot from his team-mate Willie Buchan.

Less than a minute had passed, however, when Aberdeen fashioned an equaliser. A cross from Benyon was missed by the Celtic goalkeeper Joe

The 1937 Final. Celtic v Aberdeen, the record crowd for a club match in Europe.

Kennaway and his centre-half Alex Lyon, but not by Armstrong of Aberdeen, whose shot enabled the game to stay on level terms for the next hour. The winner eventually fell to Celtic and was created by the oldest player on the field, the legendary Jimmy McGrory.

A veteran of fifteen years with his beloved Celtic, McGrory had scored in every previous round of that year's competition and was also taking part in what would be his last Scottish Cup Final before retiring from the playing side of the game. It would not have concerned him that he was unable to sustain his scoring record until the very end, rather he would have taken the view that it genuinely did not matter who scored as long as someone did for the team of your choice. On the whole McGrory's record was so remarkable as a goal scorer that his club could not honestly have backed him up on that particular piece of philosophy, however.

With nineteen minutes left for play that day, though, McGrory fed the ball to Willie Buchan and his goal took the trophy back to Parkhead after a gap of four years, although it was destined to leave there again soon after under circumstances which could have been said to be remarkably co-incidental.

The avuncular, pipe smoking McGrory left Celtic to become manager of Kilmarnock in the season which followed and took them to Hampden at the end of one of the most astonishing competitions in the tournament's history. Time was not on the side of peace but East Fife apparently enjoyed limitless hours in which to complete their epic run to the Final in which they became the first side from outwith the First Division to win the trophy.

It was a time of extraordinary happenings. The ground of Larbert Amateurs, who were to play Morton in the second round of the Cup, was found on closer inspection by the representatives of the SFA to have a bricked up boundary wall which prevented the ball from going out for a corner at one junction. Perhaps it was such a structure which was referred to when teams were said to have their backs to the wall.

They were given two weeks in which to restore their pitch to logical dimensions or risk going over the wall. In the event the tie was played at Watling Park, Falkirk. Even less time was granted to Ross County from the Highland League to put their house in order. In their case the joinery work was found to be at fault, to wit two sets of goals which had posts four inches shorter than the laws of the game permitted. The mistake was spotted before Albion Rovers eliminated them from a tournament which threatened to take up the whole of 1938 when East Fife settled down to their marathon run by taking two games to put out Aberdeen in the third round.

There were no shortage of surprises like that one. Both Hearts and Hibs, for instance, had gone out in the first round, leaving only the unfashionable St Bernard's and Edinburgh City as the standard bearers for the capital in the Cup. The biggest shock of all, though, came when Jimmy McGrory returned to Parkhead with Kilmarnock and put out the holders with a 2-1 win which came only a few weeks after the Ayrshire club had lost by eight clear goals in a League match played on the same ground. Celtic had, for the Cup-tie, adopted a new, Arsenal type strip, retaining, of course, their traditional green and white colours. The luckless jerseys were thereafter consigned to a dark recess inside Parkhead and never seen again, while Celtic men tried to tell themselves that it was no loss what a friend had received.

They found that concept less abstract and far easier to accept when

McGrory's team then had the nerve to follow up that result by eliminating Rangers in the semi-final, following a frantic match at Ibrox in which, with the score standing at one-all, there were then five goals in the last forty minutes, with Kilmarnock eventually getting the winner two minutes from the end.

Still without all that much attention being paid to them, meanwhile, East Fife, doggedly thrashing around in the undergrowth, once again required two games to put out their next opponents, Raith Rovers, with a penalty from Herd in the last minute being all that kept them from a third match.

Once safely into the semi-finals by that tortuous route, however, the East Fife players should have asked to switch from the conventional weekly wage with bonuses in order to go on to the piece work scale. Such a move could have enabled them to retire on the proceeds of this one Cup run as it began to really develop momentum.

1938 and Beaton, Noble, Kirk and Falloon of Clyde receive instruction from Mattha Gemmell, the club's trainer, prior to their quarter-final tie with Third Lanark. Gemmell served the club for 47 years.

Paired with their peers from the Second Division, the doughty St Bernard's, it would not have surprised anyone connected with East Fife that their first game should end in a draw. The real fun started, however, when three goals were disallowed in all before the replay eventually ended up with the same scoreline of one goal each. A third game was fixed for Tynecastle, only for it to be discovered that a testimonial match for the Hearts player Tommy Walker had earlier been arranged by the club for the same night.

Pushed back further on the calendar, the game seemed destined to be the first semi-final ever played after the Final itself and by now captivated watchers were keeping one eye on the vote for the unification of Austria and Germany and the other on what it would take to prise East Fife apart from St Bernard's.

Two days before their meeting, Dave McLean, the East Fife manager, as he was then permitted to do, signed on loan the Falkirk player Dan McKerrall. As anyone with a sense of the romance of the Cup will doubtless have guessed,

McKerrall then proceeded to score the winner five minutes before the end to prevent a fourth game and a possible act of Parliament to decide who went through to meet Kilmarnock in the Final. The joyfulness of the occasion was totally ruined for the manager, McLean, however, since his brother had been killed in a car crash the day before and he sat motionless and un-interested throughout the entire game.

It had taken a total of nine matches, one with extra-time, and a running schedule of fourteen hours in all to get East Fife to Hampden and it should therefore have been entirely expected that the Final would not be decided on a single day.

The first match of the 1938 Final. McKerrell of East Fife unsuccessfully appeals for a goal after charging the keeper over the line.

Even though East Fife did their level best to rid themselves of the distinction of being the arch-procrastinators in the competition by scoring through MacLeod in only sixteen minutes, it was Kilmarnock who proved to be the awkward ones. McAvoy's equaliser was not without problems for them either, though. The Cup Final replay meant that Kilmarnock, whose League form had been as bad as their play was good in the Cup, had to go back to Hampden on the Wednesday, play Morton at home on the Friday and then go to Tynecastle the day after to face Hearts. The two League games needed to yield at least two points to prevent Kilmarnock from being relegated.

In each successive round from the quarter-final stage onwards East Fife had picked up a new player on the eve of the match in which they carried the day. (Andrew Duncan of St Johnstone being the man signed in the last eight.) Perhaps feeling it would bode ill to give up on a good thing like that, the club asked for, and got, Johnny Harvey on loan from Hearts for the Final replay, even though he had not played a great deal of first team football for the Edinburgh side. The more prosaic motive was an injury to Andy Herd in the first game.

If Harvey had been subconsciously conserving his energy for this one

McAvoy's (far right) equaliser in 1938. The goal won Kilmarnock a replay but only delayed East Fife's victory.

moment, then he was a wise man from the East, sure enough. Coming to the club for whom the regulation ninety minutes was just a warm up, Harvey played his part in bringing about a two-all draw before extra-time was necessary yet again. Goals from Miller and McKerrall then took the Cup to Fife and, consequently, history was re-written, which was only fitting since the winners did everything twice in order to put their name in the record books, and took a grand total of seventeen-and-a-half hours to gain that recognition. Undaunted, Kilmarnock defeated Morton 3-0 forty-eight hours later to end an eventful, if unrewarding, first season in club management for McGrory.

The sense of anti-climax for East Fife who, in spite of their memorable achievement were still playing among the lower orders, must have been overwhelming in 1939. The holders went out of the competition meekly to Montrose in spite of having home advantage and once again the Scottish Cup was sent spinning in to the air and with no foregone conclusions by any means about who was going to snatch it and claim it as theirs.

For the first time this century, as if to underline the egalitarian nature of the competition at that stage in its life, a second successive season would pass without Celtic or Rangers appearing in the Final. They had started the year by playing each other in front of a British record crowd for a League match of 118,730 inside Ibrox. Only beginning to be noticed then was the adverse effect suffered by the Rangers pitch as a result of the staging of a military tattoo there during the Empire Exhibition in Glasgow.

Once the Rangers players were refused permission even to go on to the field wearing football boots during the week so that the playing surface could retain the look and texture of a bowling green when show time came around on a Saturday afternoon. If the ravages of horse drawn carriages had taken their toll and made the pitch a leveller, there was even worse to follow when Clyde came to Ibrox and put Rangers out of the Cup by four goals to one (Willie Martin bagging all four). Clyde, although they had appeared in two Scottish Cup Finals, had never done so at Hampden. In getting there that year it was to be a case of third time lucky since they would win the trophy to take away with

1939. Clyde's first Scottish Cup success.

them for the first time following their initiation to the national stadium.

Apart from the comparatively exotic margin of their win at Ibrox, Clyde's run was of the modest, hard working, unspectacular type held in such high esteem at the time.

The intractable Hearts, clearly intent on bringing the good name of the game into shame by blatant boastfulness, scored no less than twenty-eight goals over two games in the first and second rounds, fourteen against Penicuik and the same number against Elgin. The smelling salts were put away when they were then punished for their brazen ways after extra-time against Celtic in the third round.

Clyde's opponents in the Final were Motherwell, an elegant side of five Scottish internationalists and one Welsh (Ben Ellis) whose status as one of the best teams never to have won the Cup until then was attributable to the kind of bad luck which had, eight years earlier, seen them lead Celtic by two goals in the Final with seven minutes to go and then falter, ultimately to lose in a replay. Having disposed of Celtic, ironically, at the quarter-final stage, Motherwell may have thought fortune was to be redressed in the most apposite fashion. Two goals in the last four minutes of a replayed semi-final with Aberdeen had also swept them into Hampden on an optimistic tide.

With Hitler by then across Vienna, Prague and Lithuania it was already a race to the tape between an organised existence, including the sporting life, and the disruption of war. Clyde were the more determined to seize the time and then run for cover.

Dougie Wallace, brought to Scotland from South Africa two years previously, began what turned out to be a rout with the only goal of the first half for Clyde. It was a practised trick of the Shawfield defence to send every defensive clearance to one of their wingers and let him adopt tunnel vision until he came screeching to a halt on the bye-line in time to deliver the telling cross. On this occasion Robertson was the model, while Wallace collected his pass, pivoted around the centre-half, Blair, and unleashed a shot high into the net.

The second goal was comic-tragedy and finished off Motherwell as serious opponents. The side from Lanarkshire had used the off-side trap all season and had shown no inclination to change their ways at Hampden. When the Clyde centre-forward Martin ran into an off-side position in the second half, quickly realised his mistake and ran back on-side, no-one was in any doubt except Andrew Murray, the Motherwell goalkeeper. Out of sheer force of habit, presumably, he booted the ball out to where he had seen Martin standing, expecting to see a free kick being taken.

Before his fellow defenders could react to this sudden aberration, the Motherwell man stood perplexed as Martin gathered the ball instead and ran forward to score easily. Demoralised, Motherwell conceded another two goals to Noble and then Martin again in the last five minutes. Joy was unconfined in that part of the East End of Glasgow which houses Clyde, but they are not long, the days of wine and roses.

On the Wednesday after the Scottish Cup Final conscription was announced and five months later the words of Neville Chamberlain on the wireless signalled that Britain was at War. Set against a horrendous loss of life, the game of football pales into insignificance and there was no attempt, as there had been during the 1914-18 conflict, to pretend there was nothing going on, really.

Large groups of people forming crowds inside football stadia like so many sitting ducks was clearly not on and conscription also made team selection haphazard. There were impromptu Cup competitions and a temporary

Management 1930s style. Davie McLean (left) engineered East Fife's 1938 triumph. Beside him are Jimmy Smith and Johnny Haddow, Dumbarton's manager and trainer.

Southern League but by and large the game as people knew and loved it was a bogey.

The same people, those who were fortunate enough to survive and come back to form the spectating public, might have wondered if the same could not have been said for the type of game with which they were presented when season 1946-47 saw the re-introduction of the Scottish Cup. Celtic, for example, whose creative play was a copyright skill which had previously carried them to the heights, went out to Dundee, then in the 'B' division, and were roundly criticised by their own support for trading muscle for manoeuvrability.

Rangers fared little better, being unable even to make the last eight of the competition. And Clyde, their hard won status as the Cup-holders put in brackets after their name in the newspapers of the day for the benefit of those whose entire lives had been placed in a parenthetical state and who had forgotten about it due to a six year war, also retired without sound or fury at the first round stage.

The first post-war Cup Final was, in fact, between Aberdeen and Hibs, who had won their way there at the end of a peculiar competition which had to adapt its own rules to merge with the nation's requirements. Midweek matches were banned by order of the government and, as a consequence, replays of Cup-ties were out of the question. Ties had to be played to a finish and after a period of twenty minutes extra-time in the event of a draw further portions of overtime then took place. Each period of this extra, extra-time lasted ten minutes, or until a deciding goal was scored, whichever came soonest. Hibs' semi-final victory over Motherwell occupied all of 142 minutes.

Hibs were the coming thing in many respects. Their talented side had six players in the Scottish League pool for a match with Ireland that season and were the firm favourites to end their own annual failure in the Scottish Cup.

Showing a more prosaic approach to their work, the Aberdeen players spent the day before the Final at the Bogside race meeting. It was suggested, not altogether light heartedly, that the financial losses incurred by some on that outing were such that a Cup Final bonus was absolutely essential. After only thirty seconds of play, though, they looked to be odds against making an appearance at the pay-out window when Hibs scored. Hamilton equalised for Aberdeen, however, and shortly before half-time the Final was settled, ensuring that the Aberdeen players could go home with the housekeeping intact, when Williams scored with a cavalier shot from the bye-line which ripped through the little space between keeper and near post. The men from the Granite City could even afford to miss a penalty in the second half.

This Final was notable for two points. It was, as befitted the more intense nature of competition in the professional game, the first time the players received their medals in full view of the crowd, proving that to be seen to glory in victory was no longer a vulgarity.

Although there are references to runners-up medals in nineteenth century newspapers, it was only in 1947 that it became standard practice to have such medals struck for the losers.

Hibs were therefore the first in modern times to learn that these are generally regarded as a waste of time, dark reminders of unhappy days, better thrown in bottom drawers. Even more unfortunately for Hibs they would become all too used to taking second prize in Cup-ties.

The Benevolent Dictator

T HE IDEA OF the town of Arbroath as a reliable barometer of public opinion was always a touch fanciful but rarely was it exposed as being more inaccurate than in the immediate post-war years when the indigenous population found themselves out of step with the rest of Scotland and running contrary to every social trend within the game of football.

An advertisement appeared in the newspapers of the time inviting applications for the vacant post of manager to Arbroath FC. Perhaps in the realisation that even in the prevailing austerity the position to be filled was not the glamorous type of job likely to inspire letters by the sackful, a decision was taken with the full knowledge and consent of the ruling local administration that a council house would be immediately forthcoming to the successful applicant. Such munificence had its own reward when a total of sixty, presumably homeless, would-be chief executives at Gayfield Park put pen to paper, salivating at the prospect of becoming rate-payers in the County of Angus.

Those who already had that privilege anyway were not so moved, however, at the idea of welcoming a new managerial supremo under such profligate circumstances, liable, as they were, to undermine the moral fibre of those at an impressionable age who might think the pursuit of a career in football the only way to such undreamed of riches. A meeting of those on the voters' roll able to appreciate the gravity of the situation was called by the local Labour Party and their disgust was put down as a matter of public record in a letter sent to the Secretary of State for Scotland.

The emotional groundswell was summed up by the impassioned observation of one tremulous townsman who said that, 'The station master in Arbroath cannot get a council house and he is more of a key worker than any football manager'.

Such a phrase would never have been uttered in those parts of Glasgow and beyond where Rangers were the club held in high esteem. As well as being the period of the record crowds and the all-consuming love affair with the game, those post-war years were also twilight time in the career of Bill Struth.

Struth spoke of his club with an evangelistic zeal, as if describing something not of this world at all, defining his idea of what constituted a good Ranger as being someone who was, 'true in their conception of what the Ibrox tradition seeks from them. No true Ranger has ever failed in the mission set him'. He was already seventy-one years old when the the first post-war missionaries set out to challenge for the Scottish Cup, which they had last won in 1936. By then Struth was also a director at Ibrox and a disciplinarian who demanded unswerving loyalty from his staff.

He would not have been pleased had Willie Thornton, the centre-forward of revered memory from that era, made it known that Struth had sent the player's widowed mother two pounds every week while her son was spending the war in Egypt and Italy.

Thornton, though, had long been a particular favourite of his redoubtable manager. On the occasion of his first team debut, Thornton had been approached by Struth in the dressing room before the match at Falkirk. 'How much am I paying you, boy,' he asked in the style reminiscent of a Victorian mill-owner. '£1, sir,' replied the youngster, knowing instinctively which terminology to use. 'Anyone who can keep his boots so clean deserves double that,' Struth said, ending the brief social intercourse and being as good as his word when Thornton next collected his pay packet.

These were less sophisticated, clearly not so financially rewarding, times. Immediately after, but probably not as a direct consequence of, Rangers' win over Stranraer in the first round of the Scottish Cup in 1948, the club was taken, against the better judgement of many of the players, to Portugal to meet with the then unknown Benfica. Struth informed those who had doubts, appreciating that civil aviation was still in its infancy and sceptical about going such a long way in a Dakota, that the journey would be made in one continuous flight of three hours in duration. Eleven hours later, following a scheduled stop for re-fuelling in Bordeaux, the party arrived in Lisbon.

Struth's forte as a manager was his ability for assessing potential and having the capacity to blend the players he had gathered in effective unison. His realm of influence did not take in actually training the players, however. In the almost feudal system which was operational inside Ibrox there were three distinct classes, the ruling body who would largely dictate how the team would play, the senior professionals who would organise themselves into groups of their choosing for training, and a rank and file whose progress in an upwardly mobile direction depended upon the depth of their personal ambition.

Among the middle order was Thornton who, along with the English internationalists Stan Cullis and Tom Finney, had been the instigator of what may have been the first coaching school when they put a team together and toured extensively throughout the war years. They instructed in the Far East and Italy, occasionally trading ideas with foreign soldiers from the same professional backgrounds against whom they would play. On one occasion they were members of a British Army side which beat a team almost entirely composed of Polish internationalists in front of a crowd of forty-five thousand soldiers in Italy.

At Ibrox, though, Thornton would watch the same daily rituals observed.

If the weather was fine the players would walk in through the main door and without breaking stride do eight laps of the field in their everyday clothes. Struth, who kept a wardrobe of one dozen suits in his office upstairs, changed three times a day and could stand a little dust here and there on one of them, would accompany his staff. Those of a mind to learn further about the game itself would wait behind after a few more laps and sprints in training gear had been carried out. Those of a more lackadaisical approach would do their fastest running of all to the racecourse of the geographical location most favourable to them.

The style of play which evolved as a product of this self-tuition earned, or discredited Rangers with, the description of the 'Iron Curtain' team; a good cliché, no matter how inaccurate, never going amiss. It was true that the most forceful personalities in their team were in defence, where George Young and Willie Woodburn stood out, but this was to ignore the creative contribution of such as McColl and Cox at wing-half and the main thrust of Rangers' attack which lay in the provision of crosses from Waddell and the prolific finishing of Thornton.

Stan Williams, scorer of the winner in the 1947 Final, in action for Aberdeen v Hearts in the League Cup semi-final of the same season.

By belying the 'Iron Curtain' theory Rangers reached the Scottish Cup Final of 1948 with one such goal against Hibs in a semi-final viewed by a crowd of 143,000 at Hampden. The entire competition had been watched up until that stage by a total of 955,000 people, paying, however, just £61,106 in gate receipts.

There may be no doubt that the question of what happened to all of the sums made in these boom years, is a continual source of wonderment, as is the related issue of why certain stadia do not look appreciably different from that period when far-sighted vision and good husbandry might have made for significant structural change. Equally the attendance columns and the financial income on the other side of the ledger suggest the size of the fortunes made were not as lavish as might have been imagined.

A conscious effort was made, in fact, to keep admission charges to a minimum, since it was known that the vast majority of those who attended favoured the cheaper, standing areas. Some modern day planners within certain boardrooms have taken that habit to be a permanent condition and eschewed the notion of upgrading spectating facilities accordingly, but that is another subject.

The prices to see Rangers play Morton in the Cup Final ranged from 2s (10p) to 10s 6d (52½p). After Waddell and Thornton had gone through their telepathic understanding of each other's movements and created an equalising goal for Gillick — Morton had led from the first minute when the wind had deceived Bobby Brown in goal and carried Whyte's shot high into the net — the paying public showed their appreciation.

The following Wednesday a still record crowd for a replay of 131,975, with thousands more turned away, paid £12,234 to see Williamson score the only goal of the game in Rangers' favour.

It was the only Cup-tie he had played all season but his inclusion had been Struth's brainchild, although Thornton, who was moved to inside-forward to accommodate him, had been called into the manager's office prior to the match to see how he felt about the ploy and left the room actually believing the whole thing had been his idea — another Struth-ism.

In the main, players who celebrated an event of this magnitude, in front of crowds which would send the senses of the modern day footballer reeling along sybaritic lines, took their pleasures more phlegmatically. The last house at the Glasgow Empire and then home, as in the case of Thornton, to places like Winchburgh where, as he observed, 'It would have been impossible to get into trouble even if you had wanted to'.

At Ibrox the basic wage was £10 with a £2 bonus for a win as well as an occasional inducement of £20, an extra payment of dubious legality at the time. Outside in the real world there was a post-war effort going on and the Chancellor of the Exchequer, Sir Stafford Cripps, had asked for a voluntary wage freeze. The office bearers of the players' union in Scotland accordingly decided, early in 1949, not to press the Ministry of Labour over the question of freedom of contract, which, if achieved, would have seen their members break free of the system which bound them to one club, without legal redress, until the end of time. It would take those who succeeded that vacillating body thirty-one years to eventually bring about their members' emancipation.

Inside Ibrox Struth, the benevolent dictator, still had his way, generally keeping his men happy and compliant. On only two occasions were his fiscal policies contested. On the first of those a dressing room cabal decided the bonuses paid half yearly would go further if given free of tax, a feeling which Jock Shaw was sent to convey. Struth, voicing stentorian defiance, said merely, 'Bring me the ringleaders', and no more was ever heard from downstairs.

On the other George Young refused to join the queue of players who were told to line up and sign their annual agreements, knowing it was their turn to come in when a buzzer sounded and leaving as soon as they had appended their signature, denied sufficient time to read the terms far less the small print. Young held out during the close season but succumbed when the bugle sounded on the first day of the season, being promptly re-signed and then dropped on the same morning Rangers left to play their first fixture.

In general, players whose business acumen would have appalled the coming generation were equally happy to accept payment in kind, thankful to be in full-time employment as footballers and nothing else.

Others like the Scottish internationalist side's full-back of the time, Jimmy Stephen, were not so fortunate. Stephen, who played with Bradford City, was employed during weekdays at Norwood Green Colliery. For poor attendance at his place of employment he was recalled to the RAF to serve a further fifteen months as a reminder of the proper attitude required.

Less punitive, but more familiar, were the words spoken by the Rangers director George Brown on the occasion of Scotland losing a League International to England at Ibrox by three clear goals as the summer of 1949

1948. Rangers set out for Lisbon.

approached. 'We must find a team', he intoned slowly, 'which, even if defeated, goes down with flying colours'.

A novel method of discovering one such commodity was devised by the reigning President of the SFA, Sheriff David Gray, before the full international team played England at Wembley. If successful, the victorious eleven were to be granted a fishing holiday in Moffat on his estate.

Players anxious to sample the aristocratic way of life went down to London and applied the more working class approach to the job of demolishing England 3-1, although it is a game remembered as much for the display in goal of Morton's Jimmy Cowan as anything else. A crowd of ten thousand filled Glasgow's Central Station to welcome back the team bound for a sea food diet, a reminder of the continuing grip on the people the game and its heroes had.

A few weeks earlier 104,000 had come to Hampden for the Scottish Cup semi-final between Rangers and East Fife, a side then managed by Scot Symon, who was ultimately to enjoy better luck than he would that day, since a Thornton hat-trick put the Glasgow club into their second successive Final.

Thornton had been demobbed from the army in September of 1946 and had not missed a single game in the intervening thirty months, a testimony to his own level of fitness and an ability to withstand the type of bruises which could be inflicted with the crude, Manfield Hotspur, boots of the day. Especially so since, as one correspondent of the time remarked in his bilious account of the type of football to which he was being subjected, 'it is a spoiling grab and hold game which is draining the colour from our national pastime'. This only serves to show that each succeeding generation of spectator comes complete with a resident Jeremiah.

A crowd of 108,000, who disbelieved the people's game had turned to monochrome on them, formed the traditionally serried ranks at Hampden to watch Rangers defeat Clyde in the 1949 Final and give themselves a chance of doing what only they themselves had previously done in the history of the competition this century — win the trophy three times in succession.

Between the opportunity and the reality, incipient change was beginning to be felt in the social habits and expectations of the growing number taking advantage of a half-day off work on a Saturday, however.

When the Scottish team returned from a tour of the United States on 23 June 1949, after a six day journey spent lolling around the upper decks of the Queen Mary, still thanking their luck for having the abilities to enjoy a lifestyle the likes of which their adoring public could only share vicariously on Movietone newsreels, the seeds of that change were already being sown.

Potential consumers were becoming gradually more excited at the prospect of a transmitter being built in Birmingham which would allow them to sample the wondrous delights of television by the year 1951. The significance of that development with regard to the game of football could not possibly have been foreseen at that time unless by the clairvoyant, of which there were none employed by the SFA or the member clubs, more to the pity.

As well as the diversion to come, the general public had tired of the dubious pleasure of queueing for hours on end to buy tickets for football matches, going home to gaze at newspaper pictures of the snaked procession marked with arrows saying 'start' and 'tail'.

The government was growing restless with the practice, too. Mr Chuter Ede, the exotically named Home Secretary, had asked for the discontinuation

Willie Thornton heads what would have been his own third in the 1950 Final v East Fife. He was off-side.

of ticket sales on two grounds. The first was the unnecessary application of additional pressure on the police force, since such sales could sometimes be the source of public disorder. The other was the honourable member's assertion that the less honourable members of society should be dissuaded from indulging in 'acts of spivvery'. By the time Rangers got to the Final of the Scottish Cup in 1950 an awful lot of people would have been dead on their feet, at any rate, had they been forced to queue for tickets for all their ties.

To begin with, it had taken three games to negotiate a path around Raith Rovers in the fourth round. The team from Kirkcaldy were, like their peers in the First Division, possessed of sufficient personalities and know-how, before superior coaching and a difference in status from part-time to full-time stretched them apart, to provide the more famous with this protracted inconvenience. This was, perhaps, why so many turned out so often, to see if the smaller clubs could bloody the noses of the bigger boys.

So it was with Queen of the South, who took Struth's side to a second game in the semi-final at Hampden before Rangers set about emulating their missionary forefathers of 1934-36. The job of converting East Fife to the idea that Rangers had not come to be easily diverted from their task of the Cup treble took only one minute to perform.

It was then that Bob Findlay gave them the lead, and later Willie Thornton scored his first goal in a Scottish Cup Final for Rangers, doubling his tally before the ninety minutes had elapsed.

It is amusing to think that Thornton was still, on that day as on all the others, travelling into Glasgow from Winchburgh on the same train as that carrying his club's supporters, and walking from there to the St Enoch hotel for his pre-match meal. It is also indicative of someone knowing how to run a railway in those days that Rangers never once turned up a man, or men, short in the pre-car age for footballers.

That night, largely impervious to the depth of their achievement, the Rangers players returned to the St Enoch, took in the second house at the Empire and Thornton returned to Winchburgh still wondering how a person could stray from the straight and narrow within the village limits.

In the wider world outside a new era was on hand, as it was inside Ibrox Stadium. Bill Struth, born in Edinburgh, temporarily housed at Shawfield as a trainer with Clyde but coming to regard Ibrox as his spiritual as well as temporal home, was now elderly and in extremely poor health.

Those factors finally loosened the bond between man and club and in 1954 Struth resigned the job which had been his life's work. The club's style of play had not received universal approval but success was all their following, or Bill Struth, cared about. Although still the most formidable force in the country and with the resources to ensure their continued strength and inhibiting reputation, they were about to be more strongly challenged than they had been since the early days of his stewardship. Struth would not be alive to see it.

In 1956, aged eighty-one, he died in Glasgow. The evangelical flame had been passed on to Scot Symon, a former player with the club who had gained his managerial experience at East Fife and Preston North End. It was a mark of the competitive intensity into which he was pitched that Rangers did not win a Scottish Cup again until the sixth anniversary of Struth's resignation.

Fittingly, Struth's picture hangs to this day in the one place at Ibrox which he above all helped construct, the trophy room.

Mania from Heaven

THE QUICKEST way to gather a crowd around you at the advent of the fifties was to put two teams on a rectangular surface with goal posts at either end and play two halves, each of forty-five minutes in duration. In the immediate post-war years there was a craving for diversion and everything else apart from the irresistible attraction of reorganised club football was on ration.

As a consequence the game struck it big and the crowds boomed. Men who had not seen a game for six years came home from overseas to a job and the regular routine of working until lunch time on a Saturday afternoon and then going to a match. In so called peace-time, men, women and children were hurt when a crowd of 100,000 people queued in a state of high anxiety to get one of only 27,000 tickets available to see Bristol Rovers' home replay in the FA Cup with Newcastle in 1951.

Rangers departed the Scottish Cup before a more orderly, if no less disappointed, multitude of 102,000 at Ibrox in the second round tie with Hibs the same year.

As it remains a mystery why, throughout these golden years of the revered Famous Five in Edinburgh, Hibs managed to win three League championships but knew only constant disappointment in the Cup, in spite of Smith, Johnstone, Reilly, Turnbull and Ormond producing a spate of goals, so it was a source of frustration that this period of public addiction was not seized upon more productively to assist in the Scottish game's development.

A regrettable insularity tainted the administrators at club and international level, and a sense of inferiority out of touch with the mood of their aggressively confident sides of the day polluted the air. Scotland had, in 1950, refused the offer extended to the runners-up in the British Championship to play in the World Cup Finals being staged in Brazil, although that was at the very least a decisive step.

Four years later Scotland's administrators would give the impression of not being sure if they were indecisive or not when it came to the international scene. Club men, equally loath to risk defeat by foreigners, recoiled at the idea of broadening the domestic game's base and mouth-watering opportunities were lost to harness the fervour of a famished public standing like so many Oliver Twists in queues asking for more, but getting only the abuse he subsequently suffered.

The anxiety to spend money on the harmless recreation of football was not restricted to the main centres of the population, either. The record attendance figure for Stark's Park, Kirkcaldy was created when Hibs met Raith Rovers in the Scottish Cup of 1952, and later that same year a midweek record was also established at Motherwell when Rangers were the visiting side in the same tournament.

More ominously, there was coming along, too, that mechanism which really would seize the imagination of a public in need of colour (even its monochrome variety) after the grey days of war. By March of 1952, a total of 26,000 people in Scotland had bought receivers and gawped in fascination at television for the first time. The absence of men of vision, with noteable exceptions like the chairman of Hibs, Harry Swan, and Robert Kelly of Celtic, would see to it that, like a shaded area which takes longer to defrost, Scottish football would need more time to melt into the sunnier disposition of the rest of Europe and the World, by which time it had lost the monopoly on the attention of its audience.

Before such problems were able to be perceived, though, the pickings were rich, with the particular exception of Duns, from the Highland League, who were left to count, if that is a feasible description, gate receipts of 5s (25p) from a Qualifying Cup-tie in September 1950 with the Renfrewshire works team, Babcock and Wilcox.

As belated recompense, in the Cup itself, Duns were brought back to the West of Scotland to play Celtic. The Parkhead club had not won a match that year so far outwith the Cup and had only survived the first round against East Fife by getting a replay at Methil with only eight minutes to go and then breaking their duck in Glasgow.

If Celtic's crowds were like all others in taking on swollen proportions, there was also a highly exciteable strain running throughout their number. Celtic had not won the Cup in fifteen years, during which time reigning monarchs had changed, there had been an abdication crisis and also a World War, none of which had distracted the minds of their following from the necessity for a change in the club's circumstances. The more fanatical wing were off course, for example, when threatening letters were sent to the referee, Jack Mowat, before Celtic met Aberdeen at Parkhead in the quarter-finals.

As well as being generally regarded as the sternest official in the country and a man of implacable temperament, Mowat had been a war time squadron leader in the RAF. He was also awarded the MBE by a grateful nation for his work in testing Stirling bombers. The points of poison pens were hardly likely to bring an involuntary stoop to his straight back and Mowat handed the letters over to the police before supervising a match which Celtic won easily, in any case, with three goals to spare.

The more conventional control of the ever growing crowds was already under consideration before Celtic ultimately arrived at Hampden to play Motherwell in the Cup Final. It had been proposed, before any of the ground was covered, that a minaret-style watchtower be constructed from which a policeman would observe the crowd's formation patterns and pass on relevant information to avoid accidents. As anyone who has been in the national stadium at any time in the last thirty-four years will have no doubt noticed, this idea, like many others, never got off the ground.

The problem was attended to, thankfully, by continuing progress in the field of electronic communication. Motherwell's appearance at Hampden was the result of a stirring run which overshadowed the growing suspicion that, as a team, they could not stand comparison with some from the club's illustrious past. They had nevertheless reached the Final at the expense of the much vaunted Hibs, whose defence never exhibited the consistency of form or selection which had earned the side an envied reputation in attack.

The expectation, therefore, was of a thrilling encounter, but the Cup's history is pock-marked by numerous promises being breached by over anxiety and a surfeit of tension on the big day. Luck will often have it, too, that for one side the awkwardness of their performance is corrected on the one moment

1951. Celtic leave Glasgow Central and set off for their American tour, during which the cup was carried in a paper bag purchased from Macey's of New York.

sufficient to take the trophy, giving them the chance to reflect that the Cup is a reward for the run as a whole and not just the sprint to the finish.

In Celtic's case this happy experience began when Baillie tackled Humphries of Motherwell and swung a head high pass in the direction of the centre-forward John McPhail. A player whose abilities were frequently called into question, but rarely by the Celtic fraternity, McPhail then demonstrated his dexterity by gliding the ball past his marker, Paton, with his head and then evading another defender's challenge. Leaving the goalkeeper Johnstone with no other option but to advance from his line, McPhail then did the logical thing and chipped the ball over his head for a goal fit to win any Cup.

With a casual regard for what they had done, Celtic, who were given a send off by five thousand people when they boarded the train for Southampton and their cruise on the Queen Mary, which was taking them to tour the United States, stuffed the trophy into a paper bag and kept it there while they were away.

They sailed home into deeper water than possibly even that awesome vessel could have handled. McPhail, the hero of the Summer, returned visibly overweight and entered a sluggish period in keeping with that of the team in general and the club went into the New Year amid controversy over the misbehaviour of the crowd who watched them lose to Rangers at Parkhead.

This game led directly to a head-on confrontation between the Celtic club and the SFA. The ruling body's Referee Committee called upon Celtic to remove from the roof of their covered enclosure the flag of the Irish Free State, as gifted to them by the prime minister of the Republic, Eamon de Valera, in recognition of the club's historical ties with that island. The SFA's decision also had the approval of the Glasgow magistrates.

The SFA and the Scottish League subsequently called the flag an incitement to trouble, after discussions on the subject, and at a meeting of the SFA council a vote of 26 to 7 instructed Celtic to take down the tricolour. The club's later motion calling into question the legality of that decision was seconded by Bailie John Wilson, chairman of Rangers, and both he and his opposite number at Parkhead, Robert Kelly, left the SFA council chamber arm in arm in what must have looked a barely credible act of union over such a matter.

While so engrossed, Celtic's League form had slipped as quickly as the SFA would have liked the flag to come down the pole and with seven matches to play the club were in third bottom position, in danger of showing the offending piece of cloth to new groups of supporters who could never have imagined their sides would play at Parkhead in anything but the Cup. Celtic have a habit of reacting favourably to a highly charged atmosphere, though, and in their first home game after being told they risked being suspended from the League they defeated Queen of the South by six goals to one and so began their ascent into a healthier space. The furore over the flag later died a natural death.

Events had taken their toll of them in the Scottish Cup, however, and for the first time since season 1889-90 Celtic lost a replay in the competition, and thus the holders went out in the first round to Third Lanark at Cathkin. The Cup in 1952 was also significant for being the vehicle which introduced the 'voucher' system for fairness in all-ticket matches. It was the brainchild of Bert Herdman, the manager of Raith Rovers, who, with a foresight which could have been used in many more places, initiated the scheme by giving regular customers a promissory note as they passed through the turnstiles unsuspectingly at a League game before the tie with Hibs in which the ground's capacity was established.

When the Edinburgh side and then Rangers accompanied Celtic on to the competition's list of fallen — Motherwell had beaten the men from Ibrox for the first time in their Cup history — it became apparent the trophy's destination would be an unexpected one.

In the end the Final brought together the previous year's runners up, Motherwell, who had beaten Hearts before a crowd of 99,000 at Hampden, and Dundee, who had eliminated Third Lanark in front of a comparatively poor crowd of 23,000 at Easter Road. The lack of interest shown by the citizens of the capital ran, as do most things in their lives, contrary to the national trend and the alleged fault was that too few were interested in turning out in neutrality to watch sides other than the two resident there.

The Final, the losers would say, was decided when Dundee decided to take a risk on their centre-forward Bobby Flavell, who had been troubled by injury beforehand. Flavell had gained a certain notoriety two years earlier when he suddenly walked out on Hearts, who had paid the not insubstantial sum of £11,000 for him, and took his talents to South America for Millionarios, lured into ignoring the rule of law where minor details such as contracts were concerned by the payment of a £2,500 signing on fee and a wage of £120 a week. Such sums of money were many times the national average wage, as was the £150 Flavell was fined on his return twelve months later when he fled Bogota.

Subsequently brushed off Hearts' incorruptible shoulder on to Dundee, after serving a lengthy ban imposed by the SFA, Flavell had scored a hat-trick when the Tayside club defeated Motherwell in the semi-finals of the League Cup and was therefore risked again at Hampden on this flimsy scrap of logic. Had they but known, even greater forces were at work against Dundee in the shape of a cat by the stage name of 'Rhubarb'.

This had been the fictitious feline lead in an American film of the time, titled *Rhubarb* and starring Ray Milland, about a pussy possessed of paranormal powers used to inspire a baseball team to greater heights. The Motherwell coach, Ben Ellis, had been at the pictures in mid-January, before the Cup started, and hung a portrait of the screen character inside the dressing room at Fir Park with the inevitable results.

1952. Wilson Humphries fires in Motherwell's third in the 4-0 victory over Dundee.

Some things are simply bigger than all of us and Dundee travelled the distance from poise to panic within the short space of a minute at the start of the second half at Hampden. Watson and Redpath then established an unassailable lead for Motherwell and Humphries and Kelly later performed the same trick of scoring twice in a minute. The emphatic nature of Motherwell's win was such that it was recorded that all ninety-three of the town's policemen were pressed into service to subdue those who warmly welcomed back the new holders.

If any of that crowd had doubts about the club's long-term prospects, the events of the season which followed would bear them out with lurid clarity. Motherwell became the second holders of the trophy in successive years not to reach even the later stages when they went out at home in spectacularly awful fashion, losing by six goals to one to Aberdeen in a replay.

This was a sudden example of a more lingering problem and Motherwell were also relegated that same season. It was the first time in the club's history they had dropped out of the First Division and there is no word of what happened to the portrait of the cat named 'Rhubarb', although it must be supposed that she had used up all nine lives on Motherwell's behalf in putting their name on the Cup.

In the Elizabethan era which began with the Queen's coronation in 1953, Aberdeen have belatedly attained deserved prominence in the Scottish Cup and stand as joint holders of the distinction for having the record number of successive wins. At the outset of her majesty's reign, though, the club was to gain only an unenviable reputation for good attendance but bad luck on Hampden's prize giving day.

In the Final of 1953 they met a Rangers side in the last throes of its 'Iron Curtain' days, when the policy of not losing any goals was as important as the creation of them. Due for a period of change and re-appraisal, the club would not re-appear at Hampden in that particular competition for another seven years. Along the way that year they had encountered Celtic for the first time in a Scottish Cup-tie in a quarter of a century and quietly disposed of them with the only two goals of an incident-free game, in spite of the prolific letter writers on Celtic's behalf, who sent off the usual dire, unfulfilled threats to the Ibrox player, Sammy Cox.

Aberdeen, who had gone to replays at both the quarter and semi-final stages, clung on grimly to their hope of winning the trophy by then taking

Aberdeen fans come to Glasgow for the 1954 Final.

Rangers to a second game after Harry Yorston equalised a goal from John Prentice.

Prentice's place in the replay was taken by Billy Simpson and Rangers, appropriately, gave the Cup to their then terminally ill manager, Bill Struth, for the last time in his career, with a goal scored by the player he had transplanted into the side as a tactical change.

The game was at last being dragged, albeit screaming, into the era of the younger, more worldly and adaptable men. Scotland had agreed to participate in the 1954 World Cup Finals in Switzerland but developed an attack of over-dramatisation before departure. The SFA Selection Committee, known colloquially as the 'Big Seven' met first to choose who were, presumably, the even bigger three from their septet. This trio would then in turn choose the list of players who would represent their country's World Cup squad under the managership of Andy Beattie, a man who, perhaps just as well under the prevailing circumstances, was known to be short on words.

Even the most voluble would have been dumbstruck when it was announced that only thirteen players in all would go to Switzerland. There was not a single Rangers player among them, either. The way in which they became, in season 1953-54, the third, successive holders of the Scottish Cup to go out before the Final gave an indication, though, of their general well-being not being as well as it might have been. They fell victim, too, to one of the Cup's storybook episodes.

In the semi-final Rangers were defeated by a mammoth six goals to nil by

1954. Aberdeen centre-half Young (face down, centre), has just mis-hit an attempted clearance of a Mochan shot past his own keeper. Celtic's first goal.

Aberdeen whose forward, Joe O'Neill, scored three of them. As well as defying Rangers, O'Neill had confounded medical opinion in returning to the side for that game only three weeks after fracturing his skull.

On the day Celtic won the First Division championship, one week before they would contest the Cup Final against Aberdeen, O'Neill, showing definite signs of being the injury prone type, was hurt so badly he had to withdraw from the Hampden team and his family of six brothers and sisters were thus enabled to openly declare their affection for Celtic without any feeling of filial disloyalty.

The objects of their affection were well able to look after themselves by that stage however. As well as the League flag, Celtic also had the Coronation Cup at Parkhead, a tournament for which they had to receive an invitation but ended up winning, taking Manchester United at the penultimate stage and the invariably unlucky Hibs in the Final. Aberdeen appeared to match the inspiration this had provided. The Celtic players had been sent to watch the technique of the touring Hungarian national side, who had been drawing admiring glances from all who saw them, and a coach, George Patterson, had been introduced on to the staff at Parkhead.

Only the forbearance of Fred Martin in Aberdeen's goal kept the score level for them at half time. Neil Mochan, though, eventually put Celtic ahead, playing the percentages by scoring with a shot across the face of a crowded goal which went in off a defender. Buckley's equaliser in the very next minute raised northern hopes but they were quickly lowered again when Willie Fernie, with one of the intelligent runs for which he was noted, rolled the ball across the front of the goal to where Sean Fallon was standing in what would come to be known as the position of maximum opportunity.

Both morale and expenditure were high at Parkhead and in a commendable move to heighten their knowledge of the game the Cup-winners were taken to Switzerland to attend the World Cup tournament. They would witness at first hand only the disheartening ambivalence which Scotland's officials, if not the sorely pressed players, felt for the venture, and also the embarrassing consequences of such a half-hearted approach.

Of the thirteen players chosen, two, incredibly, were goalkeepers. The squad travelled without Scotland tracksuits and did their training in their own club jerseys like children in a public park wearing the strips of their favourite teams. When Austria's captain presented the Scotland captain with a commemorative pennant prior to the first match, there was a fittingly impoverished response when he was offered only a shake of the hand in return.

Not surprisingly the game was lost and the sense of being involved in something farcical was heightened when Scotland's manager, Andy Beattie, announced his resignation before the next match against Uruguay. The side's timing was no better on the park, unfortunately, and a humiliating 7-1 defeat followed.

These were perfect examples of the new world, in which teams only got out of the game what they were willing to put in to it. The Scottish Cup holders, Celtic, looking on with the presumed intention of absorbing such lessons, largely ignored them, strangely enough. They then entered a lengthy period of aimless stumbling before appreciating the haphazard old ways were over and done with.

All Change

PROTRACTED periods of denial from ownership where the Scottish Cup was concerned saw men with strong club affiliations driven to uncharacteristic extremes of behaviour when the famine eventually ended for them. In the case of the then assistant chief constable of Glasgow, Walter Doherty, on the night of 27 April 1955, 'driven' was the operative word.

Assuming high office within the Glasgow constabulary was clearly not the pinnacle of life's achievement for Mr Doherty. That had come many years earlier when he was a ball-boy at Shawfield, the home of his beloved Clyde. In between both those stages, when presumably pounding the beat, he had watched the club from Rutherglen, on the outskirts of Glasgow, take the Scottish Cup for the first time in their history by defeating Motherwell in the Final. He had also probably shared the unspoken feeling of guilt that this may have annoyed someone and been a contributory factor towards the outbreak of World War Two, since Clyde recorded their breakthrough only months before Neville Chamberlain's announcement from 10 Downing Street effectively terminated the competition for a period of eight years.

Joy was unconfined when Clyde proved by defeating Celtic after a replay that they could win a trophy and not trigger off the holocaust. To rejoice that this was so a police car with siren wailing and speedometer ignoring the restrictions as laid down by their superiors was pointed in the direction of 263 Main Street, Bridgeton, with Walter Doherty in the passenger seat.

The sight and sound of such a vehicle was not uncommon in that part of the city where the malevolent mores of certain sections of the community often required high velocity intervention. But this was a social call. The assistant chief constable, insensitive to the feelings of the disappointed half of Glasgow's citizenry who had been at the match, and obviously in no mood for the political implications, was at the head of a parade clearing a path for the Cup to be shown at the mouth of the tenement close wherein lived Mattha Gemmell.

Gemmell was by then an octogenarian of uncertain health, but one who had previously dedicated his life to Clyde as everything from groundsman to club trainer, being blessed with the necessary sense of humour to carry out these duties. The main prerequisite of being a Clyde man, he had once observed philosophically, was 'a heart made in a foundry'.

Clyde's success began and ended a four year period from the mid to late fifties in which those who followed Hearts and Falkirk could also claim that same physical fortitude, even if they had, while doing so, a smile on their faces which a stone mason could not have removed with a chisel. It was in those Finals that their clubs lifted the Scottish Cup for the first time in fifty and forty-four years respectively.

As corroborative evidence that, historically, your turn came round with something less than regularity, this spate of unexpected winners began when Clyde defeated Aberdeen at the penultimate stage in 1955, thus preventing a repeat of the previous year's Final between Celtic and the side from Pittodrie.

Had they met again it would only have been the third time in the tournament's then eighty-two year-old history that such a 'double' had occurred. The fact that they did not would mean the Scottish Cup would be going for all of one hundred and ten years before that distinction could be noted once again.

The year of 1955 was not a time for things remaining as they were, at any rate. A strange sub-culture known as 'Teddy boys' made their crepe-soled, drape-jacketed way out from the undergrowth to the 'monotonous, suggestive rhythms' of their rock and roll music, written off by Sir Malcolm Sargent as an art form which 'You may be sure will die before very long'.

Any self-respecting conductor of the BBC Symphony orchestra would have said that then, anyway, but Sir Malcolm's judgement was as suspect as that of those Aberdeen supporters who made it known they would boycott the Scottish Cup semi-final in protest at the decision to stage the match at Easter Road, so saving their money for the Final itself. The request for a ground switch was not pursued too vigorously by either management, however, and Aberdeen, who led the First Division at that stage, ultimately fell between the two stools and landed injuriously at the exit door for Scottish Cup departees.

If their followers left muttering darkly about the questionable wisdom of the game's administrative body, there might have been even more widespread concern, in retrospect, at the decision then taken to make Clyde versus Celtic the first Scottish Cup Final ever to be televised live.

The only criterion to be fulfilled was that at least eighty per cent of the match tickets be sold beforehand. Once this was achieved, just, Kenneth Wolstenholme was dispatched from London, incongruously, to commentate on a game between two sides of which he could only have had limited knowledge to say the least. What he did not have, either, was a regional accent, and that was good, since local dialects were anathema to the Corporation.

Nationalistic carping aside, the attendance the following year, when television rights were withdrawn, showed, interestingly, an increase of over twenty-six thousand people. With a logic bordering on the perverse, however, the cameras were welcomed back the year after that to the deafening sound of people scurrying to the 'Family Department' for some takeaway 'sustenance', the originators of that species which came to be known as the armchair fans.

What the cathode ray tube beamed in 1955 was a multi-racial Clyde team with a South African goalkeeper, Ken Hewkins, an Irish full-back, Jimmy Murphy, and nine of the local indigenous personnel. Collectively they contained no glamorous array of stars, except, perhaps, for the winger Tommy Ring, who went on to become Clyde's most capped player, appearing twelve times for his country.

Ring was part of a Clyde attack which had developed an enviable understanding of each other's play and also contained a quintet of potential match winners. Celtic, on the other hand, knew far less consistency of team selection and the anxiety of their following at this potential drawback was exemplified by the nervous blowing on various bugles during the playing of the National Anthem prior to the game's start. Their behaviour chilled the watching television audience and brought the wrath of the policemen on crowd control duty, presumably led by the aforementioned Walter Doherty, down upon their irreverent souls.

Walsh puts Celtic ahead in 1955

Those whose trumpet lip had been forced to tremble in protective custody missed a game which had an ending of infuriating anti-climax for Celtic. Leading by a Jimmy Walsh goal, and with only three minutes remaining, a corner was conceded to Clyde. If it was exasperating to hear the taker, Archie Robertson, say afterwards that he had scored directly from the award by use of his 'wrong' foot, since the left one had been injured earlier, there must have been a temptation to end it all when the corner kick which earned a replay and cost Celtic a cup was described as 'a bad one, placed too near the goalkeeper'.

Johnny Bonnar, who had, as explained, moved near enough to take preventive action, succeeded only in fumbling the ball over the line, however.

It was at this point, apparently, that eyes were closed inside Parkhead and a pin struck whimsically into a list of names to alter Celtic's tactical approach in the second game. Bobby Collins was dropped and Sean Fallon, who had not played in the first team for some months, chosen to replace him. There were two schools of thought about this native of Sligo with the accent which is to this

1955. Clyde's last gasp equaliser as Beattie mis-judges Robertson's corner.

day indecipherable to all but his compatriots. Half of those who had seen him score the winning goal in the previous year's Scottish Cup Final stoutly defended his industry and courage, if somewhat less loquacious on the subject of basic ability. Repatriation to his native Ireland would not have disappointed the rest, who frequently booed Fallon's name when any team bearing it was read out at Parkhead.

To placate those of a nervous disposition set on edge by news of Fallon's selection, the National Anthem was dropped from the sweet music discoursed as light relief beforehand. It made no difference. Tommy Ring, who came, ironically, from a Celtic-loving family, scored the only goal of the game after fifty-two minutes and the disbelief of the green bedraggled followers was made complete the morning after the night before when Bobby Collins, discarded by his club, was chosen in the Scotland party for the game with Portugal and for the summer tour to Yugoslavia, Austria and Hungary.

Representative honours were not always accepted in the spirit with which they were handed out. A wild-eyed group from the Hearts Supporters Association, led by their secretary George Wardrope, had, that same season, written an official letter of complaint to the SFA Selection Committee following the choice of four players from Tynecastle in the pool for the Scotland 'B' team to meet England at Ibrox three days before a Scottish Cup-tie. This was an indication of the intensity of disappointment felt in parts of Edinburgh over Hearts' inability to win the trophy, or even appear in a Final, since the early years of the twentieth century.

The story went of the Tynecastle fan who had been saving up to have a memorable day out at Hampden — but who died a millionaire instead. Nevertheless, the fates had conspired in 1956 to give them on either side of their legendary 'Terrible Trio' of Conn, Bauld and Wardhaugh the 'Peripatetic Pair' of Alex Young and Ian Crawford, who could flit anywhere across the forward line to create and take chances, enabling Hearts to score fifteen goals for the loss of none as they reached the Final against the resilient but still capriciously chosen Celtic.

Hearts' attendance of 54,233 for the replayed semi-final with Raith Rovers was a midweek record for a game in Edinburgh, confirming, perhaps, the suspicions of both Aberdeen and Clyde that the capital's public liked none so much as their own.

Meanwhile, a little socially gauche desperation had crept into the behaviour of the Parkhead fans suffering withdrawal symptoms after only two years without consummate success in the Scottish Cup. Before the semi-final with Clyde, a friend of Buckie Kemp, a Shawfield player, was found beaten up and a noxious note, signed 'The Bhoys', sent to Kemp stating that it would happen again if he scored against Celtic.

The bullies' timing was no better than their manners, though, and Kemp did not receive the note until after the game was over, by which time he had, ironically, become immersed in a controversy of his own making as the scorer of a belated goal which would have given Clyde an equaliser and a replay, had it not been disallowed.

Possibly deluding themselves that this was kismet, Celtic went back to the lucky dip approach to team selection for the Final, playing Billy Craig, an outside-right from St Anthony's juniors who had appeared only four times in all in Celtic's colours and never in a Cup-tie. Mike Haughney, normally a right-

John Cumming of Hearts briefly leaves the field in the first half of the 1956 Final.

back, was moved up to partner him at inside-right and the players let in on the secret two hours before the game started, with the inevitable consequences.

An estimated sixty thousand of those thought unwilling to watch outsiders play in Edinburgh gladly made the journey from there to Glasgow and watched a match of some drama as Hearts took the lead through Crawford and then had John Cumming injured so badly he spent the rest of the game wiping gore from a head wound. The pugnacious breed of onlooker, although not actually experiencing the discomfort themselves, agreed it was in the best fighting traditions of the club that Cumming play on since blood did not show up on a maroon jersey.

The inequality of the competing sides did leave its mark and further goals from Crawford and Conn, with a consolation effort from Celtic in between, gave Hearts the Cup. Normally reserved Edinburgh temporarily blew its immaculate top. Conclusive proof of a hitherto unsuspected weakness of moral fibre came, in fact, when free drink was dispensed in those of the capital city's pubs where Hearts stood for a better type of person. It was a walk on the wild side which, it is to be hoped, was enjoyed to the full since to the present day Hearts have never recovered sufficient steadiness of gait to win the trophy again.

Crawford puts Hearts two ahead against Celtic in 1956 as the Edinburgh side race to their first Cup win for fifty years.

Their hangover in the morning following the defeat of Celtic could not possibly have been any worse than that of the previous season's winners of the trophy, Clyde. A 3-1 defeat from Raith Rovers consigned them to the Second Division, a spectacular example of fluctuation in fortunes.

The market in transformations at speed, however, was to be cornered by Falkirk the following season. The club had been at the foot of the First Division for so long that previously strong men began to wilt under the strain. Bob Shankly, brother of the soon to be fabled Bill and not from retiring stock, quit his post as manager in December of 1956 and Bobby Brown, the former Rangers goalkeeper asked to be left out of the team, too, presumably to gain peace of mind in time for Christmas.

With fourteen League games left, from which, it was reckoned, they needed to average one point to avoid relegation, and the Scottish Cup about to begin, Falkirk, although far from a rich club, decided drastic steps were necessary. Turning the transfer market into a game of monopoly, they bought four players in one week: George Merchant and Andy Irvine from Dundee, Doug Moran from Hibs and Rangers' Derek Grierson. The shrewdest move of all came when they acquired themselves a new manager to re-arrange the pieces into a winning team once again.

James Christopher Reginald Smith, née Schmidt in his native East London, South Africa, had been an England internationalist full-back when with Millwall. During the war, while stationed at RAF Leuchars, he had guested for Dundee and was eventually sold to them in 1946. When Falkirk took over his services he left his then job as manager of Dundee United in the Second Division with prospects for advancement which were still highly debatable in spite of a board who continued to produce money from places where other clubs did not have places.

It took until March, with a win over Kilmarnock, for Reggie Smith, as he was popularly known, to lift Falkirk out of the League's bottom two for the first time that season but the team continued on its winning way under his inspirational guidance, although there were those within Brockville with an understandably suspicious streak who believed that a pipe band might have something to do with this undiluted success as well.

The Muirhead pipe band, then World champions in their field, constituted the pre-match entertainment at Brockville on a Saturday and, not unreasonably, since no-one else had either, had never seen the club lose under Reggie Smith.

Pedantic quibbling having no part in something which was gathering astonishing momentum, a request was made to the appropriate authority by Falkirk for approval to have the band travel to Tynecastle for the replay of the Scottish Cup semi-final against Raith Rovers. Permission was granted and the side from Kirkcaldy reeled, as it were, under Falkirk's strength of purpose, losing by two goals to nil.

The Final itself, again allowed to be televised live for the paltry sum of fifteen hundred pounds, was, as a consequence attended by twenty-four thousand people less than constituted an eighty per cent sell-out at Hampden, and the SFA were inundated by claims for loss of earnings from clubs whose League matches played that same afternoon suffered at the gate as a result of the transmission. The irony is that for the second time in two live broadcasts, no outright winner could be found without recourse to a midweek replay.

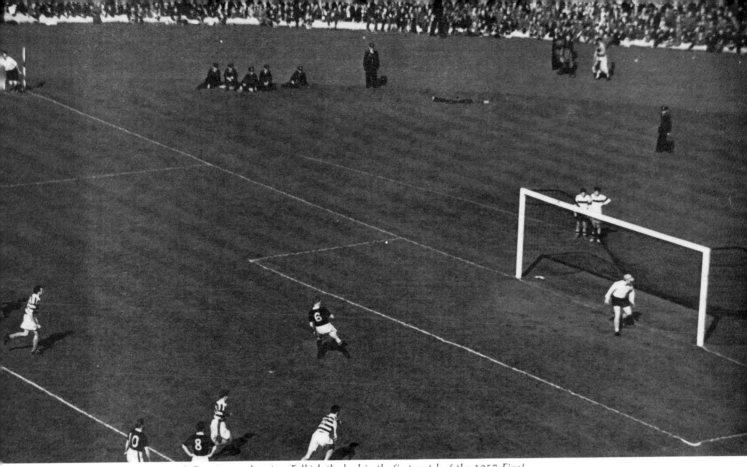

A Prentice penalty gives Falkirk the lead in the first match of the 1957 Final.

1957 replay. Merchant of Falkirk heads the game's first goal.

Although pulling back from 1-0 down, a goal scored by John Prentice from the spot, Kilmarnock displayed little of the authority expected of them and never looked like getting a winner.

Falkirk took the initiative in the second match, scoring first through George Merchant, but being taken to extra-time by an equaliser scored with just ten minutes left. In the one hundreth minute of play Doug Moran won the Cup for Falkirk before it was mathematically certain the club had avoided demotion as an unusual and unwanted accompanying distinction.

The following Friday, just forty-eight hours later, Reggie Smith, by now demonstrating powers verging on the diabolic, left out seven of his Cup-winning side and still beat Raith Rovers by three goals to two, so making virtually certain that they would remain in the First Division.

Between times the euphoria continued when Falkirk returned with the Cup to a rapturous reception from a public who turned out in such numbers as can reasonably be expected at the sight of the miraculous. There had been, the local police confirmed solemnly, a bigger crowd on the streets of Camelon than had been witnessed for the visit of Queen Elizabeth. All that remained unanswered, perhaps, was what reason there could be for a royal stop over at Camelon. The story, though, ultimately had an unhappy ending for Reggie Smith. A man of some integrity, obviously, Smith accepted full responsibility, as he assumed much of the credit for their Cup win, when Falkirk were eventually relegated two years later and resigned his post as manager.

1958. A despondent Lawrie Leslie of Hibs has just been beaten by a deflected shot. It gave Clyde the Cup.

1958. Johnny Coyle, scorer of the Final's single goal, displays the Cup at Shawfield.

For the provincial clubs like Falkirk and those in Clyde's position, liked but rarely visited cousins on the outskirts of a city with a powerful family base of its own, a less than malign conjunction of the game's changing financial structure with the redevelopment of Glasgow meant the days of the Scottish Cup shocks were to be short-circuited within the next decade.

Clyde, with a new manager in Johnny Haddow, who had replaced Paddy Travers, and a new centre-forward in Johnny Coyle, who had signed from Dundee United in the season after promotion back to the First Division, were treated to one last hurrah in 1958.

Only four of the side which had won the Cup three years earlier remained and the revised formation had recorded a remarkable run in the sectional ties of the League Cup, scoring a record thirty-eight goals in all, including twenty-five in their three home games, 8-1 against Dundee United, 7-1 against Dumbarton and a spectacular 10-0 against Stranraer.

It was a sequence more invigorating than either their comparatively prosaic run towards Hampden or the quality of the Scottish Cup Final itself, played against Hibs. Even the pre-match build up rose quickly but petered out suddenly on the eve of the great day.

Lawrie 'last minute' Reilly, whose retirement was being dreaded by the Hibs supporters, had played what was assumed to be his last game the previous Monday against Rangers in Edinburgh, helping the home club to win. A sudden whiff of impending immortality flared in the nostrils and hopes rose that he might be tempted to go out in a blaze of glory.

With the tension and uncertainty growing, a bout of tonsilitis floored Reilly at the last minute and deflated those dreams of a fateful end to his career. He missed what was a largely undistinguished Final decided by a goal from Johnny Coyle, his eighth in that year's Scottish Cup, in the first half of a game tinged only with the controversy of Hibs 'goal' from Joe Baker, who was then a stripling of seventeen.

Baker had clearly palmed the ball into the net in his excitement, however, and there was no serious attempt to disguise the deception and claim an equaliser.

That night the Scottish Cup returned quietly and without attendant, siren-wailing fuss to 263 Main Street, Bridgeton and to the quintessential Glaswegian who once said he only believed there was a Scottish Cup when he saw it in black and white, which just happened to be Clyde's colours of the period.

Mattha Gemmell, who had assumed his first duties as a Clyde groundsman the previous century while Queen Victoria was still on the throne and actually remained long enough to have two benefit matches played in his honour, one in 1924, the other in 1945, died at the age of ninety-two in 1966.

He was one of the few in the East End of Glasgow still living in his old house. Whole communities were being moved out, almost on a daily basis, to the housing schemes many miles from Shawfield. So far as that area of Glasgow was concerned, at any rate, Celtic were the team worth watching in the mid-sixties as they emerged from a deep sleep.

To the South of the city lay the ever present threat of Rangers and in the far North of the country something stirred as well. The romance of the Cup was what would go West.

A climate grew up in which the smaller clubs had to sell their best players, once they had nurtured them to a suitable state of efficiency, to their richer neighbours, just to maintain their existence. The effect was to ensure that the Scottish Cup would never again change hands with such stimulating regularity.

The strong became stronger in a more professional manner, too. No more would the players of Celtic, for example, be told the team for a Cup Final twenty minutes before they ran out at Hampden: a piece of timing which had, in 1956, still left more than quarter of an hour to while away after the managerial instruction period was over.

Proper physical preparation and tactical forethought became acceptable practices as a new breed of players turned coaches emerged, led, to Celtic's good fortune, by someone who had lived through the more haphazard days at Parkhead.

Two years of persistent injury, and the final confirmation from a Harley Street specialist that he could never play the game again, had prompted Celtic in 1957 to make their former centre-half and captain a scout for the club and then, when his exceptional abilities blossomed, a coach to the reserve team.

It would be the best day's work they had probably ever done. His name was Jock Stein.

History's Witnesses

ONE OF THE most endearing aspects of the Scottish Cup should be the pageant which goes on around the Final itself, where the adherents of the less powerful clubs from the smaller pockets of the population use the occasion as an expression of their identity. The impedimenta of the great day in its more innocent setting take in normally staid members of society wearing daft hats done out in the team colours, co-ordinated with matching rosettes.

An open topped bus is another pre-requisite in the event of a provincial dog having its day, with players who have gained localised immortality toying capriciously with the remainder of their careers by dangling precariously over the edge of the top deck with the Cup itself held aloft. Who sits downstairs in the bus on these occasions and how they got there in the first place are questions which are never contemplated in the excitement of the moment.

There then follows the obligatory balcony scene in which elected officials wearing the chains of their office stand proudly above the throng and beside those who have enhanced the life of the local community, introducing them individually by name and perhaps suspecting deep down that the players would be unable to return the compliment if the need were suddenly to arise.

Each in turn moves self-consciously towards the microphone to intone their deathless phrases only to have their oratory buried under an avalanche of cheering. Life is too short for transient glory to be taken up with speech making. In any case, oppressive licensing hours dictate that women and children, called as history's witnesses whether they wish it or not, have to be shepherded homewards before the remainder of the weekend becomes lost in a way which will be embellished with the passage of time.

None of which, however, will cause any deficiencies in memory banks so serious that the precise details of the game, the individual merits of the players concerned and the full extent of the lavish celebrations afterwards cannot be recalled with the utmost clarity decades after the event.

So it was when St Mirren brought the Scottish Cup home to Paisley in 1959, so many years after it had last been there that permanent amnesia must have been suspected when it took so long to find its way back. Not since 1926 had St Mirren caused the largest burgh in Scotland to take temporary leave of its normally hard working senses, and what seemed like the whole town appeared intent on making up for lost time.

The actual Scottish Cup trophy has remained unchanged for the last 112 years, the oldest of its kind still being played for in Great Britain. On the night of 25 April 1959, however, it came perilously close to being taken as an elaborate souvenir of someone's night in Paisley's Jail Square.

In spite of incessant rain, the special intensity of which can only be experienced in that part of Renfrewshire, the St Mirren manager Willie Reid and his bedraggled players, who might have been glad to tamper with the Cup-winning imagery and have a bus with a convertible roof, were unable to enter the town hall without a struggle greater than anything they had endured in the earlier part of the day when defeating Aberdeen easily by three goals to one.

Reasoning that they might make it with the full use of their athletic powers, but that an inanimate object had no chance of survival, the possession they had toiled for throughout the preceding months was, thankfully, thrown with all due care above the heads of the crowd and given an airborne entry into the seat of local government.

It was not a night for circumspection in any case. Davie McCrae, a member of the St Mirren side who had defeated Celtic in the Final of thirty-three years earlier had, for instance, broken the seal at last on a bottle of whisky given to him by a generous sponsor that day. The people of Paisley perhaps being imagined to be apprehensive when it came to the distribution of largesse, a television crew was dispatched with all due haste to capture the event on film for posterity.

The cameras had been prevented from filming the Final itself, a veto imposed by the clubs of the lower division who had denied approval for fear of a detrimental effect on attendances at their games played that same afternoon. It had seemed, though, that what was a very healthy crowd of 108,591 at a game involving neither member of the Old Firm was actually made up in the main of those with a vested interest in St Mirren and Aberdeen, staging a phenomenally loyal demonstration of their emotional support.

The circumstances of their being there were also exceptional. Aberdeen had helped themselves to avoid relegation by the audacious trick of beating the First Division champions, Rangers, at Ibrox by two goals to one the previous week.

St Mirren had also been third from the bottom of the League when the Cup got underway that season but a 10-0 win over Peebles Rovers in the first round inspired them into a spirited run in that tournament which was consistently contrary to their League form, a fitting contradiction in terms.

The manner in which they disposed of Celtic in the semi-finals by an imperious four goals to nil implied their moment was at hand and so it turned out. That a part-time team, as St Mirren then were, could contest the Scottish Cup Final would be considered unlikely now but the general absence of tactical planning, and the greater prevalence of individual talents then, enabled such things to happen with some regularity.

The differing levels of fitness then became the decisive factor and eight of St Mirren's side that day were aged twenty-three or under. Tommy Bryceland, who was, with Tommy Gemmell, the inspiration behind the side, scored with a header two minutes before half-time. Alistair Miller then put them two goals ahead and ten minutes from the end the bus was pointed in the direction of Paisley when Gerry Baker scored a third. Baird's goal for Aberden was no form of consolation to anyone who had to make a much longer journey home empty-handed.

With some disregard for their lack of achievement, too, the Aberdeen players then rejected a two pound increase in their weekly wage packet for the following season, offered to them the Monday after the Final. Less inclined to look a gift horse in the mouth, the players of St Mirren accepted an identical offer from a grateful management and began the next Scottish Cup competition as the highest paid semi-professionals in the League on a basic salary of sixteen pounds a week.

The sudden accumulation of wealth once again seemed to have its desired effect when it came to the defence of their trophy. In the first round the

1959. St Mirren go three up against Aberdeen through Baker.

individual scoring record in the twentieth century history of the competition was established by Gerry Baker as he had cause to take the acclaim of the Love Street crowd no fewer than ten times in what was a mismatch with Glasgow University.

The exotically named University goalkeeper Nick Saltrese had what might have been described as only an academic interest in the match, anyway, being obliged to pick the ball from the net a total of fifteen times, but no doubt being able to see the funny side of it all since the game took place, with a superb irony, on Students Charities Day.

His side's preparation for the game had been somewhere south of intensive, too, since the players had been thrown out of the gymnasium in which they normally trained prior to visiting Love Street so that their student sisters could have their weekly American dance class.

The jig was up for St Mirren soon after as well since the Cup was destined to be restored to one of its more familiar resting places, Ibrox. Rangers had set out on the road to Hampden by defeating Berwick in a game which was an ominous foretaste of even worse to come. Damage totalling one thousand pounds was caused by visiting supporters, moving the chairman of the Berwick Board of Trade, Mr R C Blackhall, to comment acidly that, 'It is the mark of the beast to leave a trail of havoc and damage'.

The Rangers Supporters Association opened a fund for its members to atone for the misdeeds of others associated with their club. One week later an inspection of the monies taken in found the fund's intake to amount to six pounds.

Even that small sum would have paid the weekly footballing wage of half the Eyemouth United team who enlivened the later stages of the tournament by becoming the first non-league club since the war to reach the quarter-finals of the Scottish Cup. On a ground they shared with local schoolboys and where fish boxes were used as turnstiles, the fishermen, who were paid one pound a week to fill another kind of net, had attained that stage by defeating Cowdenbeath.

In the same round, incidentally, Celtic had come within six minutes of suffering the most embarrassing result in their history when they trailed Elgin City by a single goal at Boroughbriggs before being spared an ignominious farewell through two late goals. In a subtle way Kilmarnock, a burgeoning force under Willie Waddell, showed they had the requisite nerve to withstand such trials by then surviving the trip to Eyemouth. The negotiation of the ordeal took them into the penultimate stages of the competition.

Discretion being the better part of the valour which would have been required to remove revellers from the foliage in the event of more provincial high jinks, the ornamental gardens of Kilmarnock were immediately fenced in after the local team had removed Clyde from their path and advanced towards Rangers in the Final. In any event, the preventive measures proved to be unnecessary. Rangers, still smarting from the considerable blow of losing by six goals to one against Eintracht Frankfurt in the first leg of the European Cup

There was little to compel attendance behind the St Mirren goal in this 1960 Cup-tie. Gerry Baker was creating a record in the competition for this century by scoring 10 of the club's goals in a 15-0 win over Glasgow University. The all-time record is held by John Petrie of Arbroath with 13 of his side's 36 against Aberdeen Bon Accord in 1885.

1960. Millar, inside the six-yard box gives Rangers the lead against Kilmarnock.

semi-final, were in no mood to accommodate anyone. Besides which, fate also had its trick ready to play on Kilmarnock.

After thirteen minutes of the Final their centre-half Willie Toner was injured and rendered ineffective in his defensive role for Kilmarnock, spending the rest of the match, in the days before substitutes, moving less purposefully elsewhere. Jimmy Millar, a Rangers centre-forward who was well qualified to handle a full complement of able-bodied men far less a depleted side, scored twice thereafter and the day passed largely without incident. Some interest, though, was to be found in the attempts of the Kilmarnock goalkeeper Jimmy Brown to salvage something from his otherwise fruitless afternoon.

Brown was the owner of a public house in Kilmarnock and erroneously thought he could balance up the loss of takings in his place of business, on a night when there was no cause of celebration, by securing the match ball at time up for later display when the mood was lighter and more conducive to alcoholic intake. The SFA, insensitive to such frivolous notions, wrote to him in the strongest possible terms and the deflated ball had to be sent back by a similarly let down Jimmy Brown.

Rangers' sense of well being turned out to be a fleeting one, though, as the Germans performed a return raid on Govan and scored another six goals in the second leg of the European Cup semi-final. This in turn set up the classic Final at Hampden between themselves and Real Madrid, the most famous club in the world and possesser of the two most admired talents, Ferenc Puskas and Alfredo di Stefano.

It was a match, won by seven goals to three by the Spaniards, which was to have a profound effect on those who patronised the Scottish game and who tested the national stadium's capacity to hold all those wishing to see how the other half lived. They left in the knowledge that they themselves were existing in a state of penury. Realising full well the impoverished state of their own traditional fare compared with the ample menu set down before them that night, the Scottish public thereafter took a more critical view of their own national competitions and wondered if there was any likelihood of getting the full value for their then admission levy of 2s 6d (12½p) for the terracing.

There was already one operating in their midst, albeit in unlikely surroundings, who would eventually ensure that they did and who would begin to demonstrate his considerable expertise in the season which followed. ✱·Jock Stein had, unheralded, left his post in charge of Celtic's reserve side on 14 March 1960 for the managership of Dunfermline. In Fife's 'Auld grey toon' Dunfermline were a struggling country club with no recognisable pretensions towards anything higher than attaining their own survival in the First Division.

The fear of relegation had been the immediate problem the then thirty-seven year old Stein had to contend with. Lending weight to a theory which would inflate as his career progressed, to the effect that Stein carried a portable wand, he had instantly instigated a winning run, which included the ending of Kilmarnock's fifteen game unbeaten run in the championship three weeks after taking up the job.

Once safety had been guaranteed he set his sights on higher things with a flawless attention to detail. Tommy McDonald, a forward, was purchased from Wolves. At McDonald's suggestion, Stein then contacted Willie Cunningham, an Irishman who had fallen out with Leicester City and had temporarily given up the game for an everyday job in Paisley. Cunningham would later be required to fulfil a role which had been clamouring for space in Stein's fertile imagination, that of a spare man as the bolt to the defensive door, a position which would later come to be defined as the sweeper.

In an era of shallow attention to tactical detail this was to demonstrate a deep knowledge of the game's potential which was to give Stein a head start over the managerial competition and ultimately take Dunfermline from obscurity to recognition on the map of the game which previous cartographers would have denied them through insufficient proof of the town's existence in that sense.

Showing a marked disinclination towards being acquired as anything other than a reward for excellence, the Scottish Cup had survived the flight through the night air in Paisley and also a break-in at its Ibrox home in the 1960-61 season. It was, however, obliged to leave there by more conventional methods when Rangers were themselves burgled downstairs from the trophy room, on the pitch outside by an impious Motherwell in a Cup replay at the second round stage.

If the removal of their historic rivals and a convincing run for their own part through the remainder of the competition had encouraged Celtic to believe the Cup would be returned to their safe keeping for the first time in seven years, there were unforeseen complications yet to be encountered.

The month of April that year was a historic one in that it marked mankind's first round trip into space as carried out by the Russian Yuri Gargarin. Three days after his momentous achievement, the whole thing might never have taken place for those who developed selective amnesia, blotting the real world out of their minds, after a similarly spectacular return to the earth's

✱ Jock Stein died at the age of 62, just after the Wales v Scotland world cup match at Ninian Park, Cardiff 10ᵗʰ September, 1985 (Heart attack)

Eddie Conachan is carried shoulder high after his performance had totally frustrated Celtic and brought Dunfermline the Cup in the 1961 replay.

atmosphere by the Scottish international side at Wembley. The weekend trip to London, for those who make the pilgrimage every two years, is an outlet, and various flights of fancy at what Scotland will do to an English side, perceived as standard bearers of the oppressors, are boarded.

The loss of the first choice goalkeeper for Scotland, Lawrie Leslie of Airdrie, disturbed no-one from their pre-occupation therefore. His understudy had, after all, played in the drawn match against England the year before and seemed to take sustenance in his times of need from an innate self-confidence, both with his country and his club, Celtic. His name was Frank Haffey.

His natural sense of optimism proved groundless on this occasion, though, as Scotland lost by a barely credible nine goals to three. Haffey, nothing if not honest when there was a need for probity under the prevailing circumstances, admitted a degree of accountability for each and every one. Many others would have withdrawn into their shell and been unable to face duty between the goalposts in a Cup Final just one week later but Haffey acted in an unabashed manner which seemed to suit his club's mood as they approached the climax to their season.

The meeting with Dunfermline in the Final was, after all, a coming together of a full-time side who, in spite of the barren years, had at least been over the course often enough to pre-suppose uncertainty would not be a problem and Dunfermline, whose first appearance at Hampden this was in a Scottish Cup Final in the seventy-sixth year of their existence.

Redressing the balance in psychological terms was a ploy for which Jock Stein had a natural aptitude, though. Dunfermline set up their training camp prior to the match at Seamill, which was, as if he didn't know, Celtic's traditional, preparatory headquarters. The manager was also practised in the art of debunking the firmly held convictions of others with an innocent look and a plausible explanation which caused the less cynical to privately remonstrate with themselves for being so gauche as to bring up such a naive topic in the first place.

In this instance it was presumed that Stein's recently enjoyed intimate knowledge of the Celtic team, ten of whom had been under his care when he was in charge of the reserve side at Parkhead, would be an influential factor in determining the outcome of the Final.

The eleventh man, Willie Fernie, had also played with Stein in the last Celtic side to win the trophy against Aberdeen in 1954, which meant he was hardly an unknown quantity, either. The very idea was dismissed out of hand by Stein who said in what would ultimately prove to be one of the great misleading statements of the time, 'My out of date knowledge of Celtic won't help us'. He said it with such emphasis, though, that there was a reluctance to bring up his almost total recall when it comes to players he has seen, especially those he had left behind thirteen months earlier.

Of the Dunfermline side which eventually came to Hampden only one, Willie Cunningham, had not been at the club prior to Stein's arrival there. The remarkable transformation in the team could only be taken to mean, therefore, that the material was there to work with and that self-belief had been the only missing ingredient. In overcoming the natural apprehension which nevertheless came with their first Final, Dunfermline were immeasurably assisted by their goalkeeper Eddie Connachan, whose virtuosity in the first game granted them a replay from a goal-less match and the opportunity to approach the second game in a more relaxed, knowing fashion.

In between Celtic lost their full-back, Jim Kennedy, because of a sudden appendicitis operation but nevertheless allowed their former captain and most experienced player, Bertie Peacock, to join up with the Northern Ireland international squad for a game in Italy. Stein, of course, rejected the idea of letting his Ulsterman, Willie Cunningham, make the same trip, although he was asked to do so.

Consequently a young Celtic side were beaten by two second half goals from Davie Thomson and Charlie Dickson, and once again had to endure the spectacle of another memorable performance from the Dunfermline goalkeeper Connachan, whose athleticism caused the game to be known as 'Connachan's Final'.

Irony piled upon irony as the trophy and medals were handed over by Robert Kelly, SFA president as well as Celtic chairman, and his wife. Dunfermline stayed up late that night while the man who was to all intents and purposes Celtic went home from his duties at the presentation and thought long and hard.

A week later in Glasgow betting shops were able to open legally for the first time since they were ruled outside the law in 1853.

Anyone who had wandered in, without looking over his shoulder for once, and placed a wager on the long range forecast that the events of the previous week at Hampden would stir Celtic to observe Stein's progress closely with a view to re-installing him at Parkhead would have shown commendable, if understandable, foresight.

Double Money, Treble Time

IT WAS ALL a question of style. The early sixties, that series of irreverent explosions fuelled by the young running riot on the fruits of national prosperity, established the footballer as the glamorous figurehead at the top of the social scale. Some of them, however, were more 'nouveau' to the game of being suddenly 'riche' than others.

Rangers won three Scottish Cups in succession between 1962 and 1964, the third time the club had claimed that distinction and also the last to date, while more than doubling the wage packets of their playing staff during the same three year period. By still retaining the traditional twice-yearly bonus payment for tangible profit on the field they brought into being an aristocratic clique within the domestic game. Some would take to self-aggrandisement as if to the manner born, others found moving up the social scale an odious period of trial and error.

There was, for example, one particularly outgoing young man who, once firmly established among the inordinately well paid at Ibrox, decided it was time his well-being was properly noticed and bought himself a bungalow in Lanarkshire. The asking price of two thousand pounds he met by turning up at the office of the appropriate estate agent and ostentatiously depositing on to the desk in front of him the exact amount in single, one pound notes, presumably pulled from a large brown envelope by his own cigar-clutching, bejewelled hand.

The one less comfortable in his role as a man of substance had suffered the scorn of the Ibrox dressing room each morning concerning the matter of his personal hygiene.

Patiently he explained that while he had also moved into the obligatory bungalow, which introduced him to the luxury of a well-appointed bathroom, it was impossible to enjoy the amenities since every time he switched on the means of supplying hot water a red light came on and he immediately switched it back off again for fear of an explosion. The workings of the immersion heater system were explained to him and he was enabled to resume a normal, odourless existence.

It was a less eccentric balance than these two players provided which meant that the profligate and the plodders were able to come together in a Rangers team which was on occasion genuinely entitled to be thought of as brilliant. Many internal factors should have conspired against that level of greatness ever being realised at all but in the end sheer ability won out and what the side of that period could have gone on to achieve, had there been a more dedicated strain evident throughout the work of some, continues to be a source of wide-eyed conjecture.

When it is considered, on the other hand, that the nucleus of the Celtic side which would create history by becoming the first British club to win the European Cup before that decade had run anything like its course was already at Parkhead, but toiling pitifully, a certain benign alignment of the fates has to be suspected for seeing to it Rangers went as far as they did.

There were the dedicated professionals like Caldow, Brand, Millar and numerous others but many illusions would have been shattered at that time had the innermost details of the internal workings at Ibrox regarding the less-disciplined been made known.

One of those who was there then can recall travelling time of one hour from his door to Ibrox's marbled front, and the same back again. This would involve leaving the house at 9.30 am and returning at 12.30 pm. Training, such as it was, was what took place in between. The joke went, in an understandably cheerful dressing room among those who were receiving large sums to maintain this less than punishing schedule, that the players were running in the same foot-prints each day, such was the questionable level of application involved.

An atmosphere of something other than intense professionalism would occasionally have to be paid for, though, and there was the memorable and anything but apocryphal tale of the internationalist who was given two aspirin to counteract the pain of a sore leg which upon more detailed examination elsewhere turned out to be broken.

No-one could come near to Rangers, however, for being endowed with the kind of good fortune which allowed them to deploy a beautifully balanced side in which the extravagant talents of Jim Baxter, all demonstrated on the ball and without recourse to running anywhere, were complemented by first Harold Davis and then John Greig doing the leg work on the other side of the park. In the forward line there was Davie Wilson, an occasionally inspired winger of limitless spirit, and the enigmatic Willie Henderson. Along with Baxter, Henderson would cause Rangers to tacitly revise the traditional outlook which had sustained them for almost a century while trying to present a monolithic image to the world outside. Henderson had signed as a professional for Rangers in January of 1961, on the date of his seventeenth birthday. Before he was eighteen he had asked for a transfer, presumably suffering from a low boredom threshold and impatient to replace Alex Scott in Rangers' first team.

The written request was held up like a piece of radioactive paper by Scot Symon and dismissed by the Ibrox manager in two sentences, which was, by repute, one more than he had ever used to comment on anything. 'No player will ever force the hand of Rangers. We are too great a club to be influenced by anything like this,' he declared. Two weeks later Henderson made his first team debut. Alex Scott would have to get used to the feeling. Having made a sizeable enough contribution to Rangers' season to gain attention, the graceful Scott's presence was welcomed in the Scotland team which played England in the week before the Scottish Cup Final of 1962. The following Saturday he was left out in favour of Henderson when Rangers played St Mirren.

The team from Paisley, who had only narrowly avoided relegation, had made it to Hampden by demonstrating form in the Cup which bore no relation to their everyday League matches, a trait never more clearly exemplified than in their five goal thrashing from Celtic on the Monday night before the two sides met in the semi-finals. At 3-0 in St Mirren's favour the following Saturday, the field at Ibrox, where the tie was played, was invaded by the intractable element among the Celtic support who found playing men with split personalities unacceptable, so ignoring the schizophrenic aspect of their own make-up. Both sides were removed to safety amid gratuitous bottle throwing and when they returned Celtic scored a late, irrelevant goal.

In losing, Celtic had passed up the chance to take part in the first Old Firm

Final since 1928 when Bill Struth had led Rangers to their first outright success in twenty-five years. The great man had once reacted volcanically to a suggestion that the club pay the necessary tax on the players' bonus payment.

Proof of the Struth era being overtaken by the materialisation of a less fearful, more mercenary type of player, though, came when, two days before the Final, an offer of thirty-five pounds a week for the coming season was rejected at Ibrox and what was always popularly known as a 'revolt' ensued inside the ground. It was a bloodless revolution with players agreeing to forget about their differences on Cup Final day and showing they could by easily defeating St Mirren by two goals to nil.

Resentment may have been able to be switched on and off like an immerser, though, and those who were hot on the Saturday turned cold at Aberdeen the following Wednesday. Rangers lost in the League at Pittodrie and therefore inadvertently gave Dundee the First Division championship after they had completed the other half of the unwitting bargain by winning at Perth against St Johnstone in their next match. The management at Ibrox would be careful after that not to underestimate those on their staff who had difficulty with domestic appliances but none at all with elementary arithmetic.

Parsimony at Ibrox in the sense of being reluctant to spend money freely on new players had, in contrast with Parkhead policies, never been a justifiable charge. Whereas Celtic had baulked at the idea of signing Billy Bremner from Leeds United when they could have had him for thirty thousand pounds, Rangers had created a then Scottish transfer record at the beginning of 1963 by buying George McLean from St Mirren after their rivals had pulled out of the chase considering such sums of money to be the stuff of make-believe. At the same time Pat Crerand, by then already capped eleven times for Scotland, was sold by Celtic to Manchester United for fifty-five thousand pounds amid anguished noises from their following. That no adequate replacement was bought to placate them was apparently considered neither here nor there, until, that is, the relevance of these dealings became all too apparent when the

1963. Celebrations following Rangers' 3-0 defeat of Celtic. Bobby Shearer is holding the Cup.

Old Firm met at last in the Scottish Cup Final at the end of that season.

No matter what, Celtic have always retained a huge support inured to pain and suffering but it is one which can demonstrate a punch drunk boxer's dubious judgement in not knowing when to stop coming back for more. The notion of making up for everything by defeating Rangers in a Cup Final acted like chloroform on their number and consumed their thoughts to the exclusion of all else.

A crowd of ten thousand turned up for a reserve match with Morton at Parkhead even though there were only four thousand tickets for the Final on sale. There was also a thriving black market on which terracing tickets priced at 3s (15p) were changing hands for 10s (50p), which would have been enough to administer chloroform of another sort at the 'doctor's' of your choice and so blot out the unpleasant past just the same. When demand exceeds supply the exponents of the free enterprise system, legitimate or otherwise, are mobilised as well and Glasgow police investigated the discovery of hundreds of forged tickets — all for Hampden's traditional 'Celtic End'.

Whether they had gained entry by fair means or foul, it was a touching demonstration of loyalty on the part of those Celtic men at Hampden who had no sound reason to suspect any reward in return against a naturally gifted Rangers team gathering momentum to the extent that the League title was all but won before the two teams came out before a crowd of 129,527.

There was, incidentally, one more interesting development prior to the game when the Celtic chairman, Bob Kelly, suggested that both teams and officials be brought together and reminded of their obligations on what was a sensitive occasion. Those who followed on from him twenty-one years later obviously viewed such matters differently.

Meanwhile, Kelly, or whoever picked the Celtic team, the matter was always the subject of speculation, kept faith with one disarming tactic of the club and produced a belated, surprise choice in their final selection. Jimmy Johnstone, then eighteen years old and a veteran of two games in Celtic's first team, neither of them a Cup-tie, played from the start. He acquitted himself very well, too, in a game which finished level at one goal each and was remembered for the outstanding goalkeeping of Celtic's Frank Haffey, trying vainly to compensate in what remained of his professional life for having lost nine goals against England at Wembley two years earlier.

The replay was delayed while a backlog of outstanding League fixtures caused by a two month shut-down in the ferociously inclement winter months was partly cleared up. It was a regrettable hold-up for Celtic since it gave those in charge time to come up with yet another tactical ploy. Before returning to Hampden, Celtic defeated Motherwell by six goals to nil with Steve Chalmers obtaining a hat-trick.

Chalmers was a highly respected and courageous centre forward who would enter the club's folklore before much longer by scoring the winning goal in the European Cup Final. In 1963 his inclusion in the team, in place of Johnstone, for the Scottish Cup Final replay meant that Celtic had altered their forward line for the thirty-ninth time that season, continuity of selection being clearly an abstract theory inside Parkhead.

The game represented a low point in the club's fortunes, at any rate. Rangers won easily with two goals from Ralph Brand and one from Davie Wilson and even the Celtic faithful in a crowd of over 120,000 deserted the

1964. Brand douses his team-mates, Shearer holds the Cup. Rangers have notched their third hat-trick of Cup Final wins.

cause long before the end as Jim Baxter closed the night on an arrogant note by secreting the match ball under his jersey and making a present of it afterwards to Ian McMillan.

Because of his artistry and larger than life persona, Baxter was the most celebrated personality in the Scottish game and someone for whom others were willing to make allowances in order to enjoy his patronage. The then owner of the Kinema Ballroom in Dunfermline was one, giving the sack to a steward for his lack of tact in refusing the player admission to those premises for not complying with the rules governing proper dress.

Baxter and the like were now earning at a rate so far in excess of ordinary mortals that they probably felt life's tedious little rules concerning such matters did not apply to them. Immediately before beating Celtic the Ibrox management, now conforming to the dictates of the world in which they found themselves, however unwillingly, had offered the Rangers players contracts which they were unable to refuse. The bonus payment which took them into 1964 was then described by one of those now wealthy beyond his most avaricious dreams as 'stunning' and there seemed little on the horizon to suggest this Rangers side could not emulate their predecessors by winning the Scottish Cup for a third consecutive time.

At the quarter-final stage the avuncular Jimmy McGrory and his Celtic side, convinced they had undergone the necessary transformation, swung back like a punch bag. The defeat of Slovan Bratislavia in Czechoslovakia the previous midweek by an aggregate 2-0 had prompted an official reception attended by thousands of men, women and children at Parkhead in honour of the club's achievement in reaching the semi-final of the European Cup Winners' Cup.

Their imperishable spirit was poorly recompensed, though, when Rangers won through easily by two goals to nil at Ibrox forty-eight hours later, their fifth consecutive win over Celtic that season. Dunfermline, managed by Jock Stein, fell in the semi-final and three days later he left to take over Hibs.

The stage was therefore set for the only Scottish Cup Final it was imagined could provide a reasonable test of Rangers' capabilities. The Dundee of Slater, Hamilton, Penman and Gilzean were formidable opponents, so much so that an occupant of the Rangers dressing room that day recalls it as it being one of the few times when the other side was discussed other than to check on the colour of their jerseys in order to avoid a clash.

Part of the reason behind this may have been the suspicion that their adversaries also had players with a good conceit of themselves. The extent of Dundee's anxiety to get a piece of the commerical action which was increasingly finding its way into the game clearly indicated that they were confident of backing up their sales talk by producing the goods on a Saturday.

Earlier in the week of the Final a training session had been disrupted at Dens Park by the appearance of cameras from Grampian Television, who had refused beforehand to pay for the privilege of capturing the celluloid drama of it all. Their presence was enough to send the players falling face downwards on the pitch on a given command as if Grampian had ordered missile strafing of the place as a reprisal.

On arrival at their base in Glasgow the faces of the Dundee players, by this time calling their grievance 'unfair exploitation', were also hidden from the cameras of newspaper photographers whose editors would not pay the sum of £1.18s per man. Commercialism still had a little way to go, you understand, and yet to appear were the personal agents who would advise on the desirability of rounding off figures to a neat two pounds, if only for the sake of the personal accountants who were also soon to emerge.

Dundee were as good as Rangers thought they might be and the game entered its last couple of minutes with the score tied at one goal all. The excitement generated was such that Davie Wilson, believing there to be at least another ten minutes left, reacted like a scalded cat when an ambulanceman on the track, who clearly had a vested interest in the game's outcome, informed him of the Final's late hour.

The attempts of he and the rest of the side to beat Bert Slater, in the Dundee goal, took on new urgency. Millar headed in his second of the game from a Henderson cross and then, only moments later, a shot from Wilson was parried out to Brand, who completed the scoring and enshrined a memorable finish in the eyes of those watching.

There seemed no limit to Rangers' potential. They had that season won the treble of League, League Cup and Scottish Cup and the Ibrox board had decided that Scot Symon should go to Spain and study coaching methods there which might help perpetuate Rangers' unchallenged supremacy in Scotland.

Rangers went to Madrid. Celtic, beaten once on Rangers' ground by St Mirren and twice by the team from Ibrox over that three year period in the Scottish Cup, went to Edinburgh for a new manager. From the following season onwards there would be no doubt that, for once, Celtic got the better part of the deal by paying less money.

A Change in the Weather

IN THE MID to late sixties the Scottish Cup acted as the catalyst for the most successful side in Celtic's history and brought about the most ignominious day in Rangers' long existence. It brought Jock Stein into Celtic Park like a blinding flash and ultimately brought down Scot Symon at Ibrox amid rolling thunder. The climate was variable, largely depending on which side of Glasgow you were on.

In the less demanding world outside the dreamier aspects of the competition brought occasional light relief from the increasing build-up of tension, as was evidenced by Elgin City's travails in the off-beat setting of Wigtownshire. The Cup draw for the preliminary rounds of 1968 which forced them into a round trip of 550 miles could hardly have been described as a fortune cookie in the first place but the long day's journey into night should have had its compensations at least in the 3-2 win over Tarff Rovers at Kirkcowan.

The biscuit was taken, though, when it was discovered the home club could not meet their financial obligations, to wit the price of fifteen return rail fares, as laid down by the SFA rules when that sum exceeds half the gate money taken. Even at that Elgin, claiming £124 10s, were out of pocket since their travelling expenses had totalled £400. But Tarff, who had collected only £75 in gate receipts, and all of it in a biscuit tin held by one man at the sole means of entrance to their ground, situated in what was clearly not one of the game's hotbeds of interest, could only send them off with that most suspicious of all assurances, 'Your cheque is in the post'.

Celtic's lengthy period of ascendancy in Scotland and, more fleetingly, in Europe was underwritten on a Sunday in January of 1965 when numerous prayers were answered and Jock Stein's appointment as manager of the club in succession to Jimmy McGrory was announced, although he did not assume control until the beginning of March.

The old club had been in a state of poor health and it was either a miracle cure, which Stein promised to bring in the eyes of the believers, or the priest who had to be sent for. Even that early in the season the Scottish Cup was all that was left for Celtic, following elimination from the League Cup and the Fairs Cup and with form in the championship so uninspiring that 1500 tickets, one quarter of Celtic's allocation, were returned to Morton for what it was thought should necessarily have been an all-ticket match at Cappielow. Purely on the strength of his coming, though, a crowd of 28,500 then watched Celtic defeat St Mirren in the first round of the Cup the Saturday after he became manager-elect.

The club had not won anything at all since defeating Rangers 7-1 in the League Cup Final of 1957, an event which may have sated forever the ambitions of the more extremist wing of the Celtic support but the receding memory of which left the side's players, and the more rational element following them, in a demoralised state.

The day before the Celtic chairman Bob Kelly introduced his new manager Celtic had, for example, dropped a brooding Jimmy Johnstone, his confidence

1965. The Celtic bus at the corner of Crown Street and Caledonia Road.

having deserted him to the extent that he felt himself unable to cross the ball, which sounded like demoralization on a horrific scale coming from that particular quarter.

Stein would sort that out by rekindling Johnstone's spirit and working valiantly to douse the more regrettable lapses in his behaviour. The player had originally gone into a depressed state after becoming the first man to be sent off in the traditional Ne'erday game with Rangers for twenty-two years, following an unseemly attack on the Icelandic player Therolf Beck.

The manager's background was checkered. Stein had drifted from his first senior club, Albion Rovers, to Welsh non-League football with Llanelli and was then bought for £2,000 by Celtic in 1951. As a player he led the club to victories in the Scottish Cup and Coronation Cup but was forced to retire from the game in 1957 with an inoperable ankle injury. Three years later he gave up the job in charge of Celtic's reserve side and took over Dunfermline, ironically winning the Fife club a Scottish Cup Final against Celtic in his first full season with them. Only ten months after he had left East End Park for the manager's job with Hibs, the irresistible call went out to him from his temporarily befuddled former employers in Glasgow.

It is said of him that Jock Stein was the man who introduced tactics into Scottish football and where Celtic were concerned he was also a talisman at work on their behalf even before he had the chance to prove the veracity of those words at Parkhead.

Two days before officially going there his last act as Hibs manager was to defeat Rangers in the quarter-finals of the Scottish Cup at Easter Road, thereby removing arguably the most serious obstacle from his own path in the competition. Two days after taking over, Stein's Celtic scored six at Airdrie, with Bertie Auld getting five of them, and stumbled only once on the way to Hampden, when it required a replay to get past Motherwell and into a meeting with Dunfermline.

It was one of the memorable finales to the competition as Dunfermline twice took the lead through Melrose and McLaughlin only for Bertie Auld, an exceptional talent beginning to rediscover himself as well under Stein, to twice equalise. The winning goal remains graphically in the mind, with the Celtic captain Billy McNeill soaring unchallenged to head a corner kick from Charlie Gallagher, who had not been in the team for three months prior to Stein's arrival, as the minutes ran away.

The period of sterility was over — even the wife of the Celtic goalkeeper that day, John Fallon, was taken from the post-match celebrations at the Central Hotel to be delivered of a son — and big Jock, the name by which everyone knew him, but not to his face, had been back just six weeks.

His presence would truly be felt in the season which followed when Celtic won the League Championship for the first time in twelve years. Life at Parkhead was never the same again for players who, it was said, had to remind themselves on a Saturday to keep running straight ahead out of the tunnel and

Billy McNeill, right arm aloft, has just headed the winner in the 1965 Final. A decade of celebrations begins for Celtic.

on to the pitch. Their more natural instinct before Stein had been to perform a right wheel and begin the endless lapping of the track which formed a training programme without the inclusion of ball work.

Stein taught them that training could be entertaining while he hammered the dents out of various crushed spirits belonging to players like Bobby Murdoch, Steve Chalmers and Bobby Lennox, who had to get used to the idea that they were once again valuable to Celtic after previously lengthy periods spent oscillating between the reserves and the first team.

Fires were also lit underneath some others who, having watched Stein guide Celtic to a Scottish Cup in record time, were willing to put up with being treated on occasion like primary seven schoolchildren, as one who was there at the time remembers it, in order to see where this man of the awesome presence would eventually lead them.

The trail led back to Hampden after a memorable first full season in which Celtic scored over one hundred League goals while taking the championship, won the League Cup and only went out of the European Cup Winners' Cup under the most contentious circumstances. A one goal win over Liverpool at Parkhead in the semi-final was discoloured by the referee inexplicably stopping the game somewhat short of the regulation ninety minutes.

The return leg at Anfield bruised Celtic's spirits even more when, in the final minute, and with Stein's side losing by two goals to nil, Lennox scored with a shot which looked to have carried Celtic into the Final on the rule which allows away goals to count double in the event of a draw. A referee with no romance in his soul and more perceptive shortcomings of an ophthalmic nature, according to those who would swear to this day that Lennox was on-side by many feet, ended the match on a sour note and left the field before he could witness violent disharmony off it.

If their disappointment was severe and their impulsive reaction excessive, it was an uncharacteristic display of aggression from a Celtic following who knew a good thing when they saw it and were turning up in remarkable numbers.

The barren years had provided sufficient shade to enable them to see the light clearly and the crowd of over 72,000, with many more thousands locked outside, who assembled for the replay of the Scottish Cup quarter-final with Hearts at Parkhead in 1966 constituted a then post-war record midweek attendance for the ground. They cheerfully watched Celtic advance by three goals to one.

Rangers, once again careering towards Celtic like a bad accident that can be foreseen but not prevented, were also involved in a memorable midweek tie of more eccentric appeal in another of the game's outposts, Dingwall. The visit of what was obviously taken to be the marauding hordes from Glasgow had aroused occasionally irrational misgivings on the part of those associated with Rangers' opponents, Ross County.

Frank Thomson, the club's chairman, took out an insurance policy worth £250,000 and covering all his players against serious injury on the field of play against Rangers, which perhaps best illustrated the kind of match they thought they were in for. At the same time Willie Munro, then district superintendent of the public houses in the locale, and a civic-minded soul, threatened the ultimate deterrent to external violence when he announced, 'I will instruct all bars to remain closed after five pm in the event of any trouble'.

1966. Willie Johnston of Rangers heads over as he is challenged by Murdoch and Young of Celtic in the first match of the 1966 Final.

With all doors and windows tightly secured, women and children evacuated to places of greater safety and an air of uneasy tension hanging over the saloon bars of Ross-shire, there was then a dreadful feeling of anti-climax when a heavy snowfall caused the game's postponement.

An anxious SFA Secretary, Willie Allan, knowing that such weather in that region can overstay its welcome, then had the temerity to suggest Ross County might instead like a day out in the bright lights of the big city with a game at Ibrox against Rangers to fulfil their Scottish Cup obligation. The very idea solicited a dramatic response from an obviously exciteable Frank Thomson to the effect that 'If Ross County go to Ibrox it will be in thirteen coffins, eleven for the team, one for the coach, Sammy Wilson, and one for me'.

A cortege from the county was averted when the climate became more temperate and Thomson's team were quietly buried 2-0 in any case by a

The century's greatest Cup shock, Sammy Reid of Berwick hits the goal which puts Rangers out of the 1967 competition.

Rangers side with more important things on their minds. Rangers had been the team of the early sixties but the growing suspicion was that Celtic now had a manager who would ensure a continuing psychological edge over them.

There is nothing even a hypo-therapist can do, however, if the majority of those under his control prove they have minds of their own, if only by simply not using them on occasion, and Celtic were not so pre-programmed as to be incapable of failing to beat Rangers at two attempts spread over four days in the Scottish Cup Final of 1966.

A marked lack of guile in attack lasted throughout the whole of the first match with Rangers and for over an hour of the replay. It was at this stage Kai Johansen created a unique double achievement. With his first goal for Rangers in Scottish football, the Dane also became the first Scandinavian ever to win a Scottish Cup-winners' medal. It was also Rangers' first period of remission since Stein had taken over at Parkhead but, in hindsight, it is clear that the Ibrox club's followers would have been better sparing themselves personal grief by leaving the country for a while thereafter, considering the price they would have to pay for their brief moment of pleasure.

Even in significant defeat like this there was no doubt that Stein was in undisputed charge at Parkhead but the same autocracy was still not common-place at either club or international level. Stein had temporarily taken over the management of Scotland from Ian McColl at the end of his first season at Parkhead but felt it was unfair to combine both tasks. The post was then turned down by both Willie Waddell and Eddie Turnbull before John Prentice accepted it and he only lasted seven months. After Stein's departure the SFA had at first advertised the job as a part-time one, which suggested that the ruling body was, in reality, unwilling to transfer total control to the individual appointed.

Overt interference with the manager's role was coming at Ibrox, too, helped into existence, ironically, by an event caused by one who would help reverse that trend one day — Jock Wallace.

Rangers were drawn against Berwick Rangers in the first round of the

Scottish Cup of 1967. It was the first time they had been there in seven years and the Glasgow side may have listened dismissively as the English club's player-manager promised that the tie would provide the shock of the year. Never one for the understated, as was discovered after that, Wallace's team took advantage of a visiting Rangers side who had within its number certain individuals who clearly felt that the whole experience of shuffling around Shielfield Park was beneath their dignity.

There are Celtic supporters with a perverted sense of history who can tell you where they were standing when they heard Rangers had lost 1-0 and such was the barely credible result that even BBC television's afternoon sports programme refused to accept it as being true in the first place.

For the first time in thirty years Rangers, then the holders of the trophy, of course, had gone out of the competition without reaching the second round and to a goal scored by a man, Sammy Reid, who had had pins inserted in a knee cap two years earlier as a last resort to allow him to continue playing the game in the lower division. Two of the Berwick players, incidentally, were sent by a manager, who was clearly trying to play down the miraculous aspect of it all, to turn out for the reserve side in a trial match against Haddington Athletic the day after, when they should have been nursing the effects of over indulgence which made speech, far less physical movement, unlikely.

Berwick's odds were cut from ten thousand to one to five thousand to one for the Cup but they went out without inflicting poverty on the bookmaking fraternity after losing quietly to Hibs in the next round. Only those whose instinctive gambling urge would have caused them in days gone by to bet their daughter's hand against the deeds to the other man's plantation would have put money on anyone but Celtic for the trophy, anyway. Immortality was at hand.

Chalmers of Celtic and the Aberdeen defence see a shot by Wallace (not in the picture) put Celtic ahead in the 1967 Final.

By now Stein had gathered around him those whose personal identities would be subjugated under the collective title of Lisbon Lions. As any child now in his teens who has his christian and surnames separated by Simpson, Craig, Gemmell, Murdoch, McNeill, Clark, Johnstone, Wallace, Chalmers, Auld and Lennox — a temporary fad which brought registrars of births to the brink of despair in 1967 — will tell you, these were the men who won everything it was possible to win, domestically and in Europe, that year.

1967. The Scottish Cup has been won and the European Cup is in prospect. Wallace and Clark are congratulated by Stein.

They also became the first British football club ever to be praised in a motion before the House of Commons, proposed by Richard Buchanan, the then Labour member for Springburn and a man who knew good public relations work when he saw it, representing as he did a constituency in which there were more readers of the *Celtic View*, the club's newspaper, than there were of *Hansard*.

That distinction followed the win over Inter Milan in the Final of the European Cup, the details of which must be automatically recalled by those who were not actually in Tibet at the time. Domestically, Celtic's highlights came, variously, on one of those days in Glasgow when the rain falls so hard it is said to bounce the height of two storey buildings, when a point from Rangers at Ibrox won them the championship, and then on a gloriously bright Saturday in the Scottish Cup Final of 1967 before a crowd of 127,117.

The pageantry of that occasion should only have been matched by the closeness of the contest. Celtic had returned from an exacting game with Dukla Prague in Czechoslovakia which put them into the European Cup Final, while their opponents, Aberdeen, were managed by an astute judge in Eddie Turnbull. He was a gruff character who was capable of facial expressions which would have stopped a clock and who possessed an aggressive enough manner to have its mechanism start up again out of fear.

His personality notwithstanding, Turnbull was a highly respected tactician and motivator of men. The day was probably lost for Aberdeen before it had begun, then, when Turnbull became unwell at the team's hotel in Gleneagles only fifteen minutes before the coach arrived to take them to Hampden. He was removed to hospital and his side went into a state of shock, turning the Final into a poor spectacle through a possibly reflexive insistence on defensive play. It had not been anticipated, either, that Jimmy Johnstone would assume a different role, playing in the position of an orthodox inside-right instead of patrolling the touchline as if tied to it like an exciteable pup on a piece of string.

The match was Celtic's fifty-eighth competitive game of the season but they were as relentlessly determined as they had been in the first and two goals from Willie Wallace, a hard but gifted striker bought earlier from Hearts, took the Scottish Cup back into Celtic's possession.

The trophy stayed at Parkhead only as long as it took to get the first round of the following season's tournament underway. In it Celtic were eliminated by Dunfermline, the last truly provincial club to gather sufficient momentum to defy their status and successfully take on all comers to have their name inscribed on the plinth.

The Fife club was managed by George Farm, another escapee from the school of charm, famed for his plain speaking and a cussed nature. Probably due to Farm it was even arranged, prior to their visiting Parkhead, that tickets be printed in advance for a replay at East End Park, an outrageous presumption under the circumstances it might have been thought.

Farm, who worked for a time as a lighthouse keeper after giving up the game, saw his side pierce through Celtic's invincible image, though, with two goals that found no reply. As if they too had experienced a premonition about the outcome of the match, the Dunfermline directors celebrated their team's achievement by taking to the dressing room the remainder of a consignment of champagne which had been held in cold storage from the Scottish Cup Final of 1960, in which they had also defeated Celtic. The action spoke volumes for the board's abstemiousness and also for the irregularity with which they had cause to pop the corks.

Another sophisticates' carry-out had to be ordered in any case because Dunfermline ultimately went on to meet Hearts in the Final. The Edinburgh club had seemingly done the hard part earlier on by eliminating Rangers to

Willie Callaghan and Tommy Traynor battle it out in the 1968 Final.

hinder the transition hoped for under Davie White, the new manager at Ibrox.

White had been brought in from Clyde in the wake of the confusion and disappointment which followed Rangers defeat in the Final of the European Cup Winners' Cup, when Scot Symon's selection was publicly criticised by his chairman, John Lawrence, and the revered manager's date of dismissal became clearer in the mind. The new man's introduction to the helm after a period as assistant manager was a turbulent one. Rangers were thrown out of the Glasgow Cup the week before losing to Hearts for refusing to play Celtic on the date stipulated by the organising committee; the implication being that Rangers had taken too many maulings from their oldest adversaries to extend their chin one more time than they absolutely had to. Worse was to follow.

On the day of the Scottish Cup Final, 56,366 went to Hampden but almost as many filled Ibrox for Rangers' last game of the season. A win over Aberdeen would have cleaned the slate and given White the prestigious prize, and the auspicious start to his career, of the championship itself.

Those from out of town who could not understand the sporadic outbursts of excited cheering around them at the Cup Final during moments of comparative calm in that match were unaware of Celtic fans with transistor radios unashamedly wallowing in news of Rangers' home defeat.

Out on the field at Hampden, Dunfermline were oblivious to all but their own sense of destiny. In spite of losing their goalkeeper Willie Duff before the game because of injury —'he was replaced by the quaintly named Dane Bent Martin — and with another player, John McGarty, playing in his first Scottish Cup-tie, they overpowered Hearts.

The Edinburgh club's preparation for the Final had been poor. In the days before the advent of the Premier Division when it was actually necessary to do your 'homework' on the opposition, since the League did not offer the same familiarity, they had played truant and were, consequently, bemused by a side to whom they had shown insufficient respect.

Hearts were already two goals behind when the dawn of realisation came up and they were given temporary hope in the form of an own goal but they were too predictable and Dunfermline, who had a more versatile approach, with Alex Edwards running things from the middle of the field, scored once more.

On paper Hearts might have been thought favourites but their League form had been mediocre, their Scandinavian forward Roald Jensen had been in a huff with the club and only decided to play in the Final at the last minute and, all things considered, they had played into their opponents' hands.

Three days later, though, Celtic exacted full revenge for their defeat in the Cup by visiting Dunfermline and winning the two points which gave them the League flag instead of Rangers.

There then appeared a story during the summer of 1968 which summed up how men could be driven to desperate measures by things like this. Three of Rangers' support, sporting club ties, had been arrested in a bar in Ndola, Zambia.

All employed by Zambian Railways, the distinctive colouring of their ties had been mistaken for those belonging to Ian Smith's ruling Rhodesian Front party and all three were placed in custody until they told their story. Release was probably on compassionate grounds, acknowledging that they had clearly suffered enough already and rightly anticipating that their ordeal was not yet over. It was that kind of time.

The fox, the lions, and the cubs

DIPLOMATIC relations between Great Britain and Sweden were not irreversibly eroded because of the incident but Harold Wilson must have been given cause just the same to revise his opinion of one section of the country's electorate when Jock Stein refused an invitation to number ten Downing Street for a reception in honour of the visiting Prime Minister, Olof Palme.

The reason given in all sincerity and solemnity from Celtic Park was that the manager was too heavily committed, since the club had an important reserve match against Rangers. Even to a phlegmatic Swede and a professional politician, who had no greater love of the game than to risk his credibility in public by admitting that he supported Huddersfield Town, this must have been hard to swallow.

It was, though, more easily assimilated by the divided citizenry of Glasgow who knew the reason for, and also shared sympathy with, Stein's order of priorities. The late sixties and early seventies were remarkable even by Old Firm standards for the intensity of feeling generated by games involving one against the other, particularly in the Scottish Cup. It was the tournament which, during this period, cost expensively bought and established players their careers at Ibrox, brought another Rangers player to the brink of a civil action against the SFA and caused that governing body to take the drastic step, without precedent before or repetition since, of calling together the players, management and officials of both clubs in order to deliver them a public dressing down for the wilder excesses of their behaviour.

The Scottish Cup has been won by only three sides since 1969 (Celtic, Rangers and Aberdeen) which is indicative of massive change in the structure of the game. The strong have become stronger, if only in the financial terms which enable them to buy up the best players from the smaller clubs, and the weak are increasingly unlikely ever to be able to work up the momentum for a little insurrection, which had been the true romance of the Cup in the less ruthlessly professional days.

Before a reply in the negative was dispatched to Mr Wilson from Celtic Park, the club's chairman became Sir Robert Kelly in the New Year's Honours list of 1969. It was a prefix the late John Lawrence privately coveted for himself at Ibrox, and which he always felt had slipped past him by inches on the night Rangers failed to emulate their greatest rivals' achievement by winning a European trophy two years earlier.

It was the whole story of Rangers' inability to get even with the widely praised and decorated Celtic, and the anxiety to change the script which put the club through some of their most trying and occasionally bizarre moments. In spite of the fact that under Davie White Rangers had many fine players, they were not getting close enough to Celtic who, apart from having the Lisbon Lions still preserved in their awesome entirety at Parkhead, also had a coming generation of extremely promising youngsters clamouring for places in the den.

Celtic even survived the unfortunate loss of the first member of the European Cup-winning side, Ronnie Simpson, the man whose birth certificate betrayed advanced years but whose physical well-being suggested there had been a registrar's misprint. Simpson was badly injured in the second round of the Scottish Cup against Clyde at Shawfield, although he did not announce his retirement officially until the following season. He had played 190 times for Celtic and managed not to concede goals on exactly half of those occasions.

Typically, Celtic survived the eighty minutes which remained of what was a goal-less draw by flamboyantly putting their colourful full-back Tommy Gemmell in goal. They then safely negotiated the intervening hurdles before finding themselves in the semi-finals, at which stage the race for the Cup was held up while the 'stewards' conducted an inquiry into alleged irregularities.

The draw had given Celtic a trip to Hampden to play Morton but Rangers objected strongly to the indignity of being sent out against Aberdeen in the other semi-final at Parkhead. It may have been the 'dear old Paradise' to those who patronised the place through choice, and christened it such because of the adjacent cemetery, but to Rangers it was no more than the powerbase of their fiercest rivals.

So unhappy were they at giving the evil spirits which hung around Parkhead a chance to work their voodoo, the Rangers board claimed not to have known the voting procedures applied when deciding choice of venue in committee. While still testing the credulity of the Association's office bearers on that one, the club also approached Bailie Frank McElhone on Glasgow's District Council and pointed out the potential hazards of these two games taking place on the same afternoon and in such proximity, prompting the knight at Parkhead to draw in and accuse Rangers of using 'outside sources' to influence the workings of the SFA.

If this was how the club reacted to the very idea of being forced to use Parkhead as a neutral venue — Davie White insisted huffily on the away dressing room, no doubt bringing cloves of garlic with him there, although Rangers scored six times, prompting mystification at what all the fuss was about in the first place — it was only to be expected that a meeting of the Old Firm in the Final itself would bring with it further heated controversy.

Colin Stein, the first player sold between two Scottish clubs for a transfer fee of £100,000 when he left Hibs for Rangers, was sent off while playing against Clyde at Ibrox, by which time, incidentally, his team was already six goals ahead and the match had only seconds remaining, suggesting a frailty of temperament on his part.

His pugnacious side was further exemplified when Stein rose to the bait thrown him by the chairman of the club Celtic had defeated in the semi-finals, and to whom the player should have reacted as cautiously as if he were approaching a hazard light, John S Thomson of Morton. Thomson, a well known eccentric, wanted to test the legality of the SFA's decision to suspend Stein for the rest of the season, in other words until the day after the Cup Final, but needed a Rangers share to act in this way. He was provided with one by the convener of the Rangers Supporters Association and both player and mentor met with a lawyer, admittedly against Rangers' better judgement, to discuss their test case.

It may be thought reasonable to assume that some internal pressure was then brought to bear on Stein, however, for forty-eight hours after that meeting the player announced he would drop his action and agreed not to get on with the game, as it were.

1969. Lennox scores for Celtic.

Ironically, Celtic, fuelling the suspicion that they had the kind of unbreakable hoodoo over Rangers which would probably have resulted in Stein being sentenced to life imprisonment had he persisted in going to court, withstood the loss of Jimmy Johnstone from the Final without a whimper after he had been suspended at the same time. A slight trembling of the bottom lip might have been excused them, though, when their other winger, John Hughes, then declared himself unfit to play on the eve of the game, but a day of memorable contrast unfolded before the last crowd of over 130,000 to witness a Scottish Cup Final.

Celtic scored in two minutes when Kai Johansen was lured away from his post at a corner kick and Billy McNeill headed unchallenged into the gap he had left. A mix-up involving Orjan Persson and Willie Mathieson of Rangers then let in Bobby Lennox to sprint half the length of the field before scoring Celtic's second a minute from half-time. It was a comedy of errors that continued only thirty seconds after when George Connelly, a teenager drafted into replace Jimmy Johnstone, dispossessed John Greig as he dawdled over a throw-out and rounded keeper Norrie Martin before scoring directly in front of a mildly hysterical crowd.

By the time Steve Chalmers scored a fourth in the second half, those not happily dazed had gone home from the other end of the ground to the darkened room. Repercussions were swift and testimony to the areas in which Rangers felt they had been let down. Alex Ferguson and Orjan Persson were put up for transfer the following Thursday and the club then left on a tour of Canada, with the restored Colin Stein, to forget about it. Stein was sent off in their first match against Spurs.

It seemed that every time the club felt the pendulum was about to swing back in their favour it only concussed them instead and, as a rule, Celtic were sitting on top of it at the point of impact. The Scottish Cup of 1970, for example, brought Rangers to Parkhead at the quarter-final stage and immersed both them and Celtic in deep recriminations after a convincing win by the home side. During Celtic's 3-1 success, Alex MacDonald of Rangers was sent off and after the match sufficiently large numbers of suitably worked-up supporters of both persuasions were arrested for the Glasgow magistrates to write to the SFA denouncing by name two players, the respective captains John Greig and Billy McNeill, for possibly inflammatory behaviour.

As a consequence twenty-four players, Jock Stein, Willie Waddell, by then the Rangers manager, and the Old Firm chairmen, Sir Robert Kelly and John Lawrence, were summoned in person to the offices of the SFA. No-one who was there that day from the playing side really believed that they were present for any other purpose than to satisfy public opinion, and that, like naughty schoolchildren, they were to be told, in the vernacular, to 'play nice'.

Not one player left with his ways mended after a meeting which lasted all of thirty-five minutes. It was hardly enough time to capture the attention of, let alone strike fear into, two dozen grown men on a charge of forming a riotous assembly.

If the differences between Celtic and Rangers had been placed on file and put in a pending tray at the SFA headquarters, however, there was also on record the £100 fine imposed on the Parkhead manager Jock Stein for what had been considered indelicate remarks to a linesman two years earlier, as reported by the referee Bobby Davidson of Airdrie. After the Scottish Cup Final involving Celtic and Aberdeen in 1970, the paperwork had to be brought up to date. By his decisions that day, Davidson was widely held to have had a direct influence on the outcome of the game, allowing Martin Buchan, at the age of twenty-one, to become the youngest Scottish Cup-winning captain of modern times.

Aberdeen had finished eighth in the First Division that year but had enjoyed a colourful run towards Hampden mainly because of the efforts of Derek Mackay, a forward who scored in every round from the quarter-final onwards, thereby causing direct embarrassment to Dundee, who had given him a free

1970. Eddie Turnbull with Joe Harper and Jim Forrest.

1971 Cup Final replay. Tom 'Tiny Wharton' administers justice to Jim Brogan.

transfer the season before. It was the referee's adjudications which remained in the minds of the Celtic officials long afterwards, though.

Aberdeen were awarded a penalty on a highly debatable hand ball decision after twenty-six minutes and Harper scored. Celtic then had two penalty claims denied them and a goal from Bobby Lennox disallowed. Derek Mackay proved preordination was at hand when he maintained his goalscoring record eight minutes from the end. Bobby Lennox then scored another goal, and was allowed to keep it, six minutes later. But Mackay, as if he had been advanced warning that he would be forgotten about by the same time the following year, went out on the equivalent of High C and produced a remarkable Final's conclusive goal seconds later.

Jock Stein's denunciation of the match official started at the top of the stairs inside Hampden's crowded foyer and did not stop until he reached the bottom, where he hinted to waiting pressmen that there ought to be an investigation into Davidson's handling of the match. It was an ugly end to the day's sport. Johnstone and Gemmell were cautioned for dissent and the Celtic players made numerous suggestions to Mr Davidson on the track as he and they watched the Aberdeen players bound up the stairs two at a time to the winners' rostrum, the least aggressive of which was that the referee should go up and get a medal himself, considering all he had done for Aberdeen.

Stein himself was later fined £10 by the SFA for his outburst, an amount so small as to encourage the notion that there were people in high places not unsympathetic to his reasons. He also had admirers at the palace and finished the season without the Scottish Cup or the European Cup (lost after another disastrous game in Milan when the club was beaten in extra-time by Feyenoord and the Celtic players, with grotesque ill-timing, chose the moment to announce the setting up of a commercial pool) but with the CBE for his services to the game.

Next to real life, medals, football and petty squabbling can stand little comparison, however, and even the Old Firm recognised this when at their New Year fixture of 1971 sixty-six perished and 145 were injured in what became known as the Ibrox Disaster. The old hostilities and prejudices were set aside in a way which was so spontaneous and civilised it is still a source of wonder that relationships between the two clubs could fall back into the more traditionally fragile peace so soon after. The Ibrox Disaster Fund found a donation of £10,000 from Celtic among its earliest contributions and the clubs joined playing forces to meet a Scotland side in a game at Hampden to further help the dependents of those killed.

Even a Catholic priest who had won the pools that day and collected £100,000 for having eight draws, one of which was the Old Firm game, gave one quarter of his winnings to the fund. Four months later the clubs met in the Scottish Cup Final and once again the spirit of reconciliation was given the day off.

1971. The Cup is won and Jimmy Johnstone prepares to mark the event.

The old order was continuously changing at Parkhead. Bertie Auld, exceptionally popular as well as a greatly appreciated talent, was freed after the Lisbon Lions took the field one last, shamelessly nostalgic time against Clyde at Parkhead as Celtic celebrated the winning of their sixth consecutive League title. Rangers, still striving to overthrow them and by now under the tutelage of Jock Wallace as first team coach at Ibrox, had been described candidly as 'rubbish' by Dave Ewing, the manager of Hibs, after the two clubs had contested a goal-less draw in their first semi-final. Unless you have about your team players who can back up such indiscreet talk against a club who take that type of speech play as an invitation to step outside, it is a foregone conclusion that the words will be force fed down your throat.

Hibs duly lost the replay, Ewing was removed from office in time for his side's next appearance at Hampden and the Old Firm got on with the business of proving Glasgow was not big enough for both of them and with the by now predictable outcome, although it took Celtic longer than expected to pull the trigger.

With four minutes left of the first game Derek Johnstone had equalised a goal from Celtic's Bobby Lennox and the sides reconvened in midweek with significant changes. Rangers lost their young full-back, Alex Miller, through injury and had to replace him in an emergency by granting a first team debut to the even younger Jim Denny, who, three months earlier, had been playing junior football with Yoker Athletic.

Celtic introduced an impertinent bundle of nervous energy called Lou Macari, a player with the physique of a jockey and the nimble staying power of a thoroughbred, who gave Celtic the lead after twenty-four minutes. Harry Hood pulled them further away two minutes later with a penalty kick. Rangers' only reply came early in the second half when Celtic's full-back, Jim Craig, had the misfortune to score an own goal.

Second place in the Scottish Cup, however, was Rangers' passport into the Cup Winners' Cup since Celtic, as League champions, would be embarking on one more quest for the European Cup itself. A year later Rangers beat Moscow Dynamo in Barcelona and, in their third Final in that competition, at last brought a European trophy to Ibrox.

Sadly, it was the riot following the match which drew the world's attention but the Rangers players, notably goalscorers Stein and Johnston, had every reason to take pride in their victory.

Celtic took their trophy to Rugby Park the week after the 1971 Scottish Cup Final and gave another of their younger players the opportunity to broaden his horizons. This one, though, was in a hurry to embark on his voyage of discovery and scored six of the team's seven goals that night in a testimonial match for Frank Beattie, the retiring Kilmarnock defender. Beattie was one of the lucky ones, he was getting out before this particular talent blossomed fully and perplexed a coming generation of defenders. His name was Kenny Dalglish.

If Dalglish was the glorification of youth — all shimmering hair, interminable running and bright-eyed finishing — Stein would provide a contrast to that before Celtic returned to Hampden the following season to

1972. Deans heads his own first and Celtic's second in the Final.

contest their fourth, successive Final by signing one of the old school, John 'Dixie' Deans.

Squat and awkward, Deans had a bad disciplinary record, a reputation as a man who lived life to the full which was the worst kept secret in the game and had also, in April 1971, been left out of Motherwell's team to play Aberdeen in a League match at Pittodrie for the simple reason that he had slept in for training on the day before the match.

He had, in fact, not turned up until mid-day which suggested he was in a coma and not a sleep. In short, Dixie Deans represented everything from which the Celtic manager should have recoiled in distaste. Making it look as if he was doing Motherwell a favour at the time, the wily Stein, who obviously saw something saveable in Deans, bought him for a fee of under £20,000 and added to his reputation as a strategist who would have given Rommel a hard time of it in the desert.

There was an immediate insight into how the manager intended to keep his wayward protege on the straight and narrow. Deans, although ineligible, was taken to Malta with the club for a European tie even before he had made his Celtic debut. In the company of both the unwaveringly diligent and also the other free spirits in the team not unlike himself in character, Deans was taken in enervating heat to a cinema on the island. The main feature was the Western 'Eldorado' which can cause the film-goer dehydration problems before the credits have finished rolling at the beginning.

The players sat in one, captive line with Stein at the end, assured that, in his players' free time, he had at least isolated any possible problems by knowing exactly what everyone was up to, which was in this case buying copious quantities of iced drinks to restore lost body fluids.

The climax to their domestic season was the game at Hampden against a Hibs side now managed by the ubiquitous Eddie Turnbull, facing up to them for the third time in five years and with a side whose best chance was to score an early goal to settle themselves against a totally assured Celtic. Instead Billy McNeill scored after two minutes and although Hibs equalised, their goal served only to set the stage on which Deans had the finest moments of his career.

A goal for him before the interval restored Celtic's lead, but it was his second and Celtic's third which lifted the game and brought the Glasgow club's support to the verge of delirium. Macari's flighted pass fell fortunately at Deans' feet, who then went around numerous defenders numerous times in a mesmeric line (or so it seemed) before scoring and going through a calisthenic routine to celebrate.

Deans went on to become only the second player in the then ninety-nine year old history of the Scottish Cup to score a hat-trick and Lou Macari also gained the more dubious distinction of scoring two goals thereafter which were almost totally forgotten about. Stein, with his at times uncanny instinct, had done it again. Celtic stood one more Cup Final victory away from winning the trophy on three successive occasions for the first time since their formation the previous century, and in the Cup's centenary year at that.

The circumstances would have been thought ready made for Stein. On the seventh of June, one month after Celtic's victory over Hibs, Jock Wallace, at the age of thirty-six, was appointed manager of Rangers. He knew nothing of preordination and cared even less about such abstract concepts, as he would soon show.

The King of the Sandcastles

THE PANJANDRUMS of the Scottish Football Association had consulted with whoever or whatever it is you consult when concerned about matters of royal protocol. There would only be six bars of the National Anthem played before the Scottish Cup Final of 1973, as is permissible when a royal personage other than the reigning monarch is in attendance.

Since it was the Final which would commemorate the centenary year of the Association's formation and was also the first at which the trophy would be presented by a member of the royal household, in the person of Princess Alexandra, it was a peculiar way of marking history when the Glasgow Orpheus Choir and the Scottish National Orchestra might have been expected at least.

The explanation lay with the competing teams and not in any nationalistic desire for revenge against England, who had come to Hampden three months earlier and smothered the celebrations at birth by defeating Scotland by the humiliating margin of five goals to nil on the ironically apposite date for a massacre of 14 February.

Rangers and Celtic matches, particularly in the Final of the blue riband of national competitions, were still events not to be wholly trusted and six bars of introduction were as much as could be hoped for before certain raucous subjects beat the band to the finish with an impatient libretto expressing their anxiousness for the hostilities to begin.

If the royal ear had to be protected from offence, the royal eye would at least feast upon a match which was fit to serve before aristocrat or commoner, however.

It was only the tenth Old Firm Final to take place out of the eighty-eight which had been played over the preceding one hundred years but also the fifth in the ten years up until then, which was indicative of the game's changing shape. Argument, which might have been the basis of every meeting between the two clubs, would rage afterwards as to whether what took place constituted the finest match between them at this exalted level.

By the very nature of these events, where the game is life's struggle in microcosm for those of a more extreme outlook who form the majority in the crowd, the intense atmosphere worked against cultured play. One participant was once moved to say it was the only game in which it was possible to get a standing ovation for winning a throw-in, and the 'greatest club game in the world' was a tribute paid only by those on the victorious side and never in unison afterwards with the vanquished.

For sustained excitement wrapped up in play of an unexpectedly high quality the centenary Final was a confection which changed all that, however fleetingly, even if there were also fifty-three deviations from the rule book in fouls committed and four players cautioned, two from each side.

It was a time of transition for both clubs. Jock Stein of Celtic remained the Scottish game's 'Godfather', a jocular reference to his all-pervasive influence, but the pressures of maintaining his team's ascendancy through numerous important changes in personnel had begun to take its toll and he had found himself at the beginning of the year in the coronary unit of a Glasgow hospital exhibiting the symptoms of exhaustion as he neared his fifty-first birthday.

Only four players remained at Parkhead from the side immortalised as the 'Lisbon Lions' when they won the European Cup six years earlier. Stein's faculties remained unimpaired, though, and the week before the Final the club had won its eighth consecutive First Division championship by defeating Hibs in Edinburgh.

If Stein was the 'Godfather' the new Rangers manager, Jock Wallace, installed at the beginning of that season, was the robust and aspiring 'Capo' of the largest rival family and the type of character Mario Puzo would have found difficult to put into words.

Once reputed to have put 'football' under the heading of 'religion' on his registration form when he signed up for active service with the King's Own Borderers, Wallace had assumed control in Rangers' centenary year. His *bona fides* were impeccable. To watch Rangers as a child he had travelled from his home in Wallyford to Edinburgh with enough money only to make that return journey. His destination of Ibrox was reached by thumbing a lift on a supporters' bus and back. Legend had it that he had once spent his travel allowance on a Rangers rosette and willingly walked home, a distance of seven miles, from the capital.

Wallace's coaching methods, in spite of his having made his name when he constructed arguably the most famous of all Scottish Cup results by knocking Rangers out of the competition in 1967 while in charge of Berwick, were ridiculed by some, if not most.

A predilection for having his teams build up their stamina with a run up and down the dunes at Gullane in particular had brought him notoriety as the 'King of the Sandcastles', but there was not one of his Rangers side of that period who would, even to this day, sneer at what he had done for them.

Those who are still playing at the highest level while in their late thirties would only say that he had increased their life expectancy in the game by making them inordinately fit. Wallace himself would not claim that he was the greatest strategist or tactician available, but neither would he stand for the implication that his Rangers team lacked skill, either.

As they approached that Final by royal appointment, Celtic having defeated Dundee after a replay, Rangers rolling over Ayr United in a single movement, the only uncontested truth was that in the prevailing playing climate of the time the only side capable of beating one half of the Old Firm at Hampden was their other half.

Nevertheless, and not for the first or last time, the Scottish Cup Final was looked upon as the game which would stave off bankruptcy for the season so far as Rangers were concerned. Celtic, their internal difficulties notwithstanding, had won the League championship. Rangers, though, had belatedly enjoyed a remarkably consistent run, dropping only two League points from early in December the previous year until the conclusion of that tournament at the end of April.

Their confidence on the day of the Final had also been bolstered by the effects of incessant rain which only subsided shortly before the kick-off, providing the type of underfoot conditions beloved of sides from Ibrox, if not by some ten thousand spectators who had not used match tickets already purchased.

1973. The winning goal in the Cup's centenary year. Tom Forsyth touches the ball into the net.

It was Celtic, though, who made what was always assumed in these matters to be the important breakthrough by scoring the first goal after twenty-five minutes. Deans had created the chance with an astute pass inside of the Rangers centre-half Derek Johnstone to Dalglish, whose finish was typically incisive.

Rangers' equalising goal came only ten minutes afterwards, however, and was made and scored by two players who, in so doing, had proved that Jock Wallace's judgement extended beyond knowing how long it should take a man to run up one side of a sand dune and down the other.

Alex MacDonald had been fashioned in the role of he who negates the effectiveness of the opposing side's creative threat, in this instance the redoubtable Bobby Murdoch. Showing there was a more positive side to his personality, however, MacDonald twice evaded the attentions of his marker and placed a perfect cross on to the head of Derek Parlane.

Parlane, too, owed his reputation to his manager, who had remodelled him from being a competent midfield player into a consistently more effective scorer of goals, thereby saving the club considerable expenditure in the process. His header past Alistair Hunter suggested it had been money well saved.

If the first half had been exhilarating, the second was to begin the excitement all over again from the very first minute. A pass from Quintin Young was converted instantly into something conclusive, detonating an explosion of blue at the Rangers end, when Alfie Conn slipped past the Celtic captain Billy McNeill and advanced at unchecked speed towards Hunter's goal, putting his side ahead for the first time in the game.

In the atmosphere of tit for tat, Celtic's equaliser came as if on cue six minutes later. Deans would have been able to claim the prize for himself but for the intervention of John Greig who, as ever, showed his wholeheartedness in a blue jersey by fisting the ball off the line and, as captain, electing to take a chance on the resultant penalty kick.

This playing of the percentages can sometimes come off when the odds against might be thought reduced by the tension of a Cup Final. Especially so when the sheer force of collective will at the 'Rangers' End' to see the gamble succeed probably has the effect of contracting the space between the goalposts in the eyes of the Celtic man attempting a defiant conversion directly in front of them.

George Connelly had not been voted the Player of the Year that season because of a susceptibility towards internal confusion under pressure on the field, however, even if his external difficulties did not always show him to be so assured, and the full cost of conceding the penalty was extracted.

It was at this point events took a bizarre and conclusive turn. In the tumult a Jimmy Johnstone goal for Celtic had been disallowed, few players having heard the referee's whistle, which had sounded well before the act of execution. Rangers were almost immediately awarded a free-kick, taken by Tommy McLean and headed on with his customary deftness by Derek Johnstone. As the ball rebounded from a post it bounced in front of a player whose presence in that proximity seemed like an apparition to both friend and foe alike as time appeared to expand to accommodate him in his moment of glory.

If there had been a sweepstake to predict the last man on the park likely to score a goal that day the name of Tom Forsyth would have come after that of the two goalkeepers and the referee. His unfamiliarity with the business of carrying out such a function was evident when he inelegantly bundled the ball over the line from a distance able only to be measured in inches after looking at first as if the magnitude of the situation in which he found himself had suddenly become all too much.

Forsyth's colleagues would admit afterwards, the man himself being reticent to the point of invisibility as a rule, that if he had not been wearing long studs to suit the going the ball would have slid under his foot and the chance would have been lost.

It is at moments like this that managers develop an overwhelming belief in the maxim that they all count, irrespective of how gauche a goal can sometimes be, and Jock Wallace had every reason to preserve that tradition. In his inaugural season he had won his first trophy as the club's manager. It had been Willie Waddell's idea to bring him to Ibrox in 1970, recalling how, when manager of Kilmarnock, Waddell himself had led the Ayrshire club to a League championship with the help of Walter McCrae, a sergeant major figure given to barrack room philosophy like 'one swallow does not a summer make' to keep his men on their toes and their minds on the job. The axiom by which the Rangers manager lived was, 'if yur no' fightin', yur marchin''.

Wallace, though, had proved himself to be a true motivator of men and had also won a Cup with no small degree of style. The outstanding testimony to the level of excellence reached in the match was the observation, offered by Rangers' Sandy Jardine later, that Celtic could honestly have made the same claim of their performance had the final result been reversed.

Celtic would take more tangible consolation from the fact that for the next two years the trophy would come to Parkhead, while their following would derive more personalised satisfaction out of Rangers failing even to make the semi-final stage on either occasion, losing twice in the earlier rounds, at Ibrox of all places.

1974. McNeill gets above Copland of Dundee United.

Much change was underway inside Parkhead, however, accelerating the end of the Stein era in which the club had developed an invincible air. Defections from the club came at a rate similar to Russian symphony orchestras which tour the West and come back as string quartets. Macari had gone in the season of Rangers' win and David Hay would leave after the emergent Dundee United were beaten by Celtic in the Final of the following season. In between George Connelly sought asylum from the problems, real or imagined, of life as a top class professional in a series of mysterious disappearances.

In the summer of 1973 Connelly, a rare talent who had yet to reach his best, was to make his full international debut for Scotland against Switzerland. While his luggage and that of the rest of the team was being loaded on to their aircraft at Glasgow airport, Connelly vanished, apparently failing even to confide in his closest friend and travelling companion, David Hay, the reasons for his actions.

In February of 1974 Connelly absented himself from training at Parkhead, again without explanation, for a week, returning only to ask for a transfer. Misbehaviour had become an unexpected and unwanted guest at the Celtic party.

Jimmy Johnstone had not played in the first team, either, for a period of three months that season, prior to his recall shortly before the Scottish Cup semi-final with Dundee. At the age of twenty-nine, such a break in his career, at a time when he might have been imagined to be at his peak, was unfortunately familiar.

The story of Scottish sport, and not just football, is liberally punctuated with examples of brilliant careers being truncated through a fascination for self-destruction. Johnstone had a decade at the very top when he might have been entitled to longer. After the defeat of Dundee, who had earlier eliminated Rangers convincingly at Ibrox, Johnstone, greatly involved in securing Celtic's safe passage to the Final, made a full confession concerning the error of his ways and declared himself to be living like a monk in a contrite attempt to make up for his past misdeeds.

So well was he doing, in fact, that there were threats to kill him in the return leg of the infamous European Cup semi-final with Athletico Madrid. Three Spanish players had been sent off and a total of nine booked in the goal-less first leg at Parkhead and the Glasgow club had only fulfilled their obligation in Spain under protest.

Although they ultimately suffered what was a distasteful defeat on aggregate, Celtic had recovered their composure to win their ninth, successive League championship, thereby equalling a world record, before facing Dundee United in the Cup Final.

It was their sixth successive Final in that competition, but the first ever in their opponent's history. The difference in stature that day was all too apparent and goals from Harry Hood, Steve Murray and Dixie Deans gave Celtic the trophy. The defeated Jim McLean would take his side away and continue the refurbishing which would eventually elevate the club far above the status of provincial cousins taken advantage of in the big city.

For Johnstone, the would-be monk, there was little time for contemplation of what would turn out to have been his last Scottish Cup appearance at Hampden. The cloistered existence ended in public disarray when he was rescued by the coastguard from the sea at Largs in the early hours of the morning while based there with the Scotland team taking part in the Home International Series. Shortly after, on a pre-World Cup visit to Norway, a nocturnal choral session led to further notoriety, but it may be of some consolation, not least of all to the man himself, to know that the much-loved and admired 'Jinky' apparently descended from the top flight while having a marvellously uninhibited time at any rate. Perhaps that is the only way he would have had it.

1975. McCann blasts Airdrie's only goal of the Final past Latchford.

The days coming along may not have been suitable to his flamboyant style, anyway. In the 1974-75 season, at the end of which Johnstone was freed from Parkhead, the eighteen members of the First Division were playing for their places in the new Premier League, a top ten elite brought about by the clamour for reconstruction to provide more meaningful matches.

Ironically, change was already on the way in any case, since Celtic's monopoly in the championship had been ended by Rangers winning the title for the first time in eleven years. Celtic's opponents in the Cup Final, Airdrie, were something of a surprise, too, as they had failed even to make the cut for the top ten. The last time the Lanarkshire club had been to Hampden on Cup Final day they had returned with the trophy. That was fifty-one years before, however, when the world of football at least was a more egalitarian one.

The haves and the have-nots were in the midst of pulling apart from each other in the mid-seventies and the part-time club, apart from one brief act of defiance when Kevin McCann repudiated his origins as a Celtic supporter and scored an equaliser, were efficiently swept aside by two goals from Paul Wilson and one from Pat McCluskey.

The day was more likely to be retained in the memory as being the occasion when Billy McNeill announced his retirement from the game at Hampden after eighteen years of unbroken and outstanding service to his club. He did not choose to finish off by returning to Hampden the following week to play in the Final of the Glasgow Cup against Rangers, preferring to bow out at the very top with the Scottish Cup above his head.

Ten years earlier this had been the first trophy he had taken delivery of as Celtic captain and the image of the successful man standing on the winners' rostrum at Hampden had been reproduced many times in the intervening years of his career. His haul of twenty-three winners' medals in major competitions may, indeed, be a world record.

1975. McNeill's last match for Celtic produces his seventh Scottish Cup-winners' medal. For McGrain, it is his first.

The Old Firm game ended in a two-all draw and it was suggested that the sides meet again the following season. It meant that with the Premier League format, which had the members playing each other four times, Rangers and Celtic were then already scheduled to meet on at least five separate occasions.

It is debatable if their tribal confrontations were ever the same after that, when familiarity bred not contempt, since the camp followers of both could hardly have had less regard for their rivals, but a condition similar to flatulence. The surfeit of Old Firm matches was an over-rich diet taking away the hunger which characterised their original state, when time had passed slowly from one meeting to the next, particularly if there was a score to be settled. More positively, the top ten would bring about radical change in other quarters and the effect would be significant not only in League football but in the Scottish Cup as well.

The Sun sets in the West

THE DIE WAS cast. The trophy had not left Glasgow for five years and it would be another six years before it journeyed beyond the city boundary. If that inanimate object could talk, it would have spoken with a pronounced West of Scotland accent and asked to be put on the coat of arms beside the bell and the tree.

The Premier Division which would eventually spawn sides who would first compete on level terms with the Old Firm and then usurp their authority in that domain was still in its infancy and resisting attempts to have its format revised by those who thought it devised by, and for, elitists. Even within the duopoly of Rangers and Celtic there was a further sub-division, though, as the Parkhead club set out without their pathfinder on the road to seeking the Scottish Cup for a third, successive time, hoping to create a piece of personal history.

The summer of 1975 had seen Jock Stein involved in a horrendous car crash which almost claimed his life and had taken him out of the game for a period of time injurious to his club. That upset had coincided with the side entering a time of transition and prior to the Cup competition beginning they had rejected a friendly with the Russian team Dynamo Kiev on the grounds that they were not ready for such a formidable challenge, a rare admission of uncertainty from that particular quarter, with its illustrious past in Europe.

Rangers, on the other hand, were no longer living on their past successes but once more looking the genuine article. The League Cup had already been taken into their safekeeping and in the midst of clubs coming to terms with their new surroundings, the side's League form demonstrated a confidence which made the championship seem an inevitability as well.

Celtic's dismissal of a little diversion against the Russians looked all the more unfortunate, too, when they had signposted their indecision by first taking a two goal lead against Motherwell and then departing the Cup at Fir Park to three at the other end.

If all around them were struggling to keep their feet, Rangers' opponents in the Cup Final would have to come from those who had made it to Hampden almost in spite of themselves. Hearts were the perfect example of the type with a Cup run which was a text book case of how not to go about things, but which also suited perfectly the mood of the time. At the outset they had been taken to a replay by a club from the lower orders, Clyde, and even then had only stumbled through with the assistance of a mis-hit shot which half-heartedly entered the net at Shawfield in the last minute of normal time. The more rigorous life in a division of only ten teams which offered no respite to the temporarily distressed had begun to take its toll of the Edinburgh club.

Floating aimlessly in the lower reaches of the League like a piece of wreckage about to go under, Hearts were given the chance to indulge in a rare piece of one-upmanship by making a retaliatory example of Montrose two rounds later. After three full games, they had still not proved themselves up to the task and the play-off at the neutral Muirton Park entered extra-time, whereupon the Hearts players finally contrived to make some sense of it all in the time added on.

The ground was a lucky one for them that season, since a single point there against St Johnstone was enough, for the time being, to prevent the club being lumbered with the doubtful distinction of reaching the Scottish Cup Final and also being relegated.

They had only reached Hampden by continuing their impression of inebriated hurdlers, negotiating the penultimate fence after their by now customary failure at the first attempt. A goal-less draw with yet another representative of the lower leagues, Dumbarton, meant a replay and the then habitual shove in the right direction when Dumbarton's Walter Smith put the ball into his own net to give the tournament's showpiece a lop-sided look.

Rangers, by the end of the season, could have fielded a team in which every player was a full Scottish internationalist, and they had also gone twenty-four straight games without defeat, the twenty-third of which had won them the League title on the Saturday before the Final. Their victims had been Dundee United, whose manager, Jim McLean, then un-used to the particular pressures of that office in an arena of intensified competition had remarked with convincing realism that the game was driving him 'mental', and that if he had enough money he would get out of the business forthwith.

His medical condition was not helped when, in their last game of the season, Dundee United went to Ibrox needing a point to avoid relegation and their colourful goalkeeper Hamish McAlpine, missed a penalty. A breakdown was averted when McAlpine showed he was better with his hands than his feet and ensured a goal-less draw which, with an irony that was to take on a familiar ring, embarrassed their civic rivals, Dundee, and put them down instead.

Meanwhile, by dint of a bewildering sequence of replays, mis-hits and own goals, Hearts fell in the front door at Hampden, whereupon they actually managed to confirm the suspicions of the onlookers by taking part in a game which was literally over before it had properly begun.

A referee who had obviously not wanted to prolong Hearts' suffering any longer than was decent put them out of their misery by beginning the match a couple of minutes before the allotted time of three o'clock. Before the hour was reached, a Derek Johnstone header had given Rangers the lead and removed what level of mystery the game might have had for those who wondered if Hearts' run might just have been so awful as to mesmerise Rangers into involuntary submission. Another goal from Johnstone and one from Alex MacDonald, who would, years later, instil a more disciplined approach in Hearts from the manager's office at Tynecastle, bettered a single score from Graham Shaw and the day was carried with the minimum of fuss.

The only non-Rangers person to leave Hampden suitably rewarded was a fourteen year old Ayrshire schoolboy by the name of Mark Reid. He won a penalty-kick competition which formed part of the pre-match entertainment, gaining a holiday in Montreal, but would get much closer to the real action in the setting of the national stadium when he grew up and signed for Celtic.

The first of Rangers' trebles under the managership of Jock Wallace nevertheless meant that Hearts ended up as Scotland's representatives in the European Cup Winners' Cup. This only heightened their ability to perplex when they put up a spirited performance there the following season and were also demoted for the first time in the club's then 103 year old history. Their

1976. Colin Jackson with Jock Wallace.

impoverished state was, on the face of it, not much worse than that of Celtic who went out of the 1975-76 season without a trophy of any description for the first time in twelve years.

The belief that the return of Jock Stein to the head of the household would rectify that temporarily dishonoured status was hard to resist.

Stein had always said up until then that he expected to get out of the game by the time he was fifty-five years old. With the customary re-evaluation of his life having been undergone while recuperating from his brush with death, Stein had changed his mind in his fifty-fourth year. His accident had not only left him time to re-appraise his ideas on when to give up doing something he obviously enjoyed and was still well able to cope with, it had also convinced him that it would be unacceptable to leave Celtic when they were so obviously in need of firm direction. A manager with a renewed sense of purpose and a team who had the hunger to re-establish themselves was an irresistible combination, and instantly successful.

Halfway through Stein's first season back in full control of team affairs the impartial arbiters of what makes horse sense in football refused to take any more money on Celtic for the championship in their betting shops.

An often noted facet of Stein's character make-up is a sense of mischief. With his powers restored fully, and his time to devote to scrupulous detail on Celtic's behalf increased because his accident had left him physically unable to indulge in his only form of relaxation, golf, he carried out a major coup as the Cup got underway. The signing of the former Rangers player Alfie Conn for Celtic induced speechless surprise in all but those employed professionally to chronicle its happening from Tottenham Hotspur, and who were forced to rummage in the superlative tray for something a little special to describe such an event.

As Rangers showed signs of going from an embarrassment of riches the season before to the ignominy of having to hand back all the silverware after a sudden descent on hard times, Stein's inspired piece of cunning was, by accident or design, and no-one was willing to fall for belief in the former, guaranteed not to help the equanimity of anyone inside Ibrox.

It was a story matched only for its capacity to produce a series of screaming headlines by the printed allegation that a group of Aberdeen players had conspired to bet against their team in a Scottish Cup tie against Dundee, and had then gone out and taken part in the club's defeat there, which cost them a place in the quarter-finals.

A bet of five hundred pounds at odds of eight to one was said to have been placed, an insinuation vigorously denied by the manager at Pittodrie, Ally MacLeod, and his board, to the extent that they co-operated fully with an investigation into the sordid tale by Grampian police. The allegations were discovered to be utterly without foundation and the club exonerated completely. The odds on Dundee probably lengthened, though, when they were eventually drawn against Celtic for the fourth time in five years at the semi-final stage, taking their customary leave of the competition at that point as Stein eyed up a suitably big trick on which to finish his return to the centre stage.

Rangers had arrived in the opposite corner as destiny had probably demanded, having once again met, and quickly disposed of, Hearts to get there. The referee chosen for the Final was, somewhat appropriately, Bob Valentine, an everyday employee of that Dundonian publishing house which specialises in the comic books which would have relished the story of Celtic and the player, Alfie Conn, whose last appearance at Hampden had been in a Rangers jersey against the green and white hoops he was now wearing.

On the Saturday before the Final, Valentine had shown his ability to move freely through the exertions of his appointment card without fear or favour by sending off the Rangers captain John Greig in a League match at Pittodrie. It was not a gesture likely to endear him to those spectators whose displeasure would reverberate from the covered terracing at the Mount Florida end of Hampden, but the referee was only warming up.

After twenty minutes play, and directly in front of their disbelieving eyes, Valentine awarded a vehemently disputed penalty kick to Celtic for handball on the goal-line by Derek Johnstone of Rangers. The Celtic full-back, Andy Lynch, gave himself a field commission to official penalty-taker and suitably justified his own faith in himself. It was to be the only goal of the game.

That French proverb which suggests that the more things change, the more they stay the same lost more than something in the translation when applied to the game of football in Scotland at that time. A constant state of flux was evident and the old order was rapidly changing. A young manager called Alex Ferguson had led his St Mirren team into the Premier Division in the company of the impudent fledgling, Clydebank, both sides winning promotion on separate occasions at Dundee's ground, and therefore at the expense of the more celebrated club.

Change was evident off the field as well, for season 1977-78 saw the first major sponsorship of the Scottish Cup competition. Scottish Brewers, under their William Younger banner, signed a three-year agreement with the SFA. Some new steps had been added to the traditional dance with commerce.

Billy McNeill, who had re-entered the mainstream when he came out of retirement and became manager of Clyde on 1 April, and had already shown enough to prove the date of his appointment was only an unfortunate coincidence, was entrusted with the job of taking over Aberdeen after just ten weeks in the administrative side of the business. His predecessor, Ally MacLeod, had left to become manager of Scotland and to take a temporarily irrational nation on an extended excursion around its own gullibility, beginning with an invasion of Wembley in the wake of a win over England which was to be the first step in taking on the world. Only later did various voices of reason queue up to eloquently put back a sense of perspective.

1977. Conn, having been part of Rangers' winning side in 1973, takes a grip on his Cup-winners' medal with Celtic.

The national interest spinning uncontrollably in the outfield, the domestic season encountered a turbulent phase both on and off the field. Intrigue and ill temper abounded, illustrated in a Scottish Cup competition which got off to a fascinating start when the draw took Rangers back to the scene of the blackest chapter in the club's history, Shielfield Park, Berwick, the same initial stage in which they had known the grotesque embarrassment of elimination eleven years earlier.

The media's frenzied interest in seeing if a similarly horrific accident would occur in the same place was fuelled when Rangers refused to accept any tickets on behalf of their supporters for the match and then asked the SFA to inspect

Berwick Rangers' ground as a potential safety hazard, which would have made it a therefore undesirable setting for such a tie. Pointing out that no such doubts had been expressed by Rangers prior to their visit in 1967, the English club cheerfully opened their door each day in any case to find itinerant Glaswegians armed only with money and deep pockets to take away the tickets they wanted. The faith of the supporters was justified as Rangers saw Berwick and lived.

In the meantime the balance of power swinging back in Rangers' favour was highlighted by Celtic going into another trough. Of the Parkhead side who held the Cup, McGrain had been forced to admit to a diabetic condition and was also afflicted by an ankle injury which was to cost him more than a year out of his career. Dalglish had at last been lured South to Liverpool. Stanton and Lynch underwent surgery and an albatross seemed to hover over the team wherever it played. Declining League status and defeat from Kilmarnock, then in the First Division, in a replay in the Cup at Rugby Park were burdens added to by the publication of a book covering the first ninety years of the club's history in which Jock Stein came under fire for the first time in his managerial career.

The motives behind the necessity for such a book so close to the more normal time for a written retrospective, the occasion of the club's centenary, were privately called into question in certain areas. Celtic failed in any case to qualify for a European competition for the first time in fourteen years and slumped to a low ebb while the other man, apart from Stein, who had been inextricably linked with their greatest achievements, Billy McNeill, showed off a natural aptitude for his chosen calling.

A League championship in his first full season in club management had only failed to materialise because Aberdeen, highly consistent though they were, had the misfortune to be in opposition to a Rangers team responding to the subtleties of Robert Russell in midfield, and which had prolific goalscorers in Gordon Smith and Derek Johnstone, able to claim over sixty between them in that particular season.

The coming together of the two sides in the Cup Final, though, was thought to be a different matter and therefore a game which bore all the hallmarks of an epic confrontation.

It was McNeill's thirteenth appearance at Hampden for the national Final and the pessimists had their most deep rooted superstitions come to fruition. On the day Aberdeen wilted under the weight of public expectation. Goals from Alex MacDonald and then Derek Johnstone were the tangible signs of Rangers' superiority before Aberdeen scored minutes from the end with a goal which summed up their day. The full-back Steve Ritchie took an inelegant swipe at the ball, causing it to somehow hang in the air and complete its mystery tour by dropping over the head of the exceptionally tall Rangers goalkeeper, McCloy. Ritchie got lucky, his team did not.

Aberdeen played a total of fifty matches that season, lost only eight of them, but won precisely nothing. McNeill, however, would not have long to dwell on how infuriatingly unpredictable the game can be.

Three weeks after the Final there occurred a turnover in managerial personnel remarkable by any standards, and begun by Jock Wallace resigning his post at Ibrox and leaving for Leicester City for reasons which have often been guessed at but never publicly explained. He was replaced within less than twenty-four hours by his former captain, John Greig, who went from the dressing room to the manager's office at the club in the face of those who disputed that such a transition could be made overnight without a little pain and suffering. Greig, a nice man, would ruefully remark years afterwards that being so was hardly a terrible affliction, but the tortured person who was forced into resignation for his own peace of mind undoubtedly bore the scars of trying to prove everyone wrong.

The Old Firm who, until then, tended to view the changing of managers as an epoch-making event, then recorded a unique double in the same month when the unthinkable occurred at Parkhead this time and Jock Stein gave way to a younger man.

Unlike John Greig, McNeill had served an apprenticeship at Clyde and Aberdeen, but his work had seemed only to have just begun at Pittodrie. He admitted as much himself when he said that he was allowing his heart to rule his head in going to Parkhead, but was unable to deny that the Celtic job was an irresistible call to his ears. If that was certainly the case, he was not exactly inheriting the ready made materials for what would nevertheless be regarded as a triumphal return.

The establishment of a new generation at Ibrox and Parkhead diverted attention momentarily from the anguish of Scotland's miserable visit to Argentina for the World Cup Finals and there was further change when McNeill's departure from the North-East made way for Alex Ferguson,

1978. John Greig, soon to be manager of the club, celebrates his last trophy success as Rangers' captain.

1979. Alex MacDonald of Rangers and Arthur Duncan of Hibs challenge for the ball in the first replay. Bremner (left) looks on.

acrimoniously separated from St Mirren, to take over Aberdeen before the new season began. Ally MacLeod, the man who once said that if he had been in the army he would have become a general, demobbed himself on his return from South America and retreated to Ayr United and club management.

The widespread changes, and their effect, were able to be calmly assessed when a severe winter brought the season shivering to a halt at the turn of the year, just as the Scottish Cup was about to get underway. Perhaps the most memorable victims of the ice encrusted hiatus were Inverness Thistle and Falkirk, whose attempts from first to last to play their first round tie took a total of forty-seven days and no less than twenty-nine separate postponements. Such was the interest caused by their efforts to play each other, the original match referee, Brian McGinlay, re-named his house 'Kingsmills' after the Highland League ground which defied all attempts to make it playable.

At one stage bonfires had even been lit on the pitch on a Sunday in order to melt the hard-packed ice which threatened to hold up the tournament indefinitely. This violation of the Sabbath was too much for a seventy-four year old minister, Ewen McQueen, who shouted over the wall of the ground in protest, predicting doom would come down upon Inverness Thistle for their wanton ways. The God-fearing among the crowd when the game was eventually able to go on would not have been surprised, then, to see the home side lose by four goals.

Although the match programme for the tie became something of a collector's item, the game was not the object of the lengthiest delay on record for the Scottish Cup, a worthless distinction held by Airdrie, whose game with Stranraer was postponed thirty-three times before there was a break in the numbing winter of 1963.

It was, however, an appropriately cheerless start to a competition that season which ended in a Final with the longest drawn out, least noticed conclusion of modern times. The protagonists, Rangers and Hibs, met against the backdrop of a public transport strike in Glasgow which conspired with the live transmission of the game to leave the Final with the lowest crowd recorded for that event since 1921, a skeletal 50,260. The game itself was similarly low key until minutes from the end when Hibs' appeals for a penalty-kick were denied when Colin Campbell was thought to have been impeded by Peter McCloy, the Rangers goalkeeper. The match finished a goal-less draw and the general public showed their appreciation of the contest when, with no live coverage of the replay, they stayed away in such numbers as to make the attendance at the first game look positively corpulent.

Yet another goal-less meeting threatened to have the trophy withdrawn for the season to save the good name of the tournament from further punishment, particularly since the continuing saga was running concurrently with a finish to the League championship which had genuinely captured the imagination.

Celtic and Rangers met at Parkhead in the home club's final game of the season knowing that a win for them would bring Celtic the title with a finish so late and from so far back that, had it been a horse race, a stewards' enquiry would have been underway before the sides came under orders that night in the East End of Glasgow.

Celtic had taken twenty-one points out of a possible twenty-six in their last thirteen matches, coming from third bottom place in the League, going into the match with a Rangers side who had yet another Cup Final replay still to contend with. There are Celtic supporters who can recall their every emotion more quickly than their children's names as Rangers took the lead and then lost it again to a side reduced to ten men by the second half. Pulling the score back to equality, Rangers ultimately lost out to a side playing with a demonic fervour and returned to Hampden so late in the season that some of their followers must have received the news of the club's eventual annexation of the trophy by postcard at the holiday resort of their choosing.

In front of a crowd which strained to reach thirty thousand, it was Hibs who actually scored first through Higgins. A goal on either side of half-time from

Police move in to quell the 1980 riot.

213

Derek Johnstone suggested a conclusive result at long last, however, if only on the basis that, when in front at that stage in the game, the Old Firm, in either guise, rarely blow up.

But a penalty-kick comfortably converted by Ally McLeod of Hibs inspired the discomforting notion that an extension to the season might be necessary at this rate to bully a winner out of the pair. It is at such a time, though, that the likelihood of an eccentric finish increases, and so it befell the luckless Arthur Duncan to misdirect the ball into his own goal and give Rangers the Cup. As had happened to their neighbours in Edinburgh, Hearts, the effect of this disappointment was to send Hibs from the heights of the Scottish Cup Final appearance into a freefall from which they were unable to recover the following season. Perversely, they experienced one of the more colourful phases in the club's history before the bang came.

By the time Hibs set out in the next Scottish Cup they had among their number a man genuinely entitled to have the word legendary placed before his name. George Best arrived at a fee of £50,000 and the promise of £2000 a game for the club, drawing large crowds of fascinated onlookers wherever he went, or did not go as was sometimes the case. Before what would have been his first Scottish Cup-tie, against Ayr United at Easter Road on a Sunday afternoon, Best allowed himself to be led astray the night before by revellers in the capital city celebrating Scotland's win over France in a rugby international at Murrayfield. A crowd of fifteen thousand were informed of his non-appearance and the player was banished by the late Hibs chairman, Tom Hart.

A reconciliation brought his wayward genius back in time for the quarter-finals against Berwick but he played only half a game before being substituted and missing the replay which Hibs won. His return for the semi-final with Celtic was not enough to prevent an emphatic defeat by five clear goals and the Irishman left Easter Road shortly after Eddie Turnbull, the manager, resigned and was replaced by Willie Ormond, who was powerless to prevent the inevitability of relegation.

The Final therefore featured Rangers and Celtic, who came to Hampden having lost the League championship to the emergent Aberdeen on the Saturday before. It would turn out to be an inglorious day in the Cup's history. The match itself was an exciting affair in which the young player Michael Conroy distinguished himself in a position at the centre of defence for which he would have been thought physically ill-equipped beforehand.

Due to the suspension of two players, McAdam and McDonald, he had been forced into the side in an emergency and his ability to subdue the dangerous Johnstone, particularly in the air, contributed hugely towards Celtic's ascendancy, although the game remained goal-less until nearing the end of extra-time. A speculative shot from Danny McGrain was then deflected by George McCluskey beyond the despairing McCloy, who had already set out in the opposite direction in response to the original attempt.

The aftermath, though, would lead even to questions being asked in the House of Commons as mounted policemen were ordered to draw their batons on the unruly factions warring all over Hampden's playing surface. No such instruction had been given in Glasgow since the General Strike of 1926. The Scottish Secretary, George Younger, drew storms of protest in the House when he directed the blame for these civil disturbances at the Celtic players caught in the act of celebrating a Cup Final win. Allegations were also made that half the policemen in attendance at the match to guard against such outbreaks of trouble had been told to go off duty before the event had ended.

If it had seemed that the bad old days had returned off the field, events on it had already begun taking a new, non-aggressive but healthily competitive tack. The outcome of the Cup Final had deprived Rangers of a national trophy, two of which had gone to Aberdeen and Dundee United. When, in the season which followed, Dundee United retained the League Cup and then eliminated Celtic from the Scottish Cup, it was apparent that the Old Firm now had more to concern themselves with than each other.

The Scottish Cup Final, for example, threw up a situation in which six of the Rangers pool had never won a medal in that particular competition, a rare sign of inexperience on their part, while the side from Tannadice, patiently built up by the manager who now had no thoughts of running madly from the game, had shown themselves to be at least the equal of their more famous opponents.

In a League match at Ibrox a few weeks before, they had, in fact, won by four goals to one, but in attempting to succeed at Hampden they had to take on the record books, history's equivalent of the tackle from behind, designed to prey on the minds of those who cannot resist looking back and wondering what relevance the past might have to the present day.

Not since 1929, when Kilmarnock won the Cup, had any side other than Celtic defeated Rangers in a Scottish Cup Final at Hampden. Dundee United, for their part, had never won a Cup-tie of any description against the men from Ibrox.

The pressure on John Greig and his team was a more up to date phenomenon, however. No longer feared as their predecessors from Ibrox had been, Rangers had survived going out of the Cup to St Johnstone at Perth in an earlier round because of a goal in the last seconds by Ian Redford. Their anxiousness might also have been their undoing at Hampden had Dundee United been able to translate their outfield strength into a single, telling goal

1981. Redford's penalty rebounds from McAlpine's legs.

1981. Jim McLean indulges in some pointed coaching. Rangers beat his Dundee United side in the replay.

against a team who had played cautiously, looking to strike on the break.

Rangers' plan might have worked, too, for they were awarded a penalty-kick in the last minute of the match when Iain Phillip impeded Robert Russell. His shot was saved by McAlpine and for the first time a crowd which was partly subsidised had been enticed back for a replay. Constantly engaged in a struggle to attract and sustain the interest of their own Dundee public, even to the extent of buying their affection when the need arose, the Dundee United directors devised a scheme whereby the club would pay half the travelling costs of those registered supporters clubs journeying by hired coach to Glasgow in midweek.

What they and everyone else who was there saw, however, was a Rangers performance so outstanding it seemed to have been choreographed to time perfectly with this finale to the club's season. Derek Johnstone and Davie Cooper, who had been left out to accommodate the less adventurous side of the first game, were recalled and within the opening twenty, inspired minutes they had helped to fashion a two goal advantage, Cooper himself and Russell being the scorers.

Dodds' goal for Dundee United gave the score a flattering appearance without any substantial promise of their getting that close to a team who were giving the night their best shot, and MacDonald restored suitable width to Rangers' lead before half-time. MacDonald scored again towards the end but by then the outcome was a formality.

Unlike the days gone by, however, such a crushing defeat would not have an adverse effect on the psyche of the losers, in this case Dundee United. If anything their proudest moment was in sight with the winning of the Premier Division championship, an incredible achievement for a club of their stature, in 1983. The emancipation of the so-called provincial clubs was at hand. At the head of the liberating forces were Jim McLean and his closest ally, Alex Ferguson.

A Light in the North

THE SCOTTISH CUP had not been kind to Alex Ferguson. In the years
when he had been building his reputation as an uncompromising centre-
forward he had, on the occasion of what should have been his first Final
appearance at Hampden, been dropped forty minutes before his then club,
Dunfermline, took on Celtic in 1965.

Four years later, the fruits of his success in establishing his reputation
having been a transfer to Rangers, Ferguson was deemed to have failed his
club by committing a tactical error which allowed their historic rivals, Celtic,
to score in the first minute of a 1969 Final they ultimately won with four goals
to spare.

The mistake cost him his career at Ibrox, in spite of his submitted plea that it
was suspect planning in the first place which had a forward two inches off six
feet delegated to mark the six feet-plus McNeill at corners. Ferguson never
played again in Rangers' first team, acting out the role of scapegoat in the
humiliating surroundings of the nearby Govan garage, where the club's third
eleven fulfilled their fixtures in the Combined Reserve League.

The Scottish Cup had colluded in the conspiracy, also connived at by the
League championship and the Scottish League Cup, to deprive him of a
winners' medal in the game's top flight. He was left scarred by memories of the
ironic forms that conspiracy could take.

There had been the day in 1968, for instance, when Rangers needed to win
their last home game of the season on the championship's final day to secure
the League title. Inside a stadium filled to capacity, and one in which Rangers
had not lost all season long (a record matched in their away form), they
inexplicably fell out of the habit of winning.

Across the city at Hampden, Dunfermline, the team Ferguson had left
behind two years earlier, finally won the Cup, against Hearts, which had
eluded them on the day they left him out against Celtic. The side which
defeated Rangers in the League at Ibrox and gave Celtic the title instead was
Aberdeen.

So it was that Ferguson brought to the job of manager at Pittodrie a hunger
for the success which had eluded him as a player, and a message to his staff that
they should never let slip carelessly the chance to win any competition for fear
of it being the only opportunity they would get.

Ferguson introduced, too, what he was fond of calling a democracy into the
Scottish game. His players learned so well from him that they won three
successive Scottish Cup Finals and helped change the complexion and shift the
balance of the domestic game, assisting in breaking the monopoly of the Old
Firm and ensuring that life, in that sense, would never be the same again.

He had taken over in the Summer of 1978, shortly after the side had tamely
lost the Cup Final to Rangers. Drastic change seemed necessary at the club and
Ferguson was the man to provide it. He had once acted as a shop steward in
leading an apprentices' strike at a factory and was certain not to baulk at the
idea of giving youth a chance. When Aberdeen returned to the Cup Final scene

four years later, only two of the men in the team had played in that failure against Rangers.

In putting this side together it had been the architect's good fortune to inherit some already possessing the necessary fibre, acquire others through careful planning and make shrewd decisions about the rest which would, had he erred, have rocked the edifice to its foundations before he had properly begun.

Jim Leighton was an ungainly looking goalkeeper, being possessed of the kind of bow legs which, in his native Renfrewshire, would have elicited the comment that he must surely have been born on a horse. Leighton could conceivably also have left Aberdeen on a free transfer following an unsatisfactory season on loan to Deveronvale in the Highland League prior to Ferguson's arrival. He was not released, however, and two games into Ferguson's managership the internationalist Bobby Clark broke his hand to attain Leighton swift promotion. It became clear that the position would soon be his on a permanent basis.

The full-backs were Kennedy and Rougvie, Kennedy being a tee-total, non-smoker of tremendous pace, the other man an imposing figure whose physical presence did not come in place of skill, but as an addendum. In between them in an awesome back four stood Miller and McLeish, around whom Aberdeen would, by and large, stand or fall. Miller was a predatory defender, blessed with a clairvoyant's gift for knowing where trouble would next crop up before even the troublemakers themselves.

Strachan had been there when he arrived at Pittodrie, although the incoming manager had been told by his board of directors that the relationship need not be a permanent one if he felt a transfer might suit both parties. The offer was declined then and Strachan placed beside Cooper and Simpson. The former had been born in India, the latter in London. Exposure to the air in the North East from infancy had added a prodigious strength to the natural delicacy of touch in their passing. Both qualities excited their mentor.

Depending upon the requirements of the occasion, Ferguson would balance this trio with Weir, who had been bought at a not insubstantial sum from his old club, St Mirren, and Bell, who had been taken from the same club on a free transfer. The contribution Bell would make led frequently thereafter to the suggestion that Ferguson had surely worn a mask and carried about his person a blunderbuss at the conclusion of this transaction.

Money in large denominations had also changed hands legitimately for McGhee from Newcastle, and every penny of it well spent, but the side was completed by Black, a teenager about whose talents his own father was so certain he telephoned Pittodrie at his own expense and craved Aberdeen's attention. The boy was played in a trial game against Formartine Juniors and taken off at half-time to the warmth of the manager's office to sign the appropriate forms, in case covetous eyes were contemplating a second-half kidnapping.

It was with this diverse grouping Ferguson strode confidently into the Scottish Cup Final of 1982 against Rangers, after first convincing himself he wanted to remain in Scotland. On the Monday before Aberdeen were due to meet Motherwell at Fir Park in the third round, Wolves had enticed him to Molineux with a view to his taking up managerial residence there. Official permission for the interview had been granted by a wise old Pittodrie

Access to the 1982 Final about to be denied.

chairman, Dick Donald, who knew his young manager would first have to see how superior his working conditions were at Pittodrie before his energies were renewed for the job.

Ferguson's head was cleared when intuition told him that at a ground where the only people working in the afternoon were the office clerical staff there was a club being held down by a dead hand.

Aberdeen, meanwhile, emerged revitalised by a working holiday in Benidorm, ready for the Scottish Cup-ties which would bring football out of an enforced hibernation caused by a particularly severe winter.

They would live dangerously at Motherwell, then managed by David Hay and undefeated in their previous 24 matches, but left content, having scored the quickest goal ever recorded in the history of the Scottish Cup, timed officially at 9.6 seconds, and even more satisfied when they looked back on Hewitt's winner as being the only serious shot at goal over the course of the remaining 89 minutes 50.4 seconds.

The removal of Celtic from their path in the next round at Pittodrie imbued the club with the belief that if the competition had been the private domain of the Old Firm in the preceding eleven years, with six victories to Celtic and five to Rangers, they were halfway towards knocking down the door on behalf of the rest of the country.

The week before the Cup Final there was a dress rehearsal as Aberdeen played Rangers at Pittodrie on the last day of the League season. They did so knowing that the title might still be theirs if they could beat the Glasgow side by five clear goals while Celtic lost to St Mirren at Parkhead that same afternoon.

Ferguson was uncertain of Celtic experiencing the kind of final day fallibility which had afflicted the Rangers team of which he had been a member years earlier. What he was sure of was that his young Aberdeen side more than had the measure of the Rangers team. Some of the Ibrox side were approaching retiral or the end of their usefulness to the club; all of them, along with their manager, John Greig, were looking to the Scottish Cup Final to bale them out of what had been a bankrupt season watched impatiently by a disaffected support.

The afternoon turned out to be the worst possible preparation as Aberdeen soon stormed four goals ahead. Only the news that Celtic were winning their match lessened the home side's hunger in the second half and prevented them from inflicting further punishment on Rangers.

The Scottish Cup Final, as one manager had graphically described it, was the day when it was supposed to be 'all paper hats and balloons'. Atmospherically, Hampden was no disappointment with Rangers' immense following giving their team one last chance for the season and the other, King's Park, end of the ground a colourful blaze of red and white scarves of those who had waited a long time for this excuse to fork out the rail fare between Aberdeen and Glasgow.

Aesthetically, the regulation ninety minutes flickered into life only now and then, mostly then, and was punctuated by the hefty challenges of men who knew exactly what was in it for both sides. Bett and Cooper of Rangers were both cautioned for the lustiness of their attempts to prevent Strachan creating a decisive breakthrough. Jardine, the elegant Rangers full-back playing in what would be his last game for the club, could not last beyond half-time following a head injury received in a tackle which earned Rougvie a place in the referee's notebook.

Against all expectations, if not the run of the play, Rangers had gone into the lead earlier with a goal headed in by John MacDonald from Dalziel's precise cross. McLeish had equalised before the interval with a swerving shot which surprised a Rangers defence grouping to deal with what they thought would be a typical defender's punt into the penalty area. The Aberdeen players who had watched McLeish do the same thing in a practice match on the eve of the Final were not so taken aback, struck only by the similarity in the situations.

The game would eventually enter extra-time, though, and it was then that all of Rangers' shortcomings were exposed in an horrific half hour during which they conceded three goals and lost another of their veteran servants, Alex Miller, with an injury sustained in trying to prevent one of them.

McGhee had put Aberdeen ahead for the first time in the match by running behind a Rangers defence beginning to show serious signs of grogginess and

Eric Black heads the only goal of the 1983 Final.

heading strongly past Stewart a ball sent over by Strachan. Miller then suffered the ankle injury which would finish his career at Ibrox when he fell in the penalty box and left McGhee needing only to thread the ball straight across the goal for Strachan to tap it over the line.

What had been a close run thing at the outset then took on elements of farce, particularly when Stewart, running from his penalty area to put a finger in yet another leak, cannoned the ball off Neale Cooper and looked back in apoplexy as the teenager gleefully knocked the ball into an empty goal and then gave a short gymnastic display in front of a disbelieving Rangers support. In doing so, he rounded off the day on which his club had vaulted to the prominent position to which they were to become addicted.

It was the fact that an excited gaggle of youngsters like Cooper, Simpson, Black and Hewitt had won something so big so early in their careers which pleased Ferguson, knowing it would instil in them a greater conviction when confronting the major milestones in the club's development which would undoubtedly lie ahead.

He was less than pleased at the lack of grace with which his side's achievement had been accepted by their opponents. It was as if, Ferguson would say afterwards, 'Rangers do not accept that Aberdeen are here to stay as one of the principal challengers for all the honours'. It would not be long before these hostilities would be resumed.

Aberdeen and Rangers had not done with each other. 1983 had only just come in, full of the annual promise of a new beginning, when the clubs fell into the bad old ways and collided in an extraordinary match at Pittodrie. In the course of a by now routine win for the home side, whose abilities cast Rangers in the unfamiliar role of underdogs whenever they met, the Ibrox player John MacDonald butted Doug Bell in the style known as the Glasgow salute, an art more usually practised outside licensed premises at the close of business.

The inflammatory effect of the incident was not dissimilar to a lighted match being placed near sweating dynamite as players turned on each other. MacDonald was sent from the field, later to be fined £200 by his club, and the SFA, appalled by the uproar as television evidence showed at least one other player guilty of the injudicious use of his head on a fellow professional, called the officials of both teams before them to take part in an inquiry into the disgraceful scenes.

Aberdeen were at the top of the Premier League, going into the fourth round of the Cup, having eliminated Hibs earlier, but their concentration began to waver in that department following a result in Europe which fuelled the notion that the club could record the audacious achievement of winning the European Cup Winners' Cup.

Bayern Munich, and in particular their West German internationalist Karl Heinz Rummenigge, had been outplayed and out-thought by Aberdeen on their own ground in the first, goal-less leg of the quarter-finals but had come to Pittodrie for the return and gone a goal ahead after only ten minutes. Such a blow is normally the signal for a collapse of the spirit so evident that defeat is an inevitability, but Neil Simpson levelled the tie on aggregate after thirty-eight minutes play. For Aberdeen to fall behind again on the hour and still win through to the semi-finals was a truly remarkable display of mental fortitude and physical courage. That the two goals should come from McLeish and Hewitt within a minute of each other served only to heighten the drama.

Ferguson was less impressed by the idea of the club's travel agent thereafter booking the team into a hotel in Gothenburg for the Final before Aberdeen had actually gone to the bother of negotiating their passage through the penultimate stage against the Belgian club Waterschei. The insult to Aberdeen's opponents was rectified when the manager issued instructions that the reservations were to be cancelled, even if the tour operator's confidence proved not to be misplaced as his clients took a 5-1 lead from the first leg with them to Belgium for what was, by then, a superfluous return meeting.

In the meantime Aberdeen had gone around Partick Thistle and into the semi-final of the Scottish Cup, where they would meet Celtic once again. The week before, another clash with Rangers ended in the now expected controversy. A surprise 2-1 defeat at Ibrox seriously impaired Aberdeen's chances of the League title and drew no words of praise for the home side from an agitated Ferguson whose post-match moods were beginning to earn him a certain notoriety.

The Rangers team in general was criticised as being a pale shadow of the sides from their illustrious past and their tactics on the day were queried to the extent that Ferguson was bereft of words to explain how they had actually succeeded. The only flaw in his argument was that Rangers had won and Ferguson, whose own talents were gaining him a growing list of admirers, had fallen into the managerial trap of occasional susceptibility to the kind of thinking which would have led him, at the post-battle de-briefing, to call Custer's last stand at the Little Big Horn a draw.

He could not have believed his good fortune the following week, though,

1983. Alex Ferguson at the conclusion of his side's 1-0 victory. He was shortly to lambast his team's performance.

when Celtic took the field at Hampden without Charlie Nicholas, a precociously gifted striker on his way to scoring over fifty goals that season. Nicholas had been injured in a training accident the day before the semi-final, a set-back which Billy McNeill would have denied to his own mother beforehand but could not cover up when the team lines eventually had to be produced, or, as it turned out, when play began.

Aberdeen won against Celtic by the only goal of the game but in the process Stuart Kennedy sustained an injury which was ultimately to finish his playing career. For Ferguson, the loss of one of the players he admired most on a personal level would always make this match a pyrrhic victory.

Even the torrential rain which fell throughout their meeting with Real

Madrid in the Cup Winners' Cup Final in Gothenburg could not remove the gloss from that night's piece of business, however, as goals from Black and Hewitt delivered the trophy into Aberdeen's possession ten days before they would have to meet their old adversaries, Rangers, in the Scottish Cup Final.

The gap between games was thought ideal for players who could recover from their playing and extra-curricular activities in ample time to provide a reminder of how they had come this far in the first place. Hibs had been systematically destroyed by five goals without reply at Pittodrie in a league match while they waited, but Ferguson grew more uneasy as the Final approached, detecting an uncharacteristic slackness in training and approach on the part of his players.

His worst fears were confirmed as Aberdeen's legs gave way underneath them and Rangers, again under extreme pressure and with a manager who, had he but known it, had only months left in the job, moved in for the kill. A laborious ninety minutes came and went without a goal, although it required a superlative save from Leighton, tipping a Bett shot over the bar, to ensure there would be extra-time.

Ferguson bolted from the dug-out to berate his players and to suggest Black revert to the outside-right role in which he had shown promise as a schoolboy, with Hewitt offering balance and width on the left, while John Greig asked his Rangers players for one last effort against an Aberdeen team displaying no traits of invincibility.

In the end Black's headed goal, from a move he instigated himself, would make Aberdeen the first team outside the Old Firm for more than a century to win the Scottish Cup in successive seasons. It was still not enough to settle the emotional turmoil Ferguson was experiencing as the frustrations of the days leading up to the Final were poured out on live television.

Excitement caused him to criticise everyone except his goalkeeper and centre-backs, Miller and McLeish. The following morning, once he had calmed down after reading his remarks as they appeared in the Sunday newspapers, he would call all his players together in the hotel at St Andrews being used for their revelries and apologise to them in public.

The same players, after all, with the addition of Stuart McKimmie, bought from Dundee to replace Kennedy, would be asked the following season to do what no club apart from Rangers had done in the preceding years of this century and win the Scottish Cup three times in a row. Even Celtic could not lay claim to that distinction and, in the Summer which came after Aberdeen's second success, Parkhead was not helped by being in a state of flux with the enforced departure of Billy McNeill from the manager's office to the same post with Manchester City.

In the days when McNeill had been in charge he had accepted that a greater spread of the major, domestic prizes was inevitable with the emergence of an exceptional Aberdeen. The history of disciplinary trouble in matches involving both clubs after he had gone suggested some of those he had left behind could not do likewise.

Under David Hay, Celtic had finished runners-up to Rangers in the League Cup Final after extra-time and taken second place to Aberdeen in the Premier Division Championship. A support always anxious for a reason to forgive and forget saw the Scottish Cup as the means by which they could again hold their heads up and Celtic attain salvation for the season.

Mindful of previously poor behaviour at games involving the two, the SFA invited Aberdeen and Celtic directors to Park Gardens on the morning of Saturday 12 May, one week before the Cup Final. Celtic, feeling this was an unprecedented and unwarranted step, drawing attention to strife on the field before anything had happened, refused to attend, thereby cancelling the meeting. Publicly Celtic expressed disquiet at the appearance of SFA Secretary Ernie Walker in the referee's room before the Final. For an event at that stage in its second year of sponsorship by the Scottish Health Education Group the rest of the afternoon was a bilious account of judgements being called into question, mainly by the Glasgow club. As ever, these were matters of personal interpretation.

Celtic fell behind to an early goal scored by Eric Black, about which they protested strongly. McGrain, the Celtic captain, had looked to be impeded as he jumped with McGhee for a headed pass from Alex McLeish, while Black, who had picked up the loose ball, seemed off-side before he shot past Bonner. Roy Aitken, a man fiercely committed to Celtic, could not contain his emotions thereafter and was sent off after a tackle on McGhee which had its origins in tactical destruction but not, the club would say later, in premeditated violence.

Nonetheless, Celtic played out the remainder of the game with ten men, Aitken being the first player since Jock Buchanan of Rangers fifty-five years earlier to be sent off in a Scottish Cup Final. The ten men battled bravely and five minutes from the end of regulation time punished a negligent Aberdeen by scoring an equaliser through Paul McStay. For a third year Aberdeen had been forced to go into extra time. The additional period was only eight minutes old when McGhee, already promised to Hamburg just as Strachan was to Manchester United, propelled a cross from the one he would accompany from Aberdeen behind Bonner for the winner. The pair had given their old club the Cup under historic circumstances as a last act.

It also gave Ferguson's side the distinction of being the only club outwith Celtic and Rangers to win the League and Cup double in one season.

1984. Roy Aitken becomes only the second player to be sent off in a Scottish Cup Final. McGarvey, McGrain and Provan look on.

Gordon Strachan, soon to leave Aberdeen, displays mixed emotions after the 1984 Final.

Celtic and Rangers both have to live now with the prospect of Alex Ferguson's Aberdeen as the dominant force in the Scottish game. In his time he has been interviewed by Wolves, linked with his former club, Rangers, when John Greig moved on, and hounded by speculation that he was to take over the managership of Tottenham Hotspur.

He remains at Pittodrie, engrossed by a challenge which would have utterly broken a weaker spirit. The loss of Rougvie, Strachan and McGhee was treated as nothing more than the chance to give further evidence of his highly imaginative talents.

He astutely judged the potential of Clyde full-back Tommy McQueen and employed an impressive turn of speed in beating Hibs for his signature. More striking still was his gamble in signing Frank McDougall from St Mirren. Most would have dismissed him as a replacement for Mark McGhee, thinking him no more than a worthy but limited journeyman. Instead, he has fitted into the Pittodrie system perfectly, his leadership of the forward line growing more astute with each passing week.

When the rich variety of the club's youngsters is also taken into account it is easy to believe that the men who left are no more than warm, but distant, memories around Pittodrie.

As the road to the 1985 Final beckons, Aberdeen top the League and have every reason to hope for a unique achievement at Hampden on 18 May, where a victory will bring a fourth successive Cup triumph. If they succeed, Aberdeen will, 112 years after the Cup's formation, and at the conclusion of the one hundreth competition, have created a new record, a new standard.

Epilogue

S O MANY SAVES, goals, fouls, tackles, cheers, boos, disputes, presentations, celebrations, wakes on from 1873, the Cup demonstrated, on Saturday 8 December 1984, that there need be no end to the cavalcade. On that day, in the first round of the 1984-85 competition, there was fresh novelty as the nation heard of the biggest defeat in living memory. Selkirk's 20-0 crushing by Stirling Albion was the largest margin of humiliation in the Cup this century.

Perhaps Selkirk did not relish the role of pathfinders in the world of nightmare but they at least could go on to a night out in Edinburgh (arranged in advance) to try and forget it all. That remedy was not available to the last side to share in so memorable a defeat. The side beaten 20-0 by Johnstone in the first round (preliminary) of the 1891-92 were Greenock Abstainers.

If the remainder of the competition is unlikely to provide so extreme an event it does, nonetheless, tantalise. Will Aberdeen set a new record, or will one of the others in the group of superpowers frustrate that ambition? Or will those teams simply succeed in knocking the stuffing out of each other, leaving the way clear for one of the less-fancied sides?

On what moment of skill, luck or clumsiness will the competition turn? The question continues to nag agreeably at the mind, just as it did for the man crossing the Clyde and heading South to Hampden on that blustery March day in 1874.

The Cup Finals

THE FOLLOWING is a brief record of the Cup Finals played to date. Those seeking fuller details should see *Scottish Cup Finals 1874-1984* by John Litster. This is available at a cost of £2 (+ p&p) from John Litster, 34 Coldstream Drive, Rutherglen, Glasgow G73 2LH.

A complete record of every Scottish Cup competition has been compiled by John Byrne and is to be published by the Association of Football Statisticians (22 Bretons, Basildon, Essex, SS15 5BY) in 1985.

It may be found that details concerning scorers and attendances for nineteenth century Finals provided in this book differ on occasion from those published elsewhere. This is the result of the conflicting accounts often given by the various newspapers of the day.

1874
21 March   First Hampden   att: 2500
Queen's Park 2 Clydesdale 0
Scorers Queen's Park: W McKinnon, Leckie
Teams Queen's Park: Dickson; Taylor, Neill; Thomson, Campbell; Weir, Leckie, W McKinnon, Lawrie, McNeil, A McKinnon

    Clydesdale: Gardner; Wotherspoon, McArley; Henry, Raeburn; Anderson, Gibb, Wilson, Lang, McPherson, Kennedy
Queen's Park beat Dumbreck (7-0), Eastern (1-0), Renton (2-0)

1875
10 April   First Hampden   att: 7000
Queen's Park 3 Renton 0
Scorers Queen's Park: A McKinnon, Highet, W McKinnon
Teams Queen's Park: Neill; Taylor, Phillips; Campbell, Dickson; McNeil, Highet, W McKinnon, A McKinnon, Lawrie, Weir

    Renton: Turnbull; A Kennedy, McKay; Scallion, McGregor; Melville, McRae, M Kennedy, J Brown, Glen, L Brown
Queen's Park beat Western (1-0), West End (7-0), Rovers (scratched), Clydesdale (0-0, 2-2, 1-0)

1876
11 March   Hamilton Crescent   att: 10,000
Queen's Park 1 Third Lanark R V 1
Scorers Queen's Park: Highet
    Third Lanark: Drinnan
Teams Queen's Park: Dickson; Taylor, Neill; Campbell, Phillips; Lawrie, McGill, Highet, W McKinnon, A McKinnon McNeil

    Third Lanark R V: Wallace; Hunter, Watson; White, Davidson; Crichton, W Drinnan, Scoular, Walker, Millar, McDonald

18 March   Hamilton Crescent   att: 6000
Queen's Park 2 Third Lanark R V 0 (replay)
Scorers Queen's Park: Highet (2)
Teams Queen's Park: Dickson; Taylor, Neill; Campbell, Phillips; Highet, W McKinnon, Hillcote, McNeil, McGill, Smith

    Third Lanark R V: (as above)
Queen's Park beat Alexandra Athletic (3-0), Northern (5-0), Clydesdale (2-0), Dumbreck (2-0), Vale of Leven (2-1)

1877
17 March   Hamilton Crescent   att: 12,000
Vale of Leven 1 Rangers 1
Scorers Vale of Leven: Paton
    Rangers: McDougall (own goal)
Teams Vale of Leven: Wood; A McIntyre, Michie; Jamieson, A McLintock; J Ferguson, R Paton, J McGregor, McDougall, J Baird, Lindsay

    Rangers: Watt; Vallance, Gillespie; Ricketts, W McNeil; M McNeil, Watson, Dunlop, P Campbell, Marshall, Hill

7 April   Hamilton Crescent   att: 15,000
Vale of Leven 1 Rangers 1 (replay, after extra time)
Scorers Vale of Leven: McDougall
    Rangers: Dunlop
Teams Vale of Leven: (as above)
    Rangers: (as above)

13 April   First Hampden   att: 8000
Vale of Leven 3 Rangers 2 (second replay)
Scorers Vale of Leven: Watson (own goal), Baird, Paton
    Rangers: P Campbell, W McNeil
Teams Vale of Leven: (as above)
    Rangers: (as above)
Vale of Leven beat Helensburgh (1-0), Vale of Leven Rovers (7-0), Third Lanark (1-0), Busby (4-0), Queen's Park (2-1), Ayr Thistle (9-0)

1878

30 March   First Hampden   att: 5000

Vale of Leven 1 Third Lanark R V 0

Scorer Vale of Leven: McDougall

Teams Vale of Leven: Parlane; A McLintock, A McIntyre; J McPherson, Jamieson; J Ferguson, McFarlane, J McGregor, James Baird, McDougall, J Baird

Third Lanark R V: Wallace; Somers, J Hunter; Kennedy McKenzie; Miller, A Hunter, Lang, Peden, McCririck, Kay

Vale of Leven beat Kilmarnock (scratched), Dumbarton (4-1), Lennox (3-0), Rangers (0-0, 5-0), Jordanhill (10-0), Parkgrove (5-0), bye

1879

19 April   First Hampden   att: 6000

Vale of Leven 1 Rangers 1

Scorers Vale of Leven: Ferguson

Rangers: Struthers

Teams Vale of Leven: Parlane; A McLintock, A McIntyre; J McIntyre, J McPherson; McFarlane, J Ferguson, James Baird, P McGregor, J Baird, McDougall

Rangers: Gillespie; A Vallance, T Vallance; J Drinnan, H McIntyre; Hill, Dunlop, Steel, Struthers, P Campbell, M McNeil

Vale of Leven were awarded the Cup after Rangers failed to turn up for a replay on 26 April. See Chapter Two.

Vale of Leven beat Alclutha (6-0), Renton Thistle (11-0), Jamestown (15-0), Govan (11-1), Beith (6-1), Dumbarton (3-1), Helensburgh (3-0)

1880

21 February   First Cathkin   att: 7000

Queen's Park 3 Thornliebank 0

Scorers Queen's Park: Highet (2), Ker

Teams Queen's Park: Graham; Somers, Neill; Campbell, Davidson; Richmond, Weir, Highet, Ker, Kay, McNeil

Thornliebank: Cadden; Jamieson, Marshall; Henderson, McFetridge; A Brannan, Clark, Wham, Anderson, Hutton, T Brannan

Queen's Park beat Rangers (0-0, 5-1), 19th L R V (14-1), Partick (5-1), Strathblane (10-1), Hurlford (15-1), bye, Dumbarton (1-0)

1881

26 March   Kinning Park   att: 10,000

Queen's Park 2 Dumbarton 1

Scorers Queen's Park: McNeil, Kay

Dumbarton: McAulay

Teams Queen's Park: McCallum; Watson, Holm; Campbell, Davidson; Anderson, Fraser, Ker, Smith, McNeil, Kay

Dumbarton: Kennedy; Hutcheson, Paton; J Miller, Anderson, Meikleham, Brown, Lindsay, McAulay, McKinnon, Kennedy

After a protest by Dumbarton, a replay was ordered. See Chapter Three.

9 April   Kinning Park   att: 10,000

Queen's Park 3 Dumbarton 1

Scorers Queen's Park: Smith (2), Ker

Dumbarton: Meikleham

Teams Queen's Park: McCallum; Watson, Holm; Campbell, Davidson; Anderson, Fraser, Ker, Smith, Allan, Kay

Dumbarton: (as above)

Queen's Park beat John Elder (7-0), Possilpark (5-0), Pilgrims (8-1), Beith (11-2), Mauchline (2-0), Central (10-0), bye

1882

18 March   First Cathkin   att: 12,000

Queen's Park 2 Dumbarton 2

Scorers Queen's Park: Harrower (2)

Dumbarton: Brown, Meikleham

Teams Queen's Park: McCallum; Watson, A Holm; Davidson, J Holm; Fraser, Anderson, Ker, Harrower, Richmond, Kay

Dumbarton: Kennedy; Hutcheson, Paton; P Miller, McKinnon; Brown, Meikleham, McAulay, Lindsay, Kennedy, J Miller

1 April   First Cathkin   att: 15,000

Queen's Park 4 Dumbarton 1 (replay)

Scorers Queen's Park: Richmond, Ker, Harrower, Kay

Dumbarton: J Miller

Teams Queen's Park: McCallum; Watson, Holm; Davidson, Campbell; Fraser, Anderson, Ker, Harrower, Richmond, Kay

Dumbarton: Kennedy; Hutcheson, Paton; P Miller, Watt; Brown, Meikleham, McAulay, Lindsay, Kennedy, J Miller

Queen's Park beat Caledonian (14-0), Cowlairs (2-2, 9-0), bye, Johnstone (3-1), Partick Thistle (10-0), Shotts (15-0), Kilmarnock Athletic (3-2)

1883

31 March   First Hampden   att: 15,000

Dumbarton 2 Vale of Leven 2

Scorers Dumbarton: Paton, McArthur

Vale of Leven: Johnston, McCrae

Teams Dumbarton: McAulay; Hutcheson, Paton; P Miller, Lang, L Keir; R Brown (I), R Brown (II), J Miller, Lindsay, McArthur

Vale of Leven: A McLintock; A McIntyre, Forbes; McLeish, McPherson; Gillies, McCrae, Johnston, Friel, Kennedy, McFarlane

7 April   First Hampden   att: 8000

Dumbarton 2 Vale of Leven 1 (replay)

Scorers Dumbarton: Anderson, Brown (I)

Vale of Leven: Friel

Teams Dumbarton: McAulay; Hutcheson, Paton; P Miller, Keir; R Brown (I), R Brown (II), J Miller, Lindsay, Anderson, McArthur

Vale of Leven: (as above)

Dumbarton beat: King's Park (8-1), Jamestown (8-1), bye, Queen's Park (3-1), Pollokshields Athletic 1-0,* 5-0)

*Dumbarton agreed to a replay because they felt the goal should not have been awarded.

1884

23 February   First Cathkin

Vale of Leven failed to turn up for the Final with Queen's Park and it was later decided to award the Cup to the Glasgow side. On the day of the match a friendly was played with Third Lanark, Queen's Park winning 4-0. It is to be presumed that the Queen's Park players in that match later received Cup-winners' medals. The team was: McCallum; Arnott, A Holm; Campbell, Gow; Christie, Allan, Smith, Harrower, Anderson, Watt

Queen's Park beat Partick (8-0), Third Lanark (4-2), Cowlairs (5-0), Partick Thistle (4-0), bye, Cartvale (6-1), Hibernian (5-1)

1885
21 February   Second Hampden   att: 2500
Renton 0 Vale of Leven 0
Teams Renton: Lindsay; Hannah, A McCall; Kelso, McKechnie; Barbour, Kelly, A McIntyre, J McCall, Thomson, Grant
   Vale of Leven: James Wilson; A McIntyre, Forbes; Abraham, J Wilson; Galloway, D McIntyre, Ferguson, Johnstone, Gillies, Kennedy

28 February   Second Hampden   att: 3500
Renton 3 Vale of Leven 1 (replay)
Scorers Renton: J McCall, McIntyre
   Vale of Leven: Gillies
Teams Renton: (as above)
   Vale of Leven: James Wilson; A McIntyre, Forbes; Abraham, McPherson; Galloway, D McIntyre, Ferguson, Johnstone, Gillies, Kennedy
Renton beat Vale of Leven Wanderers (2-1), East Stirlingshire (10-2), Northern (9-2), St Mirren (2-1), bye, Rangers (5-3), Hibernian (3-2)

1886
13 February   First Cathkin   att: 7000
Queen's Park 3 Renton 1
Scorers Queen's Park: Hamilton, Christie, Somerville
   Renton: Kelso
Teams Queen's Park: Gillespie; Arnott, Watson; Campbell, Gow; Christie, Somerville, Hamilton, Allan, Harrower, Lambie
   Renton: Lindsay; Hannah, A McCall; Kelso, McKechnie; Thomson, Grant, Barbour, J McCall, H McIntyre, Kelly
Queen's Park beat St Peter's (16-0), Pilgrims (1-0), East Stirlingshire (3-0), Airdrie (1-0), Arthurlie (2-1), bye, Third Lanark (3-0)

1887
12 February   Second Hampden   att: 10,000
Hibernian 2 Dumbarton 1
Scorers Hibernian: Smith, Groves
   Dumbarton: Aitken
Teams Hibernian: Tobin; Lundy, Fagan; McGhee, McGinn, McLaren; Lafferty, Groves, Montgomery, Clark, Smith
   Dumbarton: McAulay; Hutcheson, Fergus; Miller, McMillan, Kerr; Brown, Robertson, Madden, Aitken, Jamieson
Hibernian beat Durhamstown Rangers (6-1), Mossend Swifts (1-1, 3-0), Hearts (5-1), bye, Queen of the South Wanderers (7-2), Third Lanark (2-1), Vale of Leven (3-1)

1888
4 February   Second Hampden   att: 10,000
Renton 6 Cambuslang 1
Scorers Renton: D Campbell, McCallum, McNee, McCall (2), J Campbell
   Cambuslang: H Gourlay
Teams Renton: Lindsay; Hannah, A McCall; Kelso, Kelly, McKechnie; McCallum, J Campbell, D Campbell, J McCall, McNee
   Cambuslang: Dunn; Smith, Semple; McKay, J Gourlay, Jackson; James Buchanan, John Buchanan, Plenderleith, H Gourlay, J Gourlay
Renton beat Union (5-0), Dumbarton Athletic (4-2), Camelon (8-0), Lindertis (13-1), St Mirren (3-2), Dundee Wanderers (5-1), Queen's Park (3-1)

1889
2 February   Second Hampden   att: 17,000
Third Lanark 3 Celtic 0
Scorers Third Lanark: Oswald (jun) (2), Hannah
Teams Third Lanark: Downie; Thomson, Rae; Lochhead, Auld, McFarlane; Marshall, Oswald (jun), Oswald (sen), Hannah, Johnstone
   Celtic: John Kelly; Gallacher, McKeown; W Maley, James Kelly, McLaren; McCallum, Dunbar, Groves, Coleman, T Maley
A replay was ordered after protests concerning ground conditions. See chapter four.

9 February   Second Hampden   att: 16,000
Third Lanark 2 Celtic 1 (replay)
Scorers Third Lanark: Marshall, Oswald (jun)
   Celtic: McCallum
Teams (as above)
Teams Teams Celtic: (as above)
Third Lanark beat Whitefield (scratched), Kelvinside Athletic (8-0), Queen's Park (2-1,* 4-2), Hurlford (7-2), Abercorn (2-2, 3-1), Campsie (5-1), Renton (2-0)
*Replay ordered after Queen's Park protest about eligibility of Third Lanark player Love.

1890
Match scheduled for 8 February but postponed because of fog
15 February   First Ibrox   att: 10,000
Queen's Park 1 Vale of Leven 1
Scorers Queen's Park: Hamilton
   Vale of Leven: McLachlan
Teams Queen's Park: Gillespie; Arnot, Smellie; McAra, Stewart, Robertson; Berry, Gulliland, J Hamilton, Sellar, Allan
   Vale of Leven: Wilson: Murray, Whitelaw; Sharp, McNicol, Osborne; McLachlan, Rankin, Paton, Bruce, McMillan

22 February   First Ibrox   att: 14,000
Queen's Park 2 Vale of Leven (replay)
Scorers Queen's Park: Hamilton, Stewart
   Vale of Leven: Bruce
Teams Queen's Park: (as above)
   Vale of Leven: (as above)
Queen's Park beat Celtic (0-0, 2-1), Summerton Athletic (11-0), Vale of Leven Wanderers (8-0), Aberdeen (13-1), St Mirren (1-0), Leith Athletic (1-0), Abercorn (2-0)

1891
7 February   Second Hampden   att: 14,000
Heart of Midlothian 1 Dumbarton 0
Scorer Heart of Midlothian: Russell
Teams Heart of Midlothian: Fairbairn; Adams, Goodfellow; Begbie, McPherson, Hill; Taylor, Mason, Russell, Scott, Baird
   Dumbarton: McLeod; Watson, Miller; McMillan, Boyle, Keir; Taylor, Galbraith, Mair, McNaught, Bell
Heart of Midlothian beat Raith Rovers (7-2), Burntisland Thistle (scratched), Methlan Park (3-0), Ayr (4-3), Morton (5-1), East Stirlingshire (3-1), Third Lanark (4-1)

1892

12 March   First Ibrox   att: 40,000
Celtic 1 Queen's Park 0

Scorer Celtic: Campbell

Teams Celtic: Cullen; Reynolds, Doyle; W Maley, Kelly, Dowds; McCallum, Brady, Madden, McMahon, Campbell
    Queen's Park: Baird; Sillars, Smellie; Gillespie, Robertson, Stewart; Gulliland, Waddell, J Hamilton, Sellar, Lambie

Because of crowd encroachment it was agreed that above game be considered a friendly. See Chapter five.

9 April   First Ibrox   att: 20,000
Celtic 5 Queen's Park 1 (replay)

Scorers Celtic: Campbell (2), McMahon (2), Sillars (own goal)
    Queen's Park: Waddell

Teams Celtic: Cullen; Doyle, Reynolds; Gallacher, Kelly, Maley; Campbell, Dowds, McCallum, McMahon, Brady
    Queen's Park: Baird; Sillars, Sellar; Gillespie, Robertson, Stewart; Waddell, Lambie, Gulliland, Hamilton, Scott

Celtic beat St Mirren (4-2), Kilmarnock Athletic (3-0), Cowlairs (4-1), Rangers (5-3)

1893

25 February   First Ibrox   att: 20,000
Celtic 1 Queen's Park 0

Scorer Celtic: Towie

Teams Celtic: Cullen; Doyle, Reynolds; Dunbar, Kelly, W Maley; Campbell, McMahon, Madden, Towie, Blessington
    Queen's Park: Baird; Sillars, Smellie; Gillespie, Robertson, Stewart; Waddell, Gulliland, J Hamilton, Lambie, Sellar

Because of ground conditions it was agreed that the above game should be considered a friendly. See Chapter five.

11 March   First Ibrox   att: 15,000
Queen's Park 2 Celtic 1 (replay)

Scorers Queen's Park: Sellar (2)
    Celtic: Blessington

Teams Queen's Park: Baird; Sillars, Smellie; Gillespie, McFarlane, Stewart; Gulliland, Waddell, Hamilton, Lambie, Sellar

    Celtic: Cullen; Doyle, Reynolds; W Maley, Kelly, Dunbar; Towie, Blessington, Madden, McMahon, Campbell
Queen's Park beat Cowlairs (4-1), Kilmarnock (8-0), Heart of Midlothian (1-1, 5-2), Broxburn Shamrock (4-2)

1894 *First Old Firm*

17 February   Second Hampden   att: 15,000
Rangers 3 Celtic 1

Scorers Rangers: H McCreadie, Barker, McPherson
    Celtic: W Maley

Teams Rangers: Haddow; N Smith, Drummond; Marshall, A McCreadie, Mitchell; Steel, H McCreadie, Gray, McPherson, Barker

    Celtic: Cullen; Reynolds, Doyle; Curran, Kelly, W Maley; Blessington, Madden, Cassidy, Campbell, McMahon
Rangers beat Cowlairs (8-0), Leith Athletic (2-0), Clyde (5-0), Queen's Park (1-1, 3-1)

1895

20 April   First Ibrox   att: 13,500
St Bernard's 2 Renton 1

Scorers St Bernard's: Clelland (2)
    Renton: Duncan

Teams St Bernard's: Sneddon; Hall, Foyers; McManus, Robertson, Murdoch; Laing, Paton, Oswald, Crossan, Clelland

    Renton: Dickie; Ritchie, A McCall; Glen, McColl, Tait; McLean, Murray, Price, Gilfillan, Duncan
St Bernard's beat Airdrie (4-2), Kilmarnock (3-1), Clyde (2-1), Hearts (0-0, 1-0)

1896

14 March   Logie Green   att: 16,034
Heart of Midlothian 3 Hibernian 1

Scorers Heart of Midlothian: Baird, Walker, Michael
    Hibernian: O'Neill

Teams Heart of Midlothian: Fairbairn; McCartney, Mirk; Begbie, Russell, Hogg; McLaren, Baird, Michael, King, Walker

    Hibernian: McColl; Robertson, Macfarlane; Breslin, Neill, Murphy; Murray, Kennedy, Groves, Smith, O'Neill
Heart of Midlothian beat Blantyre (12-1), Ayr (5-1), Arbroath (4-0), St Bernard's (1-0)

1897

20 March   Second Hampden   att: 15,000
Rangers 5 Dumbarton 1

Scorers Rangers: Miller (2), Hyslop, McPherson, A Smith
    Dumbarton: W Thomson

Teams Rangers: Dickie; N Smith, Drummond; Gibson, A McCreadie, Mitchell; Low, McPherson, Miller, Hyslop, A Smith

    Dumbarton: Docherty; D Thomson, Mauchlan; Miller, Gillan, Sanderson; Mackie, W Speedie, Hendry, W Thomson, Fraser
Rangers beat Partick Thistle (4-2), Hibernian (3-0), Dundee (4-0), Morton (7-2)

1898

26 March   Second Hampden   att: 14,000
Rangers 2 Kilmarnock 0

Scorers Rangers: A Smith, Hamilton

Teams Rangers: Dickie; N Smith, Drummond; Gibson, Neil, Mitchell; Miller, McPherson, Hamilton, Hyslop, A Smith

    Kilmarnock: McAllan; Busby, Brown; McPherson, Anderson, Johnstone; Muir, Maitland, Campbell, Reid, Finlay
Rangers beat Polton Vale (8-0), Cartvale (12-0), Queen's Park (3-1), Third Lanark (1-1, 2-2, 2-0)

1899

22 April   Second Hampden   att: 25,000
Celtic 2 Rangers 0

Scorers Celtic: McMahon, Hodge

Teams Celtic: McArthur; Welford, Storrier; Battles, Marshall, King; Hodge, Campbell, Divers, McMahon, Bell

    Rangers: Dickie; N Smith, Crawford; Gibson, Neill, Mitchell; Campbell, McPherson, Hamilton, Miller, A Smith
Celtic beat 6th GRV (Dalbeattie) (8-1), St Bernard's (3-0), Queen's Park (2-1*), Port Glasgow Athletic (4-2)

First match abandoned due to poor visibility with Celtic leading 4-2.

1900

14 April   Ibrox   att: 17,000

Celtic 4 Queen's Park 3

Scorers Celtic: McMahon, Divers (2), Bell

     Queen's Park: Christie, W Stewart, Battles (own goal)

Teams Celtic: McArthur; Storrier, Battles; Russell, Marshall, Orr; Hodge, Campbell, Divers, McMahon, Bell

     Queen's Park: Gourlay; D Stewart, Swan; Irons, Christie, Templeton; W Stewart, Wilson, McColl, Kennedy, Hay

Celtic beat Bo'ness (7-1), Port Glasgow Athletic (5-1), Kilmarnock (4-0), Rangers (2-2, 4-0)

1901

6 April   Ibrox   att: 15,000

Heart of Midlothian 4 Celtic 3

Scorers Heart of Midlothian: Walker, Bell (2), Thomson

     Celtic: McOustra (2), McMahon

Teams Heart of Midlothian: Philip; Allan, Baird; Key, Buick, Hogg; Porteous, Walker, Thomson, Houston, Bell

     Celtic: McArthur; Davidson, Battles; Russell, Loney, Orr; McOustra, Divers, Campbell, McMahon, Quinn

Heart of Midlothian beat Mossend Swifts (7-0), Queen's Park (2-1), Port Glasgow Athletic (5-1), Hibernian (1-1, 2-1)

1902

26 April   Celtic Park   att: 16,000

Hibernian 1 Celtic 0

Scorer Hibernian: McGeachan

Teams Hibernian: Rennie; Gray, Glen; Breslin, Harrower, Robertson; McCall, McGeachan, Divers, Callaghan, Atherton

     Celtic: McFarlane; Watson, Battles; Loney, Marshall, Orr; McCafferty, McDermott, McMahon, Livingstone, Quinn

Hibernian beat Clyde (2-0), Port Glasgow Athletic (5-1), Queen's Park (7-1), Rangers (2-0)

1903

11 April   Celtic Park   att: 28,000

Rangers 1 Heart of Midlothian 1

Scorers Rangers: Stark

     Heart of Midlothian: Walker

Teams Rangers: Dickie; Fraser, Drummond; Gibson, Stark, Robertson; McDonald, Speedie, Hamilton, J Walker, Smith

     Heart of Midlothian: McWattie; Thomson, Orr; Key, Buick, Hogg; Dalrymple, Walker, Porteous, Hunter, Baird

18 April   Celtic Park   att: 16,000

Rangers 0 Heart of Midlothian 0 (replay)

Teams Rangers: (as above)

     Heart of Midlothian: (as above)

25 April   Celtic Park   att: 32,000

Rangers 2 Heart of Midlothian 0 (second replay)

Scorers Rangers: Mackie, Hamilton

Teams Rangers: Dickie; Fraser, Drummond; Henderson, Stark, Robertson; McDonald, Mackie, Hamilton, Speedie, Smith

     Heart of Midlothian: McWattie; Thomson, Orr; Key, Anderson, Hogg; Porteous, Walker, Dalrymple, Hunter, Baird

Rangers beat Auchterarder Thistle (7-0), Kilmarnock (4-0), Celtic (3-0), Stenhousemuir (4-1)

1904

16 April   Hampden Park 3   att: 64,323

Celtic 3 Rangers 2

Scorers Celtic: Quinn (3)

     Rangers: Speedie (2)

Teams Celtic: Adams; McLeod, Orr; Young, Loney, Hay; Muir, McMenemy, Quinn, Somers, Hamilton

     Rangers: Watson; N Smith, Drummond; Henderson, Stark, Robertson; Walker, Speedie, Mackie, Donnachie, A Smith

Celtic beat Stanley (scratched), St Bernard's (4-0), Dundee (1-1, 0-0, 5-0), Third Lanark (2-1)

1905

8 April   Hampden Park   att: 55,000

Third Lanark 0 Rangers 0

Teams Third Lanark: Raeside; Barr, McIntosh; Comrie, Sloan, Neilson; Johnstone, Kidd, McKenzie, Wilson, Munro

     Rangers: Sinclair; Fraser, Craig; Henderson, Stark, Robertson; Hamilton, Speedie, McColl, Kyle, Smith

15 April   Hampden Park   att: 40,000

Third Lanark 3 Rangers 1 (replay)

Scorers Third Lanark: Wilson (2), Johnstone

     Rangers: Smith

Teams Third Lanark: (as above)

     Rangers: Sinclair; Fraser, Craig; Henderson, Stark, Robertson; Low, Speedie, McColl, Kyle, Smith

Third Lanark beat Leith (4-1), Motherwell (1-0), Aberdeen (4-1), Airdrie (2-1)

1906

28 April   Ibrox   att: 30,000

Heart of Midlothian 1 Third Lanark 0

Scorers Heart of Midlothian: G Wilson

Teams Heart of Midlothian: G Philip; McNaught, D Philip; McLaren, Thomson, Dickson; Cooper, Walker, Menzies, D Wilson, G Wilson

     Third Lanark: Raeside; Barr, Hill; Cross, Neilson, Comrie; Johnstone, Graham, Reid, Wilson, Munro

Heart of Midlothian beat Nithsdale Wanderers (4-1), Beith (3-0), Celtic (2-1), Port Glasgow Athletic (2-0)

1907

20 April   Hampden Park   att: 50,000

Celtic 3 Heart of Midlothian 0

Scorers Celtic: Orr (pen), Somers (2)

Teams Celtic: Adams; McLeod, Orr; Young, McNair, Hay; Bennett, McMenemy, Quinn, Somers, Templeton

     Heart of Midlothian: Allan; Reid, Collins; Philip, McLaren, Henderson; Bauchope, Walker, Axford, Yates, Wombwell

Celtic beat Clyde (2-1), Morton (0-0, 1-1, 2-1), Rangers (3-0), Hibs (0-0, 0-0, 3-0)

1908

18 April   Hampden Park   att: 55,000

Celtic 5 St Mirren 1

Scorers Celtic: Bennett (2), Hamilton, Somers, Quinn

     St Mirren: Cunningham

Teams Celtic: Adams; McNair, Weir; Young, Loney, Hay; Bennett, McMenemy, Quinn, Somers, Hamilton

     St Mirren: Grant; Gordon, White; Key, Robertson, McAvoy; Clements, Cunningham, Wylie, Paton, Anderson

Celtic beat Peebles Rovers (4-0), Rangers (2-1), Raith Rovers (3-0), Aberdeen (1-0)

1909

10 April   Hampden Park   att: 70,000
Celtic 2 Rangers 2

Scorers Celtic: Quinn, Munro
          Rangers: Gilchrist, Bennett

Teams Celtic: Adams; McNair, Weir; Young, Dodds, Hay; Munro, McMenemy, Quinn, Somers, Hamilton
          Rangers: Rennie; Law, Craig; May, Stark, Galt; Bennett, Gilchrist, Campbell, McPherson, Smith

17 April   Hampden Park   att: 60,000
Celtic 1 Rangers 1 (replay)

Scorers Celtic: Quinn
          Rangers: Gordon

Teams Celtic: Adams; McNair, Weir; Young, Dodds, Hay; Kivlichan, McMenemy, Quinn, Somers, Hamilton
          Rangers: Rennie; Law, Craig; Gordon, Stark, Galt; Bennett, McDonald, Reid, McPherson, Smith

Cup withheld after riot following replay. See Chapter Eight.
Celtic beat Leith (4-2), Port Glasgow (4-0), Airdrie (3-1), Clyde (0-0, 2-0)
Rangers beat St Johnstone (3-0), Dundee (0-0, 1-0), Queen's Park (1-0), Falkirk (1-0)

1910

9 April   Ibrox   att: 60,000
Dundee 2 Clyde 2

Scorers Dundee: Blair (own goal), Langlands
          Clyde: Chalmers, Booth

Teams Dundee: Crumley; Lawson, Chaplin; Lee, Dainty, Comrie; Bellamy, Langlands, Hunter, McFarlane, Fraser
          Clyde: McTurk; Watson, Blair; Walker, McAteer, Robertson; Stirling, McCartney, Chalmers, Jackson, Booth

16 April   Ibrox   att: 20,000
Dundee 0 Clyde 0 (replay after extra time)

Teams Dundee: Crumley; Neal, Chaplin; Lee, Dainty, Comrie; Bellamy, Langlands, Hunter, McFarlane, Fraser
          Clyde: (as above)

20 April   Ibrox   att: 24,000
Dundee 2 Clyde 1 (second replay)

Scorers Dundee: Bellamy, Hunter
          Clyde: Chalmers

Teams Dundee: Crumley; Neal, McEwan; Lee, Dainty, Comrie; Bellamy, Langlands, Hunter, McFarlane, Fraser
          Clyde: McTurk; Watson, Blair; Walker, McAteer, Robertson Wyllie, McCartney, Chalmers, Wyse, Booth

Dundee beat Beith (1-1, 1-0), Falkirk (3-0), Motherwell (3-1), Hibs (0-0, 0-0, 1-0)

1911

8 April   Ibrox   att: 45,000
Celtic 0 Hamilton Academical 0

Teams Celtic: Adams; McNair, Dodds; Young, McAteer, Hay; Kivlichan, McMenemy, Quinn, Hastie, Hamilton
          Hamilton Academical: J Watson; Davie, Miller, P Watson, W McLaughlin, Eglinton; J McLaughlin, Waugh, Hunter, Hastie, McNeil

15 April   Ibrox   att: 25,000
Celtic 2 Hamilton Academical 0 (replay)

Scorers Celtic: Quinn, McAteer

Teams Celtic: Adams; McNair, Hay; Young, McAteer, Dodds; McAtee, McMenemy, Quinn, Kivlichan, Hamilton
          Hamilton Academical: (as above)

Celtic beat St Mirren (2-0), Galston (1-0), Clyde (1-0), Aberdeen (1-0)

1912

6 April   Ibrox   att: 45,000
Celtic 2 Clyde 0

Scorers Celtic: McMenemy, Gallagher

Teams Celtic: Mulrooney; McNair, Dodds; Young, Loney, Johnstone; McAtee, Gallagher, Quinn, McMenemy, Brown
          Clyde: Grant; Gilligan, Blair; Walker, McAndrew, Collins; Hamilton, Jackson, Morrison, Carmichael, Stevens

Celtic beat Dunfermline Athletic (1-0), East Stirling (3-0), Aberdeen (2-2, 2-0), Hearts (3-0)

1913

12 April   Celtic Park   att: 45,000
Falkirk 2 Raith Rovers 0

Scorers Falkirk: Robertson, T Logan

Teams Falkirk: Stewart; Orrock, Donaldson; McDonald, T Logan, McMillan; McNaught, Gibbons, Robertson, Croal, Terris
          Raith Rovers: McLeod; Morrison, Cumming; J Gibson, J Logan, Anderson; Cranston, Graham, Martin, Gourlay, F Gibson

Falkirk beat Morton (2-2, 3-1), Rangers (3-1), Dumbarton (1-0), Hearts (1-0)

1914

11 April   Ibrox   att: 55,000
Celtic 0 Hibernian 0

Teams Celtic: Shaw; McNair, Dodds; Young, Johnstone, McMaster; McAtee, Gallagher, Owers, McMenemy, Browning
          Hibernian: Allan; Girdwood, Templeton; Kerr, Paterson, Grossert; Wilson, Fleming, Hendren, Wood, Smith

16 April   Ibrox   att: 36,000
Celtic 4 Hibernian 1 (replay)

Scorers Celtic: McColl (2), Browning (2)
          Hibernian: Smith

Teams Celtic: Shaw; McNair, Dodds; Young, Johnstone, McMaster; McAtee, Gallagher, McColl, McMenemy, Browning
          Hibernian: (as above)

Celtic beat Clyde (0-0, 2-0), Forfar (5-0), Motherwell (3-1), Third Lanark (2-0)

1920

17 April   Hampden Park   att: 95,000
Kilmarnock 3 Albion Rovers 2

Scorers Kilmarnock: Culley, Shortt, J Smith
          Albion Rovers: Watson, Hillhouse

Teams Kilmarnock: Blair; Hamilton, Gibson; Bagan, Shortt, Neave; McNaught, M Smith, J Smith, Culley, McPhail
          Albion Rovers: Short; Penman, Bell; Wilson, Black, Ford; Ribchester, James White, John White, Watson, Hillhouse

Kilmarnock beat Alloa (2-0), Queen's Park (4-1), Armadale (2-1), Morton (3-2)

1921

16 April   Celtic Park   att: 28,294

Partick Thistle 1 Rangers 0

Scorers Partick Thistle: Blair

Teams Partick Thistle: Campbell; Crichton, Bulloch; Harris, Wilson, Borthwick; Blair, Kinloch, Johnston, McMenemy, Salisbury

Rangers: Robb; Manderson, McCandless; Meiklejohn, Dixon, Bowie; Archibald, Cunningham, Henderson, Cairns, Morton

Partick Thistle beat Hibernian (0-0, 0-0, 1-0), East Stirling (2-1), Motherwell (2-2, 0-0, 2-1), Hearts (0-0, 0-0, 2-0)

1922

15 April   Hampden Park   att: 75,000

Morton 1 Rangers 0

Scorers Morton: Gourlay

Teams Morton: Edwards; McIntyre, R Brown; Gourlay, Wright, McGregor; McNab, McKay, Buchanan, A Brown, McMinn

Rangers: Robb; Manderson, McCandless; Meiklejohn, Dixon, Muirhead; Archibald, Cunningham, Henderson, Cairns, Morton

Morton beat Vale of Leithen (4-0), Clydebank (1-1, 3-1), Clyde (4-1), Motherwell (2-1), Aberdeen (3-1)

1923

31 March   Hampden Park   att: 80,100

Celtic 1 Hibernian 0

Scorers Celtic: Cassidy

Teams Celtic: Shaw; McNair, W McStay; J McStay, Cringan, McFarlane; McAtee, Gallagher, Cassidy, McLean, Connolly

Hibernian: Harper; McGinnigle, Dornan; Kerr, Miller, Shaw; Ritchie, Dunn, McColl, Halligan, Walker

Celtic beat Lochgelly United (3-2), Hurlford (4-0), East Fife (2-1), Raith Rovers (1-0), Motherwell (2-0)

1924

10 April   Ibrox   att: 59,218

Airdrieonians 2 Hibernian 0

Scorers Airdrieonians: Russell (2)

Teams Airdrieonians: Ewart; Dick, McQueen; Preston, McDougall, Bennie; Reid, Russell, Gallacher, McPhail, Sommerville

Hibernian: Harper; McGinnigle, Dornan; Kerr, Miller, Shaw; Ritchie, Dunn, McColl, Halligan, Walker

Airdrieonians beat Morton (2-1), St Johnstone (4-0), Motherwell (5-0), Ayr United (1-1, 0-0, 1-1, 1-0), Falkirk (2-1)

1925

11 April   Hampden Park   att: 75,137

Celtic 2 Dundee 1

Scorers Celtic: Gallagher, McGrory
       Dundee: D McLean

Teams Celtic: Shevlin; W McStay, Hilley; Wilson, J McStay, McFarlane; Connolly, Gallagher, McGrory, Thomson, A McLean

Dundee: Britton; Brown, Thomson; Ross, W Rankine, Irving; Duncan, A McLean, Halliday, J Rankine, Gilmour

Celtic beat Third Lanark (5-1), Alloa (2-1), Solway Star (2-0), St Mirren (0-0, 1-1, 1-0), Rangers (5-0)

1926

10 April   Hampden Park   att: 98,620

St Mirren 2 Celtic 0

Scorers St Mirren: McCrae, Howieson

Teams St Mirren: Bradford; Findlay, Newbiggin; Morrison, Summers, McDonald; Morgan, Gebbie, McCrae, Howieson, Thomson

Celtic: Shevlin; W McStay, Hilley; Wilson, J McStay, McFarlane; Connolly, Thomson, McGrory, McInally, Leitch

St Mirren beat Mid-Annandale (4-0), Arbroath (0-0, 3-0), Partick Thistle (2-1), Airdrie (2-0), Rangers (1-0)

1927

16 April   Hampden Park   att: 80,070

Celtic 3 East Fife 1

Scorers Celtic: Robertson (own goal), McLean, Connolly
    East Fife: Wood

Teams Celtic: J Thomson; W McStay, Hilley; Wilson, J McStay, McFarlane; Connolly, A Thomson, McInally, McMenemy, McLean

East Fife: Gilfillan; Robertson, Gillespie; Hope, Brown, Russell; Weir, Paterson, Wood, Barrett, Edgar

Celtic beat Queen of the South (0-0, 4-1), Brechin City (6-3), Dundee (4-2), Bo'ness (5-2), Falkirk (1-0)

1928   FIRST 100,000+

14 April   Hampden Park 5 att: 118,115

Rangers 4 Celtic 0

Scorers Rangers: Meiklejohn (pen), McPhail, Archibald (2)

Teams Rangers: T Hamilton; Gray, R Hamilton; Buchanan, Meiklejohn, Craig; Archibald, Cunningham, Fleming, McPhail, Morton

Celtic: J Thomson; W McStay, Donoghue; Wilson, J McStay, McFarlane; Connolly, A Thomson, McGrory, McInally, McLean

Rangers beat East Stirlingshire (6-0), Cowdenbeath (4-2), King's Park (3-1), Albion Rovers (1-0), Hibs (3-0)

1929

6 April   Hampden Park   att: 114,708 (2)

Kilmarnock 2 Rangers 0

Scorers Kilmarnock: Aitken, Williamson

Teams Kilmarnock: Clemie; Robertson, Nibloe; Morton, McLaren, McEwan; Connell, Smith, Cunningham, Williamson, Aitken

Rangers: T Hamilton; Gray, R Hamilton; Buchanan, Meiklejohn, Craig; Archibald, Muirhead, Fleming, McPhail, Morton

Kilmarnock beat Glasgow University (8-1), Bo' ness (3-2), Albion Rovers (1-0), Raith Rovers (3-2), Celtic (1-0)

1930

12 April   Hampden Park   att: 107,475 (3)

Rangers 0 Partick Thistle 0

Teams Rangers: T Hamilton; Gray, R Hamilton; Buchanan, Meiklejohn, Craig; Archibald, Marshall, Fleming, McPhail, Nicholson

Partick Thistle: Jackson; Calderwood, Rae; Elliot, Lambie, McLeod; Ness, Grove, Boardman, Ballantyne, Torbet

16 April   Hampden Park   att: 103,686 (4)
Rangers 2 Partick Thistle 1 (replay)
Scorers Rangers: Marshall, Craig
       Partick Thistle: Torbet
Teams Rangers: T Hamilton; Gray, R Hamilton; McDonald, Meiklejohn, Craig; Archibald, Marshall, Fleming, McPhail, Morton
      Partick Thistle: (as above)
Rangers beat Queen's Park (1-0), Cowdenbeath (2-2, 3-0), Motherwell (5-2), Montrose (3-0), Hearts (4-1)

1931
11 April   Hampden Park   att: 105,000 (5)
Celtic 2 Mothewell 2
Scorers Celtic: McGrory, Craig (own goal)
      Motherwell: Stevenson, McMenemy
Teams Celtic: J Thomson; Cook, McGonagle; Wilson, McStay, Geatons; R Thomson, A Thomson, McGrory, Scarff, Napier
      Motherwell: McClory; Johnman, Hunter; Wales, Craig, Telfer; Murdoch, McMenemy, McFadyen, Stevenson, Ferrier
15 April   Hampden Park   att: 98,579
Celtic 4 Motherwell 2 (replay)
Scorers Celtic: Thomson (2), McGrory (2)
      Motherwell: Murdoch, Stevenson
Teams Celtic: (as above)
      Motherwell: (as above)
Celtic beat East Fife (2-1), Dundee United (3-2), Morton (4-1), Aberdeen (4-0), Kilmarnock (3-0)

1932
16 April   Hampden Park   att: 111,982 (6)
Rangers 1 Kilmarnock 1
Scorers Rangers: McPhail
      Kilmarnock: Maxwell
Teams Rangers: Hamilton; Gray, McAuley; Meiklejohn, Simpson, Brown; Archibald, Marshall, English, McPhail, Morton
      Kilmarnock: Bell; Leslie, Nibloe; Morton, Smith, McEwan; Connell, Muir, Maxwell, Duncan, Aitken
20 April   Hampden Park   att: 104,695 (7)
Rangers 3 Kilmarnock 0 (replay)
Scorers Rangers: Fleming, McPhail, English
Teams Rangers: Hamilton; Gray, McAuley; Meiklejohn, Simpson, Brown; Archibald, Marshall, English, McPhail, Fleming
      Kilmarnock: (as above)
Rangers beat Brechin City (8-2), Raith Rovers (5-0), Hearts (1-0), Motherwell (2-0), Hamilton Academical (5-2)

1933
15 April   Hampden Park   att: 102,339 (8)
Celtic 1 Motherwell 0
Scorers Celtic: McGrory
Teams Celtic: Kennaway; Hogg, McGonagle; Wilson, McStay, Geatons; R Thomson, A Thomson, McGrory, Napier, H O'Donnell
      Motherwell: McClory; Crapnell, Ellis; Wales, Blair, Mackenzie; Murdoch, McMenemy, McFadyen, Stevenson, Ferrier
      Celtic beat Dunfermline Athletic (7-1), Falkirk (2-0), Partick Thistle (2-1), Albion Rovers (1-1, 3-1), Hearts (0-0, 2-1)

1934
21 April   Hampden Park   att: 113,403 (9)
Rangers 5 St Mirren 0
Scorers Rangers: Nicholson (2), McPhail, Main, Smith
Teams Rangers: Hamilton; Gray, McDonald; Meiklejohn, Simpson, Brown; Main, Marshall, Smith, McPhail, Nicholson
      St Mirren: McCloy; Hay, Ancell; Gebbie, Wilson, Miller; Knox, Latimer, McGregor, McCabe, Phillips
Rangers beat Blairgowrie (14-2), Third Lanark (3-0), Hearts (0-0, 2-1), Aberdeen (1-0), St Johnstone (1-0)

1935
20 April   Hampden Park   att: 87,286
Rangers 2 Hamilton Academical 1
Scorers Rangers: Smith (2)
      Hamilton Academical: Harrison
Teams Rangers: Dawson; Gray, McDonald; Kennedy, Simpson, Brown; Main, Venters, Smith, McPhail, Gillick
      Hamilton Academical: Morgan; Wallace, Bulloch; Cox, McStay, Murray; King, McLaren, Wilson, Harrison, Reid
Rangers beat Cowdenbeath (3-1), Third Lanark (2-0), St Mirren (1-0), Motherwell (4-1), Hearts (1-1, 2-0)

1936
18 April   Hampden Park   att: 88,859
Rangers 1 Third Lanark 0
Scorers Rangers: McPhail
Teams Rangers: Dawson; Gray, Cheyne; Meiklejohn, Simpson, Brown; Fiddes, Venters, Smith, McPhail, Turnbull
      Third Lanark: Muir; Carabine, Hamilton; Blair, Denmark, McInnes; Howe, Gallacher, Hay, Kennedy, Kinnaird
Rangers beat East Fife (3-1), Albion Rovers (3-1), St Mirren (2-1), Aberdeen (1-0), Clyde (3-0)

1937
24 April   Hampden Park   att: 147,365 (10)
Celtic 2 Aberdeen 1   HIGHEST
Scorers Celtic: Crum, Buchan   CUP ATTENDANCE
      Aberdeen: Armstrong
Teams Celtic: Kennaway; Hogg, Morrison; Geatons, Lyon, Paterson; Delaney, Buchan, McGrory, Crum, Murphy
      Aberdeen: Johnstone; Cooper, Temple; Dunlop, Falloon, Thomson; Benyon, McKenzie, Armstrong, Mills, Laing
Celtic beat Stenhousmuir (1-1, 2-0), Albion Rovers (5-2), East Fife (3-0), Motherwell (4-4, 2-1), Clyde (2-0)

1938
23rd April   Hampden Park   att: 80,091
East Fife 1 Kilmarnock 1
Scorers East Fife: McLeod
      Kilmarnock: McAvoy
Teams East Fife: Milton; Laird, Tait; Russell, Sneddon, Herd; Adams, McLeod, McCartney, Miller, McKerrell
      Kilmarnock: Hunter; Fyfe, Milloy; Robertson, Stewart, Ross; Thomson, Reid, Collins, McAvoy, McGrogan
27 April   Hampden Park   att: 92,716
East Fife 4 Kilmarnock 2 (replay, after extra time)
Scorers East Fife: McKerrell (2), McLeod, Miller
      Kilmarnock: Thomson (pen), McGrogan
Teams East Fife: Milton; Laird, Tait; Russell, Sneddon, Harvey; Adams, McLeod, McCartney, Miller, McKerrell
      Kilmarnock: (as above)
East Fife beat Airdrie (2-1), Dundee United (5-0), Aberdeen (1-1, 2-1), Raith Rovers (2-2, 3-2), St Bernard's (1-1, 1-1, 2-1)

235

1939
22 April   Hampden Park   att: 94,799
Clyde 4 Motherwell 0
Scorers Clyde: Wallace, Martin (2), Noble
Teams Clyde: Brown; Kirk, Hickie; Beaton, Falloon, Weir; Robertson, Noble, Martin, Wallace, Gillies

Motherwell: Murray; Wales, Ellis; Mackenzie, Blair, Telfer; Ogilvie, Bremner, Mathie, Stevenson, McCulloch
Clyde beat St Johnstone (2-0), Dundee (0-0, 1-0), Rangers (4-1), Third Lanark (1-0), Hibernian (1-0)

1947
19 April   Hampden Park   att: 82,140
Aberdeen 2 Hibernian 1
Scorers Aberdeen: Hamilton, Williams
Hibernian: Cuthbertson
Teams Aberdeen: Johnstone; McKenna, Taylor; McLaughlin, Dunlop, Waddell; Harris, Hamilton, Williams, Baird, McCall

Hibernian: Kerr; Govan, Shaw; Howie, Aird, Kean; Smith, Finnigan, Cuthbertson, Turnbull Ormond.
Aberdeen beat Partick Thistle (2-1), Ayr United (8-0), Morton (1-1, 2-1), Dundee (2-1), Arbroath (2-0)

1948
17 April   Hampden Park   att: 129,176 (11)
Rangers 1 Morton 1 (after extra time)
Scorers Rangers: Gillick
Morton: Whyte
Teams Rangers: Brown; Young, Shaw; McColl, Woodburn, Cox; Rutherford, Gillick, Thornton, Findlay, Duncanson

Morton: Cowan; Mitchell, Whigham; Campbell, Miller, Whyte; Hepburn, Murphy, Cupples, Orr, Liddell

21 April   Hampden Park   att: 131,975 (12)
Rangers 1 Morton 0 (replay after extra time)
Scorers Rangers: Williamson
Teams Rangers: Brown; Young, Shaw; McColl, Woodburn, Cox; Rutherford, Thornton, Williamson, Duncanson, Gillick

Morton: (as above)
Rangers beat Stranraer (1-0), Leith Athletic (4-0), Partick Thistle (3-0), East Fife (1-0), Hibs (1-0)

1949
23 April   Hampden Park   att: 108,435 (13)
Rangers 4 Clyde 1
Scorers Rangers: Young (2 pens), Williamson, Duncanson
Clyde: Galletly
Teams Rangers: Brown; Young, Shaw; McColl, Woodburn, Cox; Waddell, Duncanson, Thornton, Williamson, Rutherford

Clyde: Cullan; Gibson, Mennie; Campbell, Milligan, Long; Davies, Wright, Linwood, Galletly, Bootland
Rangers beat Elgin City (6-1), Motherwell (3-0), bye, Partick Thistle (4-0), East Fife (3-0)

1950
22 April   Hampden Park   att: 118,262 (14)
Rangers 3 East Fife 0
Scorers Rangers: Findlay, Thornton (2)
Teams Rangers: Brown; Young, Shaw; McColl, Woodburn, Cox; Rutherford, Findlay, Thornton, Duncanson, Rae

East Fife: Easson; Laird, Stewart; Philp, Finlay, Aitken; Black, Fleming, Morris, Brown, Duncan
Rangers beat Motherwell (4-2), Cowdenbeath (8-0), bye, Raith Rovers (1-1, 1-1, 2-0), Queen of the South (1-1, 3-0)

1951
21 April   Hampden Park   att: 131,943 (15)
Celtic 1 Motherwell 0
Scorers Celtic: McPhail
Teams Celtic: Hunter; Fallon, Rollo; Evans, Boden, Baillie; Weir, Collins, J McPhail, Peacock, Tully

Motherwell: Johnstone; Kilmarnock, Shaw; McLeod, Paton, Redpath; Humphries, Forrest, Kelly, Watson, Aitkenhead
Celtic beat East Fife (2-2, 4-2), Duns (4-0), Hearts (2-1), Aberdeen (3-0), Raith Rovers (3-2)

1952
19 April   Hampden Park   att: 136,304 (16)
Motherwell 4 Dundee 0 HIGHEST POST
Scorers Motherwell: Watson, Redpath, Humphries, Kelly
Teams Motherwell: Johnstone; Kilmarnock, Shaw; Cox, Paton, Redpath; Sloan, Humphries, Kelly, Watson, Aitkenhead

Dundee: Henderson; Follon, Cowan; Gallagher, Cowie, Boyd; Hill, Patillo, Flavell, Steel, Christie
Motherwell beat Forfar Athletic (4-0), St Mirren (3-2), Dunfermline Athletic (1-1, 4-0), Rangers (1-1, 2-1), Hearts (1-1, 1-1, 3-1)

1953
25 April   Hampden Park   att: 129,861 (17)
Rangers 1 Aberdeen 1
Scorers Rangers: Prentice
Aberdeen: Yorston
Teams Rangers: Niven; Young, Little; McColl, Stanners, Pryde; Waddell, Grierson, Paton, Prentice, Hubbard

Aberdeen: Martin; Mitchell, Shaw; Harris, Young, Allister; Rodger, Yorston, Buckley, Hamilton, Hather

29 April   Hampden Park   att: 112,619 (18)
Rangers 1 Aberdeen 0 (replay)
Scorers Rangers: Simpson
Teams Rangers: Niven; Young, Little; McColl, Woodburn, Pryde; Waddell, Grierson, Simpson, Paton, Hubbard
Aberdeen: (as above)
Rangers beat Arbroath (4-0), Dundee (2-0), Morton (4-1), Celtic (2-0), Hearts (2-1)

1954
24 April   Hampden Park   att: 129,926 (19)
Celtic 2 Aberdeen 1
Scorers Celtic: Young (own goal), Fallon
Aberdeen: Buckley
Teams Celtic: Bonnar; Haughney, Meechan; Evans, Stein, Peacock; Higgins, Fernie, Fallon, Tully, Mochan

Aberdeen: Martin; Mitchell, Caldwell; Allister, Young, Glen; Leggat, Hamilton, Buckley, Clunie, Hather
Celtic beat Falkirk (2-1), Stirling Albion (4-3), Hamilton Academical (2-1), Motherwell (2-2, 3-1)

1955
23 April   Hampden Park   att: 106,111 (120)
Clyde 1 Celtic 1
Scorers Clyde: Robertson
Celtic: Walsh
Teams Clyde: Hewkins; Murphy, Haddock; Granville, Anderson, Laing; Divers, Robertson, Hill, Brown, Ring

Celtic: Bonnar; Haughney, Meechan; Evans, Stein, Peacock; Collins, Fernie, W McPhail, Walsh, Tully

27 April   Hampden Park   att: 68,735
Clyde 1 Celtic 0
Scorers Clyde: Ring
Teams Clyde: (as above)
    Celtic: Bonnar; Haughney, Meechan; Evans, Stein, Peacock; Walsh, Fernie, Fallon, W McPhail, Tully
Clyde beat Albion Rovers (3-0), Raith Rovers (3-1), Falkirk (5-0), Aberdeen (2-2, 1-0)

1956
(2.1)

21 April   Hampden Park   att: 133,399
Heart of Midlothian 3 Celtic 1
Scorers Heart of Midlothian: Crawford (2), Conn
    Celtic: Haughney
Teams Heart of Midlothian: Cuff; Kirk, Mackenzie; Mackay, Glidden, Cumming; Young, Conn, Bauld, Wardhaugh, Crawford
    Celtic: Beattie; Meechan, Fallon; Smith, Evans, Peacock; Craig, Haughney, Mochan, Fernie, Tully
Heart of Midlothian beat Forfar Athletic (3-0), Stirling Albion (5-0), Rangers (4-0), Raith Rovers (0-0, 3-0)

1957

20 April   Hampden Park   att: 81,057
Falkirk 1 Kilmarnock 1
Scorers Falkirk: Prentice (pen)
    Kilmarnock: Curlett
Teams Falkirk: Slater; Parker, Rae; Wright, Irvine, Prentice; Murray, Grierson, Merchant, Moran, O'Hara
    Kilmarnock: Brown; Collins, J Stewart; R Stewart, Toner, Mackay; Mays, Harvey, Curlett, Black, Burns

24 April   Hampden Park   att: 79,785
Falkirk 2 Kilmarnock 1 (replay after extra time)
Scorers Falkirk: Merchant, Moran
    Kilmarnock: Curlett
Teams Falkirk: (as above)
    Kilmarnock: (as above)
Falkirk beat Berwick Rangers (2-1), Aberdeen (3-1), Clyde (2-1), Raith Rovers (2-2, 2-0)

1958

26 April   Hampden Park   att: 95,123
Clyde 1 Hibernian 0
Scorers Clyde: Coyle
Teams Clyde: McCulloch; Murphy, Haddock; Walters, Finlay, Clinton; Herd, Currie, Coyle, Robertson, Ring
    Hibernian: Leslie; Grant, McClelland; Turnbull, Plenderleith, Baxter; Fraser, Aitken, Baker, Preston, Ormond
Clyde beat Dumbarton (5-0), Arbroath (4-0), Celtic (2-0), Falkirk (2-1), Motherwell (3-2)

1959
(22)

25 April   Hampden Park   att: 108,591
St Mirren 3 Aberdeen 1
Scorers St Mirren: Bryceland, Miller, Baker
    Aberdeen: Baird
Teams St Mirren: Walker; Lapsley, Wilson; Neilson, McGugan, Leishman; Rodger, Bryceland, Baker, Gemmell, Miller
    Aberdeen: Martin; Caldwell, Hogg; Brownlie, Clunie, Glen; Ewan, Davidson, Baird, Wishart, Hather
St Mirren beat bye, Peebles Rovers (10-0), Motherwell (3-2), Dunfermline Athletic (2-1), Celtic (4-0)

1960
(23)

23 April   Hampden Park   att: 108,017
Rangers 2 Kilmarnock 0
Scorers Rangers: Millar (2)
Teams Rangers: Niven; Caldow, Little; McColl, Paterson, Stevenson; Scott, McMillan, Millar, Baird, Wilson
    Kilmarnock: Brown; Richmond, Watson; Beattie, Toner, Kennedy; Stewart, McInally, Kerr, Black, Muir
Rangers beat Berwick Rangers (3-1), Arbroath (2-0), Stenhousemuir (3-0), Hibs (3-2), Celtic (1-1, 4-1)

1961
(24)

22 April   Hampden Park   att: 113,618
Dunfermline Athletic 0 Celtic 0
Teams Dunfermline Athletic: Connachan; Fraser, Cunningham; Mailer, Williamson, Miller; Peebles, Smith, Dickson, McLindon, Melrose
    Celtic: Haffey; McKay, Kennedy; Crerand, McNeill, Clark; Gallagher, Fernie, Hughes, Chalmers, Byrne

26 April   Hampden Park   att: 87,866
Dunfermline Athletic 2 Celtic 0 (replay)
Scorers Dunfermline Athletic: Thomson, Dickson
Teams Dunfermline Athletic: Connachan; Fraser, Cunningham; Mailer, Miller, Sweeney; Peebles, Smith, Thomson, Dickson, Melrose
    Celtic: Haffey; McKay, O'Neill; Crerand, McNeill, Clark; Gallagher, Fernie, Hughes, Chalmers Byrne
Dunfermline Athletic beat Berwick Rangers (4-1), Stranraer (3-1), Aberdeen (6-3), Alloa (4-0), St Mirren (0-0, 1-0)

1962
(25)

21 April   Hampden Park   att: 126,930
Rangers 2 St Mirren 0
Scorers Rangers: Brand, Wilson
Teams Rangers: Ritchie; Shearer, Caldow; Davis, McKinnon, Baxter; Henderson, McMillan, Millar, Brand, Wilson
    St Mirren: Williamson; Campbell, Wilson; Stewart, Clunie, McLean; Henderson, Bryceland, Kerrigan, Fernie, Beck
Rangers beat Falkirk (2-1), Arbroath (6-0), Aberdeen (2-2, 5-1), Kilmarnock (4-2), Motherwell (3-1)

1963
(26)

4 May   Hampden Park   att: 129,527
Rangers 1 Celtic 1
Scorers Rangers: Brand
    Celtic: Murdoch
Teams Rangers: Ritchie; Shearer, Provan; Greig, McKinnon, Baxter; Henderson, McLean, Millar, Brand, Wilson
    Celtic: Haffey; McKay, Kennedy; McNamee, McNeill, Price; Johnstone, Murdoch, Hughes, Divers, Brogan

15 May   Hampden Park   att: 120,263
(27)
Rangers 3 Celtic 0 (replay)
Scorers Rangers: Brand (2), Wilson
Teams Rangers: Ritchie; Shearer, Provan; Greig, McKinnon, Baxter; Henderson, McMillan, Millar, Brand, Wilson
    Celtic: Haffey; McKay, Kennedy; McNamee, McNeill, Price; Craig, Murdoch, Divers, Chalmers, Hughes
Rangers beat Airdrie (6-0), East Stirlingshire (7-2), Dundee (1-1, 3-2), Dundee United (5-2)

1964
25 April — Hampden Park — att: 120,982 (28)

Rangers 3 Dundee 1

Scorers Rangers: Millar (2), Brand
Dundee: Cameron

Teams Rangers: Ritchie; Shearer, Provan; Greig, McKinnon, Baxter; Henderson, McLean, Millar, Brand, Wilson
Dundee: Slater; Hamilton, Cox; Seith, Ryden, Stuart; Penman, Cousin, Cameron, Gilzean, Robertson
Rangers beat Stenhousemuir (5-1), Duns (9-0), Partick Thistle (3-0), Celtic (2-0), Dunfermline Athletic (1-0)

1965
24 April — Hampden Park — att: 108,800 (29)

Celtic 3 Dunfermline Athletic 2

Scorers Celtic: Auld (2), McNeill
Dunfermline Athletic: Melrose, McLaughlin

Teams Celtic: Fallon; Young, Gemmell; Murdoch, McNeill, Clark; Chalmers, Gallagher, Hughes, Lennox, Auld
Dunfermline Athletic: Herriot; W Callaghan, Lunn; Thomson, McLean, T Callaghan; Edwards, Smith, McLaughlin, Melrose, Sinclair
Celtic beat St Mirren (3-0), Queen's Park (1-0), Kilmarnock (3-2), Motherwell (2-2, 3-0)

1966
23 April — Hampden Park — att: 126,552 (30)

Rangers 0 Celtic 0

Teams Rangers: Ritchie; Johansen, Provan; Greig, McKinnon, Millar, Wilson, Watson, Forrest, Johnstone, Henderson
Celtic: Simpson; Young, Gemmell; Murdoch, McNeill, Clark; Johnstone, McBride, Chalmers, Gallagher, Hughes

27 April — Hampden Park — att: 98,202

Rangers 1 Celtic 0 (replay)

Scorers Rangers: Johansen

Teams Rangers: Ritchie; Johansen, Provan; Greig, McKinnon, Millar, Henderson, Watson, McLean, Johnstone, Wilson
Celtic: Simpson; Craig, Gemmell; Murdoch, McNeill, Clark; Johnstone, McBride, Chalmers, Auld, Hughes
Rangers beat Airdrie (5-1), Ross County (2-0), St Johnstone (1-0), Aberdeen (0-0, 2-1)

1967
29 April — Hampden Park — att: 127,117 (31)

Celtic 2 Aberdeen 0

Scorers Celtic: Wallace (2)

Teams Celtic: Simpson; Craig, Gemmell; Murdoch, McNeill, Clark; Johnstone, Wallace, Chalmers, Auld, Lennox
Aberdeen: Clark; Whyte, Shewan; Munro, McMillan, Petersen; Wilson, Smith, Storrie, Melrose, Johnston
Celtic beat Arbroath (4-0), Elgin City (7-0), Queen's Park (5-3), Clyde (0-0, 2-0)

1968
27 April — Hampden Park — att: 56,366

Dunfermline Athletic 3 Heart of Midlothian 1

Scorers Dunfermline Athletic: Gardner (2), Lister (pen)
Heart of Midlothian: Lunn (own goal)

Teams Dunfermline Athletic: Martin; W Callaghan, Lunn; McGarty, Barry, T Callaghan; Lister, Paton, Gardner, Robertson, Edwards, Sub: Thomson (not used)
Heart of Midlothian: Cruikshank; Sneddon, Mann; Anderson, Thomson, Miller; Jensen (sub Moller), Townsend, Ford, Irvine, Traynor
Dunfermline Athletic beat Celtic (2-0), Aberdeen (2-1), Partick Thistle (1-0), St Johnstone (1-1, 2-1)

1969
26 April — Hampden Park — att: 132,870 (32)

Celtic 4 Rangers 0

Scorers Celtic: McNeill, Lennox, Connelly, Chalmers

Teams Celtic: Fallon; Craig, Gemmell; Murdoch, McNeill, Brogan (sub Clark); Connelly, Chalmers, Wallace, Lennox, Auld
Rangers: Martin; Johansen, Mathieson; Greig, McKinnon, Smith; Henderson, Penman, Ferguson, Johnston, Persson, Sub: Jardine (not used)
Celtic beat Partick Thistle (3-3, 8-1), Clyde (0-0, 3-0), St Johnstone (3-2), Morton (4-1)

1970
11 April — Hampden Park — att: 108,244 (33)

Aberdeen 3 Celtic 1

Scorers Aberdeen: Harper (pen), McKay (2)
Celtic: Lennox

Teams Aberdeen: Clark; Boel, Murray; Hermiston, McMillan, M Buchan; McKay, Robb, Forrest, Harper, Graham, Sub: G Buchan (not used)
Celtic: Williams; Hay, Gemmell; Murdoch, McNeill, Brogan, Johnstone, Wallace, Connelly, Lennox, Hughes, (Sub: Auld)
Aberdeen beat Clyde (4-0), Clydebank (2-1), Falkirk (1-0), Kilmarnock (1-0)

1971
8 May — Hampden Park — att: 120,027 (34)

Celtic 1 Rangers 1

Scorers Celtic: Lennox
Rangers: D Johnstone

Teams Celtic: Williams: Craig, Brogan; Connelly, McNeill, Hay; Johnstone, Lennox, Wallace, Callaghan, Hood, Sub: Macari (not used)
Rangers: McCloy; Miller, Mathieson; Greig, McKinnon, Jackson; Henderson, Penman (sub D Johnstone), Stein, A MacDonald, W Johnston

12 May — Hampden Park — att: 103,297 (35)

Celtic 2 Rangers 1 (replay)

Scorers Celtic: Macari, Hood (pen)
Rangers: Craig (own goal)

Teams Celtic: Williams; Craig, Brogan; Connelly, McNeill, Hay; Johnstone, Macari, Hood (sub Wallace), Callaghan, Lennox
Rangers: McCloy; Denny, Mathieson; Greig, McKinnon, Jackson; Henderson, Penman (sub D Johnstone), Stein, A MacDonald, W Johnston
Celtic beat Queen of the South (5-1), Dunfermline (1-1, 1-0), Raith Rovers (7-1), Airdrie (3-3, 2-0)

1972
6 May — Hampden Park — att: 105,909 (36)

Celtic 6 Hibernian 1

Scorers Celtic: McNeill, Deans (3), Macari (2)
Hibernian: Gordon

Teams Celtic: Williams; Craig, Brogan; Murdoch, McNeill, Connelly; Johnstone, Deans, Macari, Dalglish, Callaghan, Sub: Lennox (not used)
Hibernian: Herriot; Brownlie, Schaedler; Stanton, Black Blackley; Edwards, Hazel, Gordon, O'Rourke, Duncan, (sub Auld)
Celtic beat Albion Rovers (5-0), Dundee (4-0), Hearts (1-1, 1-0), Kilmarnock (3-1)

1973 (37)

5 May Hampden Park I O att: 122,714
Rangers 3 Celtic 2
Scorers Rangers: Parlane, Conn, Forsyth CARS
Celtic: Dalglish, Connelly (pen)
Teams Rangers: McCloy; Jardine, Mathieson; Greig, Johnstone, A MacDonald; McLean, Forsyth, Parlane, Conn, Young, Sub: Smith (not used)
Celtic: Hunter; McGrain, Brogan (sub Lennox); Murdoch, McNeill, Connelly; Johnstone, Deans, Dalglish, Hay, Callaghan
Rangers beat Dundee United (1-0), Hibs (1-1, 2-1), Airdrie (2-0), Ayr United (2-0)

Lost 100+

1974

4 May Hampden Park att: 75,959
Celtic 3 Dundee United 0
Scorers Celtic: Hood, Murray, Deans
Teams Celtic: Connaghan; McGrain (sub Callaghan), Brogan; Murray, McNeill, McCluskey; Johnstone, Hood, Deans, Hay, Dalglish, Sub: Lennox (not used)
Dundee United: Davie; Gardner, Kopel; Copland, D Smith (sub Traynor), W Smith; Payne (sub Rolland), Knox, Gray, Fleming, Houston
Celtic beat Clydebank (6-1), Stirling Albion (6-1), Motherwell (2-2, 1-0), Dundee (1-0)

1975

3 May Hampden Park att: 75,457
Celtic 3 Airdrieonians 1
Scorers Celtic: Wilson (2), McCluskey (pen)
Airdrieonians: McCann
Teams Celtic: Latchford; McGrain, Lynch; Murray, McNeill, McCluskey; Hood, Glavin, Dalglish, Lennox, Wilson, Subs: Callaghan, McDonald (neither used)
Airdrieonians: McWilliams; Jonquin, Cowan; Menzies, Black, Whiteford; McCann, Walker, McCulloch (sub March), Lapsley (sub Reynolds), Wilson
Celtic beat Hibs (2-0), Clydebank (4-1), Dumbarton (2-1), Dundee (1-0)

1976

1 May Hampden Park att: 85,250
Rangers 3 Heart of Midlothian 1
Scorers Rangers: Johnstone (2), MacDonald
Heart of Midlothian: Shaw
Teams Rangers: McCloy; Miller, Greig; Forsyth, Jackson, A MacDonald; McKean, Hamilton (sub Jardine), Henderson, McLean, Johnstone, Sub: Parlane (not used)
Heart of Midlothian: Cruikshank; Brown, Burrell (sub Aird); Jeffries, Gallagher, Kay; Gibson (sub Park), Busby, Shaw, Callaghan, Prentice
Rangers beat East Fife (3-0), Aberdeen (4-1), Queen of the South (5-0), Motherwell (3-2)

1977

7 May Hampden Park 5-5 att: 54,252
Celtic 1 Rangers 0
Scorers Celtic: Lynch (pen)
Teams Celtic: Latchford; McGrain, Lynch; Stanton, McDonald, Aitken; Dalglish, Edvaldsson, Craig, Conn, Wilson, Subs Doyle, Burns (neither used)
Rangers: Kennedy; Jardine, Greig; Forsyth, Jackson, Watson (sub Robertson); McLean, Hamilton, Parlane, A MacDonald, Johnstone, Sub: Miller (not used)
Celtic beat Airdrie (1-1, 5-0), Ayr United (1-1, 3-1), Queen of the South (5-1), Dundee (2-0)

1978

6 May Hampden Park att: 61,563
Rangers 2 Aberdeen 1
Scorers Rangers: MacDonald, Johnstone
Aberdeen: Ritchie
Teams Rangers: McCloy; Jardine, Greig; Forsyth, Jackson, A MacDonald; McLean, Rusell, Johnstone, Smith, Cooper (sub Watson), Sub: Robertson (not used)
Aberdeen: Clark; Kennedy, Ritchie; McMaster, Garner, Miller; Sullivan, Fleming (sub Scanlon), Harper, Jarvie, Davidson, Sub: McLelland (not used)
Rangers beat Berwick Rangers (4-2), Stirling Albion (1-0), Kilmarnock (4-1), Dundee United (2-0)

1979

12 May Hampden Park att: 50,260
Rangers 0 Hibernian 0
Teams Rangers: McCloy; Jardine, Dawson; Johnstone, Jackson, A MacDonald (sub Miller); McLean, Russell, Parlane, Smith, Cooper, Sub: Urquhart (not used)
Hibernian: McArthur; Brazil, Duncan; Bremner, Stewart, McNamara; Hutchison (sub Rae), McLeod, Campbell, Callachan, Higgins, Sub: Brown (not used)

16 May Hampden Park att: 33,508
Rangers 0 Hibernian 0 (replay, after extra time)
Teams Rangers: McCloy; Jardine, Dawson; Johnstone, Jackson, A MacDonald; McLean (sub Miller), Russell, Parlane, Smith, Cooper, Sub: Urquhart (not used)
Hibernian: McArthur; Brazil, Duncan; Bremner, Stewart, McNamara; Rae, McLeod, Campbell, Callachan, Higgins (sub Brown), Sub: Hutchison (not used)

28 May Hampden Park att: 30,602
Rangers 3 Hibernian 2 (second replay, after extra time)
Scorers Rangers: Johnstone (2), Duncan (own goal)
Hibernian: Higgins, McLeod (pen)
Teams Rangers: McCloy; Jardine, Dawson; Johnstone, Jackson, Watson (sub Miller); McLean (sub Smith), Russell, Parlane, A MacDonald, Cooper
Hibernian: McArthur; Brazil, Duncan; Bremner, Stewart, McNamara; Rae, McLeod, Campbell, Callachan (sub Brown), Higgins (sub Hutchison)
Rangers beat Motherwell (3-1), Kilmarnock (1-1, 1-0), Dundee (6-3), Partick Thistle (0-0, 1-0)

1980 12

10 May Hampden Park CLRS att: 70,303
Celtic 1 Rangers 0 (after extra time)
Scorers Celtic: McCluskey
Teams Celtic: Latchford; Sneddon, McGrain; Aitken, Conroy, MacLeod; Provan, Doyle (sub Lennox), McCluskey, Burns, McGarvey, Sub: Davidson (not used)
Rangers: McCloy; Jardine, Dawson; Forsyth (sub Miller), Jackson, Stevens; Cooper, Russell, Johnstone, Smith, J MacDonald (sub McLean)
Celtic beat Raith Rovers (2-1), St Mirren (1-1, 3-2), Morton (2-0), Hibs (5-0)

1981

9 May　　　　　　Hampden Park　　　　att: 53,000

Rangers 0 Dundee United 0 (after extra time)

Teams Rangers: Stewart; Jardine, Dawson; Stevens, Forsyth, Bett; McLean, Russell, McAdam (sub Cooper), Redford, W Johnston, (sub J MacDonald)

　　Dundee United: McAlpine; Holt, Kopel; Phillips (sub Stark), Hegarty, Narey; Bannon, Milne (sub Pettigrew), Kirkwood, Sturrock, Dodds.

12 May　　　　　　Hampden Park　　　　att: 43,099

Rangers 4 Dundee United 1

Scorers Rangers: Cooper, Russell, MacDonald (2)
　　Dundee United: Dodds

Teams Rangers: Stewart; Jardine, Dawson; Stevens, Forsyth, Bett; Cooper, Russell, D Johnstone, Redford, J MacDonald, Subs: McLean, McAdam (neither used)

　　Dundee United: McAlpine; Holt, Kopel; Phillip (sub Stark), Hegarty, Narey; Bannon, Milne, Kirkwood, Sturrock, Dodds, Sub: Pettigrew (not used)

Rangers beat Airdrie (5-0), St Johnstone (3-3, 3-1), Hibs (3-1), Morton (2-1)

1982

22 May　　　　　　Hampden Park　　　　att: 53,788

Aberdeen 4 Rangers 1 (after extra time)

Scorers Aberdeen: McLeish, McGhee, Strachan, Cooper
　　Rangers: MacDonald

Teams Aberdeen: Leighton; Kennedy, Rougvie; McMaster (sub Bell), McLeish, Miller; Strachan, Cooper, McGhee, Simpson, Hewitt (sub Black)

　　Rangers: Stewart; Jardine (sub McAdam), Dawson; McClelland, Jackson, Bett; Cooper, Russell, Dalziel (sub McLean), Miller, J MacDonald

Aberdeen beat Motherwell (1-0), Celtic (1-0), Kilmarnock (4-2), St Mirren (1-1, 3-2)

1983

21 May　　　　　　Hampden Park　　　　att: 62,979

Aberdeen 1 Rangers 0 (after extra time)

Scorers Aberdeen: Black

Teams Aberdeen: Leighton; Rougvie (sub Watson), McMaster; Cooper, McLeish, Miller; Strachan, Simpson, McGhee, Black, Weir (sub Hewitt)

　　Rangers: McCloy; Dawson, McClelland; McPherson, Paterson, Bett; Cooper (sub Davis), McKinnon, Clark, Russell, J MacDonald (sub Dalziel)

Aberdeen beat Hibs (4-1), Dundee (1-0), Partick Thistle (2-1), Celtic (1-0)

1984

19 May　　　　　　Hampden Park　　　　att: 58,900

Aberdeen 2 Celtic 1 (after extra time)

Scorers Aberdeen: Black, McGhee
　　Celtic: P McStay

Teams Aberdeen: Leighton; McKimmie, Rougvie (sub Stark); Cooper, McLeish, Miller; Strachan, Simpson, McGhee, Black Weir (sub Bell)

　　Celtic: Bonnar; McGrain, Reid (sub Melrose); Aitken, W McStay, MacLeod; Provan, P McStay, McGarvey, Burns, McClair (sub Sinclair)

Aberdeen beat Kilmarnock (1-1, 3-1), Clyde (2-0), Dundee United (0-0, 1-0), Dundee (2-0)

1985

18 May　　　　　　Hampden Park　　　　att: 60,346

Celtic 2 Dundee United 1

Scorers Celtic: Provan, Mc Garvey.
　　Dundee United: Beedie

Teams: Celtic: Bonnar, W. Mc Stay, McGrain, Aitken, McAdam, MacLeod; Provan, P. McStay, Johnston, Burns, McGarvey. Subs: O'Leary, McClair.
Dundee United: McAlpine; Malpas Beedie, Gough, Hegarty, Narey; Bannon, Milne, Kirkwood, Sturrock, Dodds. Subs: Holt, Coyne.
Referee: B. McGinley (Balfron)
Celtic beat Hamilton (2-1) Inverness Thistle (6-0) Dundee (1-1, 2-1) Motherwell (1-1, 3-0)
Dundee United beat Hibs (3-0) Queen of the South (3-0) St Mirren (2-1) Aberdeen (0-0, -2-1)

1986

10 May　　　　　　Hampden Park　　　　att: 62,841

Aberdeen 3 Hearts 0

Scorers Aberdeen: Hewitt (2) Stark
Teams Aberdeen: Leighton, McKimmie, McQueen, McMaster, McLeish, W. Miller, Hewitt, Cooper, McDougall, Bett, Weir. Subs-Stark, J. Miller
Hearts: Smith, Kidd, Whittaker, Jardine, Berry, Levein, Colquhoun, Black, Clark, G. Mackay, Robertson Subs-W. Mackay, Cowie.
Referee-H. Alexander (Kilmarnock)
Aberdeen beat Montrose (4-1) Arbroath (1-0) Dundee (2-2, 2-1) Hibernian (3-0)
Hearts beat Rangers (3-2) Hamilton (2-1) St Mirren (4-1) Dundee United (1-0)